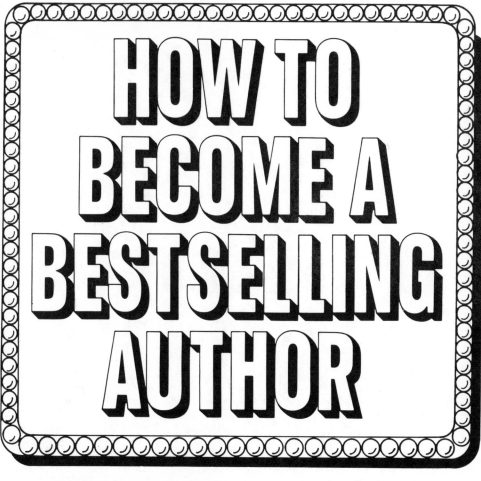

HOW TO BECOME A BESTSELLING AUTHOR

STANLEY J. CORWIN

Writer's
Digest
Books

Cincinnati, Ohio

The coupons, sales forms, and offers that appear in this book are merely illustrations and are not valid offers.

Library of Congress Cataloging in Publication Data

Corwin, Stanley J.
    How to become a bestselling author.
    Includes index.
    1. Authorship. I. Title.
PN151.C65   1984   808'.02   84-5285
ISBN 0-89879-129-4

To my wife, Donna, whose inspiration and love made this book a reality.

●
Acknowledgments

I would like to thank my daughters, Donna and Ellen, and my mother, Faye Corwin, who provided the love and the faith; my editor, Carol Cartaino, who provided the wisdom and the nurturing; my assistant, Carol Presti, who provided the dedication and the research; and beginning writers who provided the motivation. Without them this book would never have been possible.

Thank you.

Contents

Foreword

Reading Mr. Corwin's book has certainly proved very illuminating—even to *me*. I had to learn from painful experience.

For instance, I sure wish that I could have read a book such as this when *I* was still a hopeful, neophyte author. I was so excited at having a manuscript accepted that I would have signed anything right away (and did, unfortunately) without looking at or understanding what all the fine print in that long, three-page contract *really* meant.

I particularly recommend "first-time-around" authors study Chapter Nine on contracts, and Chapter Twenty: dealing with subsidiary rights.

This book taught me a lot, especially about having some control over dust jackets and blurbs. I have absolutely *hated* most of the ones on *my* books!

There is much to be learned from Mr. Corwin's book. But as in the case of all learning there are things that one accepts and things one cannot accept.

I, for instance, cannot accept the "formula" theory—perhaps because I have always written, almost compulsively, since I was eight years old. I write from my head and from within myself and would continue to write whether published or not because of what I feel.

As a writer of novels (romantic at times, but not Romances by any means!) who was fortunate enough to have an over-the-transom novel (*Sweet Savage Love*) accepted for publication the first time around, all I can say is it took a lot of hard work, a lot of rewriting, and—Stanley Corwin, where were you when I needed just this kind of book to direct me? All I had was belief, faith, and *chutzpa*, I guess!

Rosemary Rogers

●●●●●●●●●●●●●●●●●●●●
Author's Note

While I was writing this book and lecturing on *How to Become a Best-selling Author,* an extraordinary publishing event made newspaper and TV headlines across America. It was one of the most unique stories of the making of a best-seller in the history of American book publishing.

An eighty-eight-year-old woman living in a nursing home had written an epic novel about small town life. After a half century in its creation *...And Ladies of the Club* had been discovered as the most heralded writing property since *Gone with the Wind.*

This remarkable story began in the early 1920s when Helen Santmyer was a young writer living in Xenia, Ohio. She was disturbed by Sinclair Lewis's controversial best-seller *Main Street,* which depicted the drab complacency of small town American life. Miss Santmyer had published two novels in the 1920s and in the late twenties she began to write her response to *Main Street. ...And Ladies of the Club* used a ladies' literary club as a metaphor for America and centered on two indomitable women's lives and relationships during the growth of industrial America from 1868 to 1932. It was about small town life and about the human spirit and values that personified America.

With her companion and editor Mildred Sandoe at her side, Helen Santmyer wrote and wrote and wrote, until in 1981 she had finished her novel—almost 1400 pages. By now she was in her eighties. Her reflections on Ohio life, *Ohio Town,* had been published by Ohio State University Press, so she submitted her novel there. OSU Press printed a limited number primarily for sale to Ohio libraries. This edition, priced at $35.00, sold approximately 200 copies and probably would have experienced a short, obscure literary life if not for an extraordinary, fortuitous series of events.

In early 1983 Grace Sindell, a lovely literary woman who lives in Northern Ohio, was waiting in line at her local library. The wom-

| "All the News That's Fit to Print" | # The New York Times | **Weather:** New York, mostly sunny, remaining cold. Midwest, widespread snow showers, cold. South, mostly fair. West and Southwest, fog in the north, some snow in the mountains. Details are on page 10. |

VOL.CXXXIII... No. 45,921   Copyright © 1984 The New York Times   NEW YORK, THURSDAY, JANUARY 12, 1984   Y   50 CENTS

Happy Ending for Novel 50 Years in the Making

By EDWIN McDOWELL

A 1,344-page novel about life in small-town Ohio, begun more than 50 years ago by an author who is now 88 years old and lives in a nursing home, has been made a main selection of the Book-of-the-Month Club.

"There is no way we won't sell more than 100,000 copies of that book," said Edward E. Fitzgerald, chairman of the book club. "It is an absolutely stunning story." Book-of-the-Month Club has 15 main selections each year.

The book is "... And Ladies of the Club" by Helen Hooven Santmyer. G. P. Putnam's Sons plans to publish a minimum of 50,000 copies in August, and has established a $250,000 floor, or minimum, on the sale of paperback rights.

The book, begun in the late 1920's as Miss Santmyer's answer to Sinclair Lewis's unflattering portrait of small-town America in his 1920 novel "Main Street," takes place in southwestern Ohio and covers the period between 1868 and 1932. The title refers to members of the local women's literary club, through whom the town's political, cultural and social changes are related.

"I remember feeling ready to contradict everything Sinclair Lewis had said," Miss Santmyer said yesterday in a telephone conversation from Hospitality Home East in Xenia, Ohio. "It was a good book but it was prejudiced. Not all small towns are wonderful, but I'd rather live in a small town than a big city, any day." She added that she was "surprised" that anyone was interested in "... And Ladies of the Club."

Miss Santmyer is a native of Xenia, a town she returned to in 1929 after about 15 years, during which she graduated from Wellesley, worked in New York as a secretary to the editor of Scribner's magazine and earned a bachelor of letters degree at Oxford University — a degree that she said was "invented for American students who already had their bachelor's."

In the 1920's Miss Santmyer wrote

Dayton Newspapers, Inc./Charles Steinbrunner
Helen Santmyer autographing her book in Xenia, Ohio.

two novels: "Herbs and Apples," published by Houghton Mifflin in 1925, and "The Fierce Dispute," published by Scribner's in 1929. From 1935-53 she was dean of women and head of the English department at Cedarville College in Ohio. Later she was a reference librarian in Dayton, Ohio.

"... And Ladies of the Club," written entirely in longhand in a book-

keeper's ledger, was originally published in 1982 by Ohio State University Press, which in 1963 had published "Ohio Town," a book of Miss Santmyer's reminiscences. But only a few hundred copies of the $35 book were ever sold, most of them to libraries. A private person all her life, Miss Santmyer refused until yesterday to allow anyone to take her photograph. Nor did she submit one to Ohio State for use in its publicity for the book.

The book gained a new lease on life when Grace Sindell, a resident of Shaker Heights, Ohio, overheard a woman tell a librarian that ". . . And Ladies of the Club" was the best novel she had ever read. Intrigued, Mrs. Sindell checked the book out and finally persuaded her son, Gerald, a Los Angeles director, writer and producer, to read it.

"Usually by the time my parents give me a book, it's already been bought for movies or television," Mr. Sindell said yesterday. "I couldn't find the book here in Los Angeles, so I finally had to get it from Ohio State."

Mr. Sindell showed it to Stanley Corwin, a Los Angeles producer who formerly was president of Pinnacle Books and a vice president of Grosset & Dunlap and of Prentice-Hall.

"I hadn't read very far when I realized this was a special kind of book and that it needed to come out as a book that other than librarians would see," Mr. Corwin said yesterday. He and Mr. Sindell flew to Ohio and acquired from Ohio State University Press all world publication, television and motion-picture rights to the book.

Mr. Corwin contacted his college classmate and friend, Owen Laster, the head of the literary department at the William Morris Agency in New York City, and the agent for James A. Michener, Gore Vidal and Robert Penn Warren.

'Overwhelmed' by Quality

Mr. Laster also thought the book was special. "When I heard about how Miss Santmyer had been working on it for so many years, I knew that this was a book that had some wonderful things surrounding it," he said. "But when I read it, I was overwhelmed with its quality, and I sensed that this book could have a second life and I wanted to help give it that."

Mr. Laster took the book to Phyllis Grann, president and publisher of Putnam's, who was initially concerned about the book's bulk. "But not after I had read the first 25 pages," she said. "After that I knew I just could not *not* buy it."

Mrs. Grann, who edits such authors as Frank Herbert, Robin Cook and Dick Francis, said that she made the decision to acquire the book solely on the basis of its literary merit. "Even before we sold it to Book-of-the-Month, I felt it was such a mesmerizing book that we had to do it," she said. "Publishers can't always worry about money, and if you do pay attention to the bottom line, you have the luxury every once in a while of indulging your taste."

Putnam's expects to price the book — which in its Ohio State edition weighs four pounds, and which a Putnam's spokesman said "is another novel thicker than 'Gone With the Wind' " — between $17.95 and $19.95.

TV Mini-Series Planned

Mr. Sindell and Mr. Corwin are planning to adapt the book for a television mini-series. "Ohio State gets the lion's share of the proceeds that come in from the book and any other income," Mr. Sindell said. "And Miss Santmyer gets half of that. She participates in every source of income."

Weldon Kefauver, director of the Ohio State University Press, which holds the copyright to the book, said that Miss Santmyer interrupted work on ". . . And Ladies of the Club" to write "Ohio Town."

"She would write and tell me about the novel, because by then she had pretty much severed her ties with New York publishers," Mr. Kefauver said. "When she finished it and asked my advice, I asked her to send it to me, and she did — in 11 boxes."

But Mr. Kefauver also became so absorbed in the book that, even though Ohio State had published only one other novel, a surrealistic work, "I hoped we would do it," he said. "To my great satisfaction, our editorial board agreed."

Miss Santmyer said yesterday that she submitted it first to Mr. Kefauver because of her satisfaction with his handling of "Ohio Town." "I felt under obligation to him," she said.

Miss Santmyer, who never married, wrote the book at her home in Xenia. Mr. Kefauver asked her to trim some of the manuscript in 1976, but by then she began the first of her periodic stays in hospitals and nursing homes. Undaunted, she dictated changes from her bed to Mildred Sandoe, her friend since 1926 who has a room down the hall from Miss Santmyer's room in Hospitality Home East.

Janine Montgomery, assistant administrator of the nursing home, which has 100 residents, said that Miss Santmyer has been in the home eight times since June 1976, but has been there permanently since last April. She is quiet and soft-spoken, and tires very quickly because of her emphysema. "If this had happened to Miss Santmyer 50 years ago, she would have been much more excited, I'm sure," Mrs. Montgomery said. "But she seems to be taking it in stride — although everyone else here is extremely excited and happy for her."

Nevertheless, last week, in celebration of the book's rebirth, the 88-pound author got what she described as the first and last permanent in her life.

'I Used to Travel

Miss Santmyer, who is blind in one eye and has a cataract in the other, said that she still spends part of each day reading books that friends from the local Greene County public library bring around, and her favorite authors remain Charles Dickens, Mark Twain and Agatha Christie. "I used to travel a lot," she recalled. "After I retired, I visited New England with Miss Sandoe, where we have very many friends, and every spring for quite a long time we went to Mexico. We're crazy about Mexico." But she never went back to Europe, after returning from Oxford. "I haven't had the money," she said.

Miss Santmyer yesterday described her first two novels as "youthful," adding, "I would just as soon forget them." But she admitted satisfaction with ". . . And Ladies of the Club." She said one reason it took so long was that she could only write part time. "That was the trouble, I always had to earn a living while I wrote," she said.

Then she added: "Here, time just doesn't matter, but I'm not doing any writing now. I think age excuses me from making any more effort."

an in front of her plunked down the 1400-page university press edition of ... *Ladies* and declared, "This is the best book I've ever read!" Her interest piqued, Grace took the book home. After a week's worth of reading, she agreed with the woman's assessment. Several months later she had finally convinced her son Gerry in Los Angeles to read a copy of the book. Gerry was a very creative film writer, producer, and director who viewed the book as a unique vehicle for television or the movies. Gerry and I are close friends and he asked me to substantiate his enthusiasm for the work.

I was initially incredulous about the size and scope of this mammoth novel. It had an elegiac, religious quality and it encompassed the entire sweep of American small town life from the Civil War to the Depression. It was superbly written and organized, but it was also simple and absorbing—very different from the quick pulp-plotted novels that filled the racks in the 1980s. This was literature, reminiscent of a late nineteenth-century novel by Fielding or Thackeray or of the novels we were made to read in high school and college literary courses, by Dreiser and Melville and their peers.

...*And Ladies of the Club* was an extraordinary literary achievement, written by a woman who sat down to write what she had to say, without worrying about getting an agent, finding the right publisher, or gearing her book to paperback or a TV mini-series. But was it commercial in today's best-seller marketplace?

After I read 200 pages I knew that the human interest story behind the book and the work itself were so special that I had to be involved with them.

Subsequently Gerry and I acquired all world publication, TV, and motion picture rights to the novel from Helen Santmyer and Ohio State University Press. Our initial plans were to sell paperback reprint rights and then develop the book for television. But then I decided to forget that the book had been previously published and to treat it as an original book—a literary discovery. We were hoping to create a different kind of national best-seller and perhaps, with a little luck, a publishing event. Nothing in our wildest fantasies would prepare us for what was about to happen across America.

I flew to New York and sought out my friend Owen Laster. Owen had risen through the ranks of the William Morris Agency to become head of their literary department, representing such authors as James Michener, Gore Vidal, Morris West, and Rosemary Rogers. When I began to tell him about a ninety-year-old lady in a nursing home in Ohio who for the last fifty years has been writing "the great American novel," he was mesmerized. "Stan," he exclaimed, "if the novel is anywhere as good as the story you just told me, we've got something here!" It was, and Owen responded enthusiastically and convincingly after reading the book.

Owen conducted a very private mini-auction on the book. Phyllis Grann, now president of Putnam, realized that she had also just discovered "something." Phyllis had a reputation for recognizing and nurturing potential best-sellers. Her track record in launching them included books by Frank Herbert and Robin Cook. Putnam acquired U. S. publication rights from Gerry and me. The best-seller launch had begun and it would never lose momentum.

We knew that Putnam would submit *Ladies* to the editorial board of Book-of-the-Month Club for summer 1984 main selection consideration. The judges would vote on January 4, 1984, for their summer choice. This would be the most pivotal date in the new life of the book. A BOMC selection was the highest literary accolade that could be bestowed upon a book prior to publication. And I predicted that they would take it. They would not likely encounter an author and literary work like this ever again.

I was on the tennis courts in Los Angeles on January 4 when Owen Laster called to tell me that the judges had unanimously chosen *Ladies* as a main selection. It was perhaps the most thrilling experience in my publishing career. And it was the first time in anyone's memory that BOMC had taken a previously published book as a main selection. A national publishing event was about to happen.

Soon after that, Putnam in association with Gerry and me issued a publicity release on the novel and its author, and how we discovered the property. Edwin McDowell, who covers publishing news for *The New York Times,* would break the story. He interviewed all the participants and on January 12, 1984, this incredible literary discovery was revealed on the front page of *The New York Times.*

In the ensuing two weeks, the human interest story of Helen Santmyer and her novel was featured in almost every major newspaper in America, in the *International Herald Tribune,* and in *Time* and *Newsweek* magazines. It was highlighted on *Good Morning America, The Today Show, CBS Morning News,* the *McNeil-Lehrer Report* on PBS, and it was covered by Dan Rather and Tom Brokaw on their respective nightly news shows. Gerry and I were inundated with phone calls and congratulatory letters. The book had become a national news story, the most talked-about literary property in decades. The New York publishing community, the Hollywood film world, and people on the street were talking about the "nice old lady in the nursing home in Ohio." And they talked about *...And Ladies of the Club.* It had become "That Book." We had created a national publishing event.

As this book goes to press, Putnam will publish *Ladies* in June 1984 with a first printing of 100,000 copies, an advertising/promotion budget of $100,000, and expectations that all of literary America will soon be reading the book that sold 200 copies in its previous life. British rights have been sold for a high advance; American paperback rights will be auctioned for hundreds of thousands of dollars; and, of course, the BOMC selection is scheduled for summer of 1984. Gerry Sindell and I have announced plans to produce it as a major TV mini-series.

Gerry and I went back to Ohio in late January to visit Helen Santmyer and her friend Mildred Sandoe and to tour the town of Xenia. It was a wonderful day, less hectic than the media blitz that had descended on the Hospitality Home East Nursing Home the past weeks. In quiet, reflective moments we took pictures and we talked to Helen about her life, her book, and her fictional town of Waynesboro, Ohio. She sat in her wheelchair, very frail and tired, discussing the values that had indelibly carved out the American spirit. She was beaming because she was proud of her achievement. It had taken her a lifetime to write her epic novel but she had done it.

I asked Helen Santmyer what message she could give to aspiring writers. "Believe in what you are writing," she answered, "and finish it." This indomitable woman had devoted her life to writing a book that she believed in. And she had never given up. It was the most important lesson that I or any writer could ever remember.

•••••••••••••••••••••••

Introduction

Everyone wants to become a best-selling author. I think I've met all of you over the last twenty years. You were the housewife in Bloomington, Indiana; the cab driver at JFK airport; the waitress in Pompano Beach, Florida; and the college professor in La Jolla, California. You all dreamed of having your book reviewed in the Sunday *New York Times;* appearing on *Good Morning America;* and "soon being a major motion picture." You had an idea, a hope, a manuscript in the back of an old desk drawer or in the back of your mind. Wayne Dyer did it! Judith Krantz did it! You could, too.

Chances were you'd never get to play center field for the New York Yankees. Someone else was selected over you to star in the newest TV series. You were either too old or too young to be President of the United States. But a best-selling author! You *could* be a best-selling author. Joseph Wambaugh (*The Onion Field*) was a policeman. Bel Kaufman (*Up the Down Staircase*) was a teacher. James Herriot (*All Things Bright and Beautiful*) was a veterinarian. And Patricia Matthews was an assistant librarian. But how? Whom do you have to know? Where do you begin? How do you go about it?

People just like you all across America have asked me, "How can I become a best-selling author?" Having been involved in the initial publication successes of such best-selling authors as Patricia Matthews (*Love's Avenging Heart*), Dr. Irwin Stillman (*The Doctor's Quick Weight Loss Diet*), and Bel Kaufman, I shared their dreams of bestsellerdom and saw their fantasies and ambitions become reality. I've worked with authors like Norman Mailer (*Marilyn*), James Jones (*World War II*), and Don Pendleton (*The Executioner* series), and I've felt their intense desires to sustain *their* best-selling roles.

C205/HOW TO BECOME A BEST SELLING AUTHOR

Beverly Hills

Course Fee: $45

The publishing industry in America has dramatically changed in recent years. Books are now packaged, promoted and hyped like other products. Authors are expected to adapt to these changes. In this topical course, you will learn how to conceive a marketable idea, choose a bestselling title and subject, promote through mail order, negotiate contracts for royalties and subsidiary rights, move into film and television tie-ins, and more. By the end of the course you will know how to effectively work with any publisher on editorial decisions. If you're serious about wanting to sell what you write, don't miss this one. (Enroll early—class space is limited.)

Stanley J. Corwin is the President of Stan Corwin Productions, Ltd., producing films, TV programs and books in association with major film companies and book publishers in Los Angeles and New York. He has been the president and chief executive officer of Pinnacle Books, vice-president of publishing development at Grosset & Dunlap, and vice-president of Prentice-Hall, Inc.

Sec A Sat

July 16   9:30am-3:30pm

In my West Coast seminars and lectures and throughout my years of publishing experience, aspiring authors have asked me how to get a book published. What is the market looking for? What are the ingredients for a best-seller? What is the secret formula? Do I need an agent? Who is the best publisher? How do I prepare a book proposal?

I've been fortunate enough to discover some best-selling books and authors; edit some extraordinary titles; market books all over the world; sell books to the movies and television, for paperback reprint, and as special-edition premiums to a breakfast cereal company; and run a $20 million paperback publishing company. I know the hype and the hyperbole, the contacts and the contracts in the publishing business. I can understand *why* you want to be a best-selling author but, more important, I know *how* you can become one. I cannot guarantee that it will happen, but whether you're writing a first novel or a nonfiction book, similar rules and formulas for creating a best-seller still apply. Books have been written on how to get your book published and how to write a manuscript. But no book like this one has ever been written before. I'm dedicating *my* best-seller to you. *You* can become a best-selling author! I'm going to tell you how!

Stanley J. Corwin
Beverly Hills, California

•••••••••••••••••••
First, You Need a
Great Idea

1. What's *your* idea for a best-selling book? You must ask yourself some very basic questions before you begin to write a "best-seller." If your idea concerns a new diet created by the Eskimos or describes the river regions of Colorado, it will interest only a narrow audience concerned with this specific subject. You limit your chances of becoming a best-selling author if your idea is esoteric, specialized, or lacking in broad appeal to the general public. Few nonfiction best-sellers were ever created or manufactured from remote subjects. You should also make sure your idea merits publication as a *book,* as opposed to a magazine or newspaper article. Can you find enough substantive material to write about your idea so that the public will pay from five to fifteen dollars to read about it? Are there enough innovative, original ideas to fill over 150 or 200 pages of a book?

Ask yourself initially: Does my idea have commercial appeal? Should it be published in book form? You must answer these two questions affirmatively before you proceed to the next phase of creating a best-seller.

The best bets for best-selling nonfiction (the never-fail *formula* subjects) are the generally accepted subjects that *everybody* wants to read about: sex, money, health, diet, and self-improvement. They fulfill a reader's desire to look better, feel better, have a better sex life, make more money, save money, live longer, lose weight, be a better person, or improve some aspect of his or her life. Recent best-

NEW NATIONAL BESTSELLER

"A remarkably effective diet, and healthy as well."
—*Family Circle*

AUDREY EYTON'S
Extraordinary

F-PLAN
DIET
LOSE WEIGHT FAST
AND LIVE LONGER

The world's best selling diet!

The book that's sweeping the country—
The magical new formula that will help you lose weight safely—and lose weight faster than ever before!

Audrey Eyton's F-Plan Diet* has been making headlines everywhere! This extraordinary new diet adds FIBER RICH FOOD AND GOODNESS TO YOUR DIET.

*As seen in *Newsweek*, *People*, *Family Circle*, *Us*, the *Star*, *Self*.
$12.95 at bookstores everywhere
over 150,000 copies in print

• WATCH FOR AUDREY EYTON ON HER NATIONWIDE AUTHOR TOUR NOW
• NATIONWIDE ADVERTISING

Photo by Robert Belton

CROWN PUBLISHERS Inc

sellers like *Life Extension, The F-Plan Diet, Nice Girls Do, Thin Thighs in 30 Days,* and *Mary Ellen's Best of Helpful Hints* have fulfilled these best-selling promises with extraordinary sales figures.

All these titles pertained to formula subjects at the outset. The subjects reflect the best-selling ideas you had initially for your book. They appealed to people's basic needs and provided answers or a course of action to improve or change some part of a person's life. These books were more likely to become best-sellers than more limited topics.

Your idea is the most important ingredient in creating a best-selling book. Fill a need; pick a subject that most book buyers will respond to readily. Choose your subject before you begin to write. The subjects aforementioned do not preclude writing about other generally popular subjects, such as gardening, real estate, collectibles, hobbies, humor, love, participation sports, biographies, first-person experiences that others would want to read about, new lifestyles, or "how-to" subjects that could fit the best-selling formula. The more you limit your market (to women, or tennis players, or Texans) the less likely you are to achieve a *national* best-seller.

Obviously you should choose a subject with which you are familiar. A doctor's name on a diet book is a stronger recommendation than a lawyer's. If you've made a million dollars in land speculation, your credentials are far better than those of someone who has had no experience in buying and selling real estate.

The "how-to" subjects have enormous popular appeal, and have worked as formula subjects. They are appealing because they promise something and because the books cost less than therapy or the price of a seminar or a course on a particular subject. Books on how to make money in the stock market can provide invaluable information quickly and cheaply. *How to Make Love to a Man* or *How to Make Love to a Woman* could be the quick, easy answer to all your lovemaking problems and questions. Those book subjects are timely, provocative, and instant, and they promise a great deal.

The inspirational book is a popular offshoot of the "how-to." These books enable you to *Be the Person You Were Meant to Be;* to achieve *Living, Loving, and Learning;* and to answer the question, *Why Do I Think I'm Nothing without a Man?*

In recent years, another popular best-seller formula idea has been the "nonbook," which you enjoy rather than read from cover to cover, and the "parody" book, a parody of an existing best-seller. The nonbook is exemplified by the Nothing Books, small books with absolutely no text inside so that you can write your own book or your own notes. The Music Nothing Book and other creations are a spinoff from the original Nothing Book. Other recent examples of nonbooks include *Thin (Anything and Everything) in 30 Days, Murphy's Law, How to Eat Like a Child,* and the *Truly Tasteless* and *Gross Jokes* books.

Successful parody books include *Items from Our Catalog* (a de-

lightful takeoff on the well-known L.L. Bean Catalog); *Plain Jane Works Out* (a spoof of the best-selling Jane Fonda *Workout* Book); and *The One Minute Lover* (a parody of *The One Minute Manager*). These books are often very cleverly written.

Many of the recent parody books were unsuccessful, particularly in the overdone areas of cubes, preppies, and cats, because they were too numerous, too late, and not funny. Generally, the first and the cleverest ones make the best-seller lists.

After you've chosen a formula subject you know something about, you must answer another basic question: "Who will buy my book?" The broad national audience you are aiming for should include all sexes, ages, ethnic groups, and, if possible, geographic markets. (The typical book buyer is an educated man or woman over 25 who lives in an urban center.) A "woman's" book on pregnancy will not sell to the male book buyer. A book on improving your putting strokes in golf will restrict your audience to golfers. But if *everyone* will buy your book, you've chosen a universal subject. The popular best-seller, *Be the Person You Were Meant to Be,* appealed to *you* regardless of age or sex or geographical boundaries. *Life Extension* appealed to everyone. So, generally, did *Personhood* and *The Joy of Sex.*

What's the competition for your book? If seventeen books have been written recently on How to Live Forever, the marketplace has no real desire to buy another one. Be selective in your choice of an idea for your best-seller. It should appeal to everybody, but not if everybody has already bought or read three books on the same subject. A sudden rash of titles on running, walking, tennis, racquetball, cubes, or cats can dilute a market that was once receptive to books on those subjects. The competition increases and the stores are inundated with instant "best-sellers" on subjects that everyone is publishing simultaneously. It is a simple matter of oversaturation. So be selective; be original in your choice of a subject. The market may not need any more. This does not mean there is no room for one more cat book. But generally, if the market is oversaturated with a genre or category (romance or science fiction, for example), it is fruitless to add to it.

Ask clerks at several different bookstores what is selling at the present and what is not. This will help you determine excessive publication of a subject. Also, visit your local library and look in *Subject Guide to Books in Print, Forthcoming Books in Print,* and the spring and fall forecast issues of *Publishers Weekly* (the book industry's weekly magazine) to see whether competing books on your subject will be published in the near future.

It is hard to gauge market oversaturation of a subject in an exact, scientific manner. Four books on cats or three movies on swords and sorcery may be commercially successful, and the next may be the one the public resists. A review of current trends and best-selling lists, research at your bookstore and library, and talking (if possible) to knowledgeable publishing people or authors are the best indicators of competition for your book idea. Your prospective publisher is also guesstimating market trends based on empirical sales and editing data and on his or her "experienced intuition" of what will sell *next year.*

Through the years, I have been asked, "What is next year's big trend?" I have answered very sincerely, "A: I don't know, and B: if I did I certainly wouldn't tell anybody else."

Years ago someone facetiously imagined that a book combining the most popular subjects would have to be a best-seller. Since dogs, doctors, and President Lincoln have always been popular, why not market a book entitled *Lincoln's Doctor's Dog?* In recent years, other broad popular titles might have been *Running With Passion's Cat* and *The One-Minute Preppy Lover.*

If you choose to write a novel rather than nonfiction, a similar formula applies. The market is presently oversaturated with historical and hysterical romances, multigeneration sagas, and occult literature (although the better ones and the heavily promoted ones can still become best-sellers). This does not necessarily mean that another *Exorcist, Thorn Birds,* or Harlequin romance would not be a huge best-seller if written well and commercially. But it would have to be better than its competition. Readers always enjoy and respond to an evocative love story, an episodic saga, or a spine-tingling gothic or horror tale, when written well. It is essential that you select a fiction subject that you are capable of writing (perhaps based on your own experiences) and for which there already exists a responsive market (based on the recent best-seller lists). Best-selling authors like King, Cook, Ludlum, Steel, and Follett write commer-

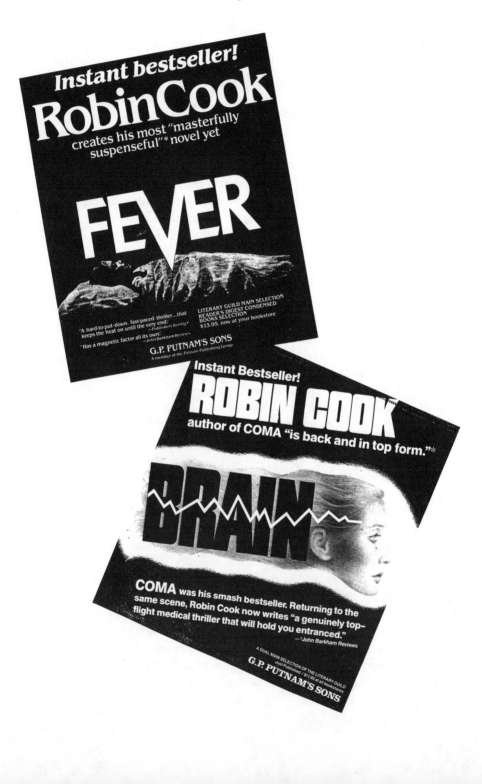

cial fiction that appeals consistently to a general audience. Fiction has less stringent requirements than nonfiction; no rigid outline is needed because the content emanates from your imagination rather than from a formula subject. But not everyone can turn out a best-selling book. Your novel must hold the reader's interest from beginning to climax.

When I first published the best-selling historical romances of Patricia Matthews, we were confident that our (and her) formula was specifically responsive to the reading tastes of the marketplace at that time. Because of the success of the Harlequin romances and because of the large TV audience that watched afternoon soap operas, we felt that America would be receptive to more fiction in this particular genre. The time seemed ripe for a big, lusty, historical romance.

Patricia Matthews is an avid reader of all the romances on the market and an assiduous researcher of her historical settings and events. She also learned to heighten reader interest by ending each chapter with a miniclimax. Her plot formulas, characterizations, and episodic historical adventures generated an enormous response from a growing number of devotees. Like her predecessors, Barbara Cartland and Kathleen Woodiwiss, Patricia Matthews became a famous best-selling author in this genre by providing formula entertainment to a highly receptive audience. She chose her subject well; her timing for publication was perfect; and she delivered all that she promised.

In recent years, other examples of formula fiction that became extraordinary best-selling novels were *Coma* and *Godplayer* by Robin Cook and *The Man from St. Petersburg* and *Eye of the Needle* by Ken Follett. Both novelists read and researched all the novels in their genres to find the best-selling ingredients that worked. They chose fictional subjects that readers particularly enjoy, and they followed an exciting plot formula that had been successful in the past.

Fictional subjects such as horror, the occult, space fantasy, love and sex relationships, spy and espionage novels, sagas, Hollywood, psychological thrillers, crime, big business, and fictionalized biographies are very popular with the mass of readers who enjoy escape reading. Obviously, new writers of fiction try to emulate the style and successful formulas of the master contemporary novelists—

Robbins, Wallace, Sheldon, Forsythe, Shaw. Several have material-ized as best-selling novelists in recent years. They include Ken Fol-lett, Judith Krantz (heir apparent to Jacqueline Susann), Stephen King, John Saul, Danielle Steel, Rosemary Rogers, and V.C. An-drews.

Often, best-selling nonfiction books are derived from successful formulas. Since *The Joy of Cooking* has enjoyed perennial success, it was logical for Alex Comfort to borrow the title's catchwords to launch *The Joy of Sex*. Another current best-seller is *The Joy of Photography*, with Eastman-Kodak as the editors. This formula could lead to such literary creations as *The Joy of Jogging* and *The Joy of Hooking*. In any event, it is a most commercially viable for-mula, which doesn't yet seem overdone. But the next spinoff book could be the one that doesn't sell. It is often only a matter of luck and timing. Your "in" idea may be too early or too late.

You can research your ideas by perusing the best-seller lists and by being aware of current events and trends. Observers of the latest fads and "in" trends in America can often perceive a best-selling idea at the most propitious time. Such cases produced best-sellers on subjects like Pac-Man, Rubik's Cube, and Valley Girls.

Several years ago, a Los Angeles rock group approached me with a book idea about an emerging new California phenomenon— Valley Girls. It was the "bitchin'," "grodiest," "ragin' " latest trend to come out of the San Fernando Valley shopping malls. Surely what began in California as a freak fad would soon go national.

I quickly packaged this idea in physical form with pictures of Valley Girls and Valley Dudes and text about their language and lifestyle. I brought this topical book idea to New York to show to a major paperback publisher because they could print and publish such a topical book faster than a hardcover house.

But I was too late. Several Valley Girl submissions had begun to make the rounds of New York publishers, and it was already be-coming an overcrowded category. A month earlier, this topical fad would probably have been unknown to most of America.

As it turned out, the first book published on the subject—*The Valley Girls' Guide to Life,* from Dell—became an instant best-sell-er. The four or five imitative books that followed were not success-ful, and the fad "vegged out" soon after it began.

Ideas for this publishing year might revolve around the Olympics, the Presidential election, or 1984 from an Orwellian perspective. Ideas abound from the news, the trends, and the world around us.

In summary, subject is the vital ingredient in a best-seller. At the outset you will have to research your subject and the competition for it in the marketplace to find the formula that will appeal to a general readership. Publishers today evaluate the idea before they see the actual writing. Is it commercial? Is it original? Does it follow a proven successful formula? Are there already too many recently published books on this subject? Will it still be topical by the time they publish it? Publishers make money on books that become best-sellers, not just by publishing a list of books. If an idea is different and potentially commercial, they will publish it. Too many books have been published in recent years in search of this magic best-seller formula, but the publishers keep trying because one hit could make a year. So first, you need a great idea. Second, you need a great title, which leads us into the next chapter.

●
Get a Fantastic Title Before You Start

2. Now that you have a great commercial idea for your book, the next logical step would be to research and write it and worry about a title after you've completed a first draft.

I disagree. Editors and authors of "How to Publish Your Book" books generally advise beginning writers to choose an appropriately commercial title *after* they've written their book, or they tell writers not to worry about a title because the prospective publisher will choose it for them. But over my years of publishing experience and working with potential best-selling authors, I have found that it makes good sense to pick a title *before* you begin. It may change later in the manuscript-development stage, but I would start with a title.

Why? You will have greater motivation and inspiration to write your book and to think about it as a best-seller. You will be able to plan and talk about your book as a specific title, rather than referring to your "manuscript." You will be excited about your titled book and will have a greater incentive to produce a best-seller. Your title will help you to fulfill the promise and the goal you established for yourself at the outset. Remember, you can always change the title.

Titles are part of the hype that sells books—and ultimately sells *you* to the marketplace. Great titles have sold millions of books. Author Wayne Dyer conceived the title *Your Erroneous Zones,* which evoked a market response. People were curious about this expression and what their "erroneous zones" were. It had a sexual connotation that titillated the reader. Dyer effectively marketed a title that became part of our lexicon. Many people were stimulated to improve a psychological region of their moods that they didn't even know existed or hadn't previously cared about. In his sequel, *Pulling Your Own Strings,* Dyer once again marketed an evocative title. Robert Ringer's extraordinary title *Looking Out for #1* helped the book to become a best-seller. It would obviously have not generated the same response had he titled it "Looking Out for #5." It was about *you,* the #1 person in your life.

How to Be Your Own Best Friend was a 56-page pep pill that could be read and assimilated in less than an hour. Written by a prominent husband-and-wife psychiatrist team, it carried the simple message, "like yourself," and reminded you that you are a pretty decent person, worthy of your own friendship. It became a phenomenal best-seller—because of its title. The book gave the reader perfect advice and delivered its entire premise in the title.

When author Terry Garrity and publisher Lyle Stuart conceived the best-selling title, *The Sensuous Woman,* and subsequently *The Sensuous Man,* they cleverly introduced a magic adjective that *sounded* sensual and sexy. Women and men were previously rich, slim, and healthy in book titles, but this was the first book that promised sensuality. It couldn't miss, and it didn't.

A title makes your book more real to you and provides an initial inspiration to begin writing your prospective best-seller. It was probably a motivating force for the author of *Zen and the Art of Motorcycle Maintenance.*

Another important reason to come up with a title first is that titles help sell publishers who buy. You are likely to attract the immediate attention of an editor or publisher if you include a catchy title at the top of your query letter or manuscript proposal. Often a "best-selling" book can then be written to fulfill the promise of a title. *The One Minute Manager, A Whack on the Side of the Head, The Neverending Story,* and *Real Men Don't Eat Quiche* are vivid examples of titles that ultimately became best-selling books.

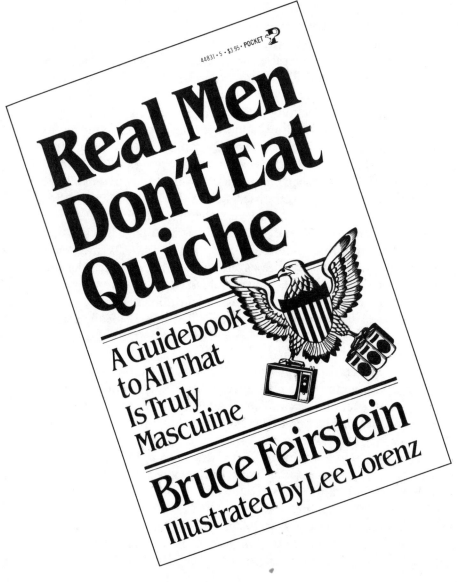

Titles pique curiosity and appeal to a publisher. If a manuscript title and an accompanying well-written and commercial proposal are passed around to key people in a publishing house, and if they evoke a favorable response, publishers reason that the response indicates its reception in the marketplace.

The famous catch phrase, "It's a Catch-22 situation," might have been a "Catch-18 situation." That was the title of *Catch-22* before the publisher felt that it conflicted with Leon Uris' *Mila 18*. Hemingway's classic, *The Sun Also Rises,* was originally titled *The Lost Generation*.

Titles sell books to people who buy. If *I'm OK, You're OK* had been titled "A Guide To Transactional Analysis," I doubt that it would have sold the millions of copies that it did. The author chose an appealing, commercial title for a clinical subject, and people responded to a new catch phrase. Many successful titles don't feature a gimmick or cutesy phrase or handle; they just state clearly what the book is about. Examples of effective titles include *Creating Wealth, Getting Organized, How to Flatten Your Stomach,* and *The Only Investment Guide You'll Ever Need*—simple titles that tell you exactly what you're buying.

When Dr. David Reuben was writing *his* best-seller, it was untitled. Just before the book went to press, the publisher and the author still did not have a commercial title. The publisher wrote to Reuben and asked him to describe his book in a sentence. Reuben wrote back that he still didn't have a title, but that his book was essentially "everything you always wanted to know about sex but were afraid to ask."

This catch phrase became such a part of our language that it led inevitably to imitative "best-sellers" featuring everything you wanted to know about real estate, dieting, tennis, etc. Some were derivative best-sellers, but many were not.

Inner Tennis was another gimmick handle that led to almost everything from Inner Sex to Inner Scrabble. It had an allure beyond learning how to play the game. Fortunately, the cross-fertilization of title ideas has not yet led to The Inner Dinner Diet or Sensuous Tennis. Still, some best-selling titles have had such great appeal that they have spawned a flock of imitators: *Real Dogs Don't Eat Leftovers; When Bad Dogs Happen to Good People;* and *Tough Times*

Don't Last, Tough People Do; and *Real Cats Don't Do Talk Shows.*

Years ago, when I first discovered and published Dr. Irwin Stillman, we chose a title to fit the exact message we were selling. The magic selling words were "doctor" (medically sound), "quick" (fast), and "diet" (how to lose weight). We combined these special words and ingredients into one of the best-selling titles of all time— *The Doctor's Quick Weight Loss Diet.* It has sold over 15 million copies to date in all editions. *The Complete Scarsdale Medical Diet* was another phenomenal best-seller. The reference to a prestigious community gave this diet book an elite tone that impressed the public. *The Beverly Hills Diet* worked because of its celebrated address. The implication was that beautiful people lived at these famous addresses, and that you, too, could be beautiful just by reading this book. I doubt that an Indianapolis Diet would have enjoyed similar success on the best-seller lists.

The imitative title is often effective, if it is not overdone. As president of Pinnacle Books, I successfully published the *Book of Sports Lists,* a compilation of original lists of sports trivia provided by celebrity contributors. It was blatantly intended as a derivative of the enormously successful *Book of Lists,* by the entire Wallace family. The title imitation worked because the "list" fad had not yet begun to proliferate, and our idea was another commercial variation. *Truly Tasteless Jokes* led, of course, to *Truly Tasteless Jokes II,* and *III* and then to other publisher's titles—*Gross Jokes* and *Gross Limericks.*

Books are often bought for publication *because* of a title. If that is the case, then you may insist in your contract that the title cannot be changed or shall be agreed upon mutually. But you should not make this demand if the publisher is also buying your story and your idea.

Although your publisher will invariably have the ultimate veto power over a title, books are often bought because of a particular title. You may insist as a contractual point that the title remain. An untitled manuscript may be titled by the publisher, but your title can be contractually the book that is bought.

Title words that contain the word "you" work particularly well—*Be the Person You Were Meant to Be; I'm OK, You're OK; What Color Is Your Parachute?; How to Survive in Your Native*

Land. The use of a famous name in the title is also helpful: Jane Fonda's *Workout Book,* and the Mary Kay *Guide to Beauty,* and Linda Evans' *Beauty and Exercise* book are recent best-selling examples. Other effective buzz words in titles include "best," "complete" and "successful."

Long titles for nonfiction books have often caused problems for publishers' jacket designers, but have generated positive reaction in the bookstores. *Megatrends: Ten New Directions Transforming Our Lives* and *The Love You Make: An Insider's Story of the Beatles* filled up a good portion of the jacket, but also filled a lot of cash registers with dollars.

Titles are often derived from famous quotations. John Donne's memorable lines, " . . . never send to know for whom the bell tolls; it tolls for thee" became the inspiration for Hemingway's classic novel, *For Whom The Bell Tolls.* Other words from famous quotations that became best-selling titles include *East of Eden* and *The Fire Next Time.*

Titles often appeal to our psychological, physical, and emotional needs, and use sexy words or an alluring phrase to titillate us. Books are often bought because their titles "turned us on" in some way. *Nice Girls Do, Men Are Just Desserts,* and *Vaginal Politics* evoked our sexual reactions. *Life Extension, Think and Grow Rich, When Bad Things Happen to Good People, In Search of Excellence,* and *Passages* appealed to certain thoughts and feelings we all have about our lives. *The Peter Pan Syndrome* and *The Cinderella Complex* reached us on an emotional, sociological level.

It is important for the new author to be familiar with best-selling titles and to practice "title awareness." The best way to do this is by subscribing to *Publishers Weekly* or by reading a weekly book review, preferably the *New York Times.* Also, visit your bookstore to study the latest titles of new releases, particularly those on the best-seller list. You might also brainstorm title ideas with friends or associates if you're not afraid they'll steal your title.

Your publisher is also attuned to the marketplace of titles. If a fresh, new, exciting title comes his way, he will share it with colleagues. Often, enthusiasm for a title can spread throughout a publishing house. If the complete or partial manuscript can deliver what the title promises, publishers will begin to dream of a potential

The Indispensable Guide
by One of the Media's
Most Popular Psychologists

This is a provocative book that can change the life of every woman courageous enough to read it. "What women need to learn is that men are just desserts; they are not the main course," asserts Dr. Sonya Friedman, who clearly and forcefully shows how every woman can resolve her inner conflicts and become an autonomous and self-reliant person. A popular radio and TV psychologist, Sonya Friedman has an audience of twenty-five million. Like its predecessors, *My Mother/My Self* and *The Cinderella Complex*, Sonya Friedman's *Men Are Just Desserts* is an invitation to real liberation, to a full and satisfying life, and to a loving and lasting relationship with a man.

$50,000 advertising/promotion campaign featuring an author tour to 20 major markets and nationwide newspaper and magazine advertising

Sonya Friedman

Men
Are
Just
Desserts

How Learning to Be
a Woman
with a Life of Your Own
Can Enrich the Life You Share
with a Man

Men Are Just Desserts
May $14.50 PPT
5¼ x 8¼ 256 pages
Initial printing: 50,000 copies
Serial rights sold to *Cosmopolitan*

WARNER
BOOKS

best-seller. *The One Minute Manager* had this effect on William Morrow publishers.

● ● ●

When I published and marketed the Patricia Matthews romantic novels at Pinnacle, we adhered to a common and continuing pattern of titles. Book One was entitled *Love's Avenging Heart,* and it was such a runaway best-seller that we adopted the "Love's" formula in all her subsequent titles. We were establishing a brand identification for Pat Matthews; *Love's Wildest Promise, Love's Daring Dream,* and others followed the first best-seller.

This pattern of continuing to use a successful title has been effective for the Harry Kemelman titles—*Friday the Rabbi Slept Late* (and so on to Saturday, Sunday, and the other days of the week); for the Fletch detective titles—*Fletch and the Man Who* (Fletch and . . .), and for the Bantam sagas about different states—*Nebraska, Dakota, Texas,* and the rest.

In planning your own best-seller, you may be thinking about a sequel or series. An appropriate beginning title would be desirable if you contemplate using similiar words in future titles. We did this at Pinnacle with the "Windhaven" saga. The initial title was *Windhaven Plantation,* followed by *Storm over Windhaven* and *Legacy of Windhaven.*

The first national best-seller in which I was proud to take part was a book originally titled *Notes from a Teacher's Wastebasket,* by a New York City school teacher. In the transition from manuscript to publication, the book was renamed *Up the Down Staircase,* a title that became a part of our vocabulary. This phrase, which was used in the novel, had an appealing, special quality. Several of us began to use it in conversation because it had a magical ring. Why not make it the title of this original book?

A book that I recently and successfully published first came my way with a unique title but little manuscript organization. *All the Good Ones Are Married,* by Hollywood screenwriter Marion Zola, is popular sociology about women's affairs and relationships with married men. The title premise was so intriguing that I believed instantly in the project. Then we had to work to construct a manuscript that would deliver the promise of the title.

With fiction it is obviously harder to predict title success at the outset. The writing and the plot, not the title, determine reader response. Not many people had ever heard of Mario Puzo, Colleen McCullough, and John Irving before *The Godfather, The Thorn Birds,* and *The World According to Garp* reached the best-seller lists. In retrospect, they were interesting, unusual, and appropriately titled books, but the stories and the commercial impact created their title recognition.

Charming stories with "charming" titles have become legendary best-selling novels in recent years. *Jonathan Livingston Seagull* and *Watership Down* are two warm and wonderful examples. Titles of novels are now less staid than they were in the past. Bizarre

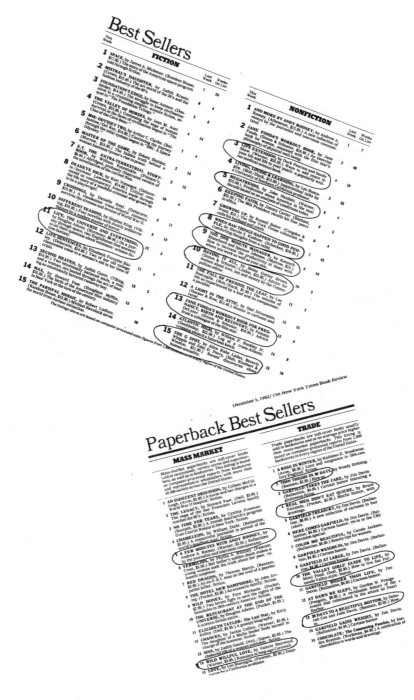

space fantasy titles like *The Restaurant at the End of the Universe,* which followed *The Hitchhiker's Guide to the Galaxy,* appeal to a youthful generation that grew up on "way out," strangely titled novels by Kurt Vonnegut and Richard Brautigan.

Recent evocative best-selling novel titles include *Dinner at the Homesick Restaurant, The Little Drummer Girl, The Executioner's Song,* and *A Confederacy of Dunces.* Shorter fictional titles are also alluring—*August, Final Payments, Sophie's Choice, Heartburn,* and *Hollywood Wives.*

Numerous best-selling novelists have adhered to successful title formulas. Robin Cook uses single dramatic words—*Coma, Brain.* Robert Ludlum uses a name followed by a noun. The titles of his best-sellers—*The Bourne Identity, The Chancellor Manuscript, The Parsifal Mosaic*—follow the same pattern. (For more on the business of titling novels, see "How Novels Get Titles" in the Appendix.)

Titles can be misleading, intentionally or otherwise. When I lectured at the University of Colorado several years ago, I stayed at the home of a conservative, religious, middle-American couple. The wife told me with great consternation that at the Denver airport she had recently spotted a book she thought could cure her phobia about traveling by air. *Fear of Flying* did not fulfill her objective.

So I recommend that you choose *your* book title *now.* Change it later if you like, but motivate and inspire your writing by working with a book that has a name with an implied premise. It's fun, personal, and sounds commercial. It may be the beginning of *your* bestseller, and it may become a famous American expression.

How Do I Begin to Write This Best-Seller?

3. After you have your proposed idea and subject and you've chosen your tentative title, you must begin to put your future best-seller on paper. At the outset it's easy to be enthusiastic about your prospective book, and later you will experience an author's high from appearing on talk shows and speaking at publishers' sales conferences. It's the in-between that is so difficult—actually writing the book. As the late, legendary sportswriter Red Smith once said, "There's nothing to writing. All you do is sit down at a typewriter and open a vein." It's also been said that a lot of people want *to have written* a book—not necessarily to write it.

Organization and common-sense planning are the key to the writing process. There is no such thing as too much planning and organization before you begin, but at some point you must begin *to write*.

An outline is essential. It will serve as your guide in the planning and writing stages of your manuscript. I generally recommend that your first outline for a nonfiction book should list all the topics and subject matter that will go into your book. Your first list should include everything you want to write about. You can eliminate the extraneous topics later. The first outline for an instructional tennis book, for example, would list serving, volleying, overhand strokes, backhand, forehand, and similar topics.

Step Two would be to organize your subject chronologically or in sequence. If you were writing a biography, your initial outline would highlight the major events of your subject's life. Your second outline would assemble this material in chronological order, and the third outline would be a listing of chapters. Outline #1 of a nonfiction book on staying slim or getting rich would include all the relevant topics you wish to include in your book. The second step would be to place these topics in sequence as they will appear in the book. Next, list your chapters and subheadings, numbering them appropriately. Examine other nonfiction books, particularly books on your subject, to see how the table of contents has been organized.

For a short, topical nonfiction book or a parody book, as opposed to a biographical, historical, or reference book, it is often practical to lay out a "dummy." Books are generally printed in signatures of 16 or 32 pages each, but offset signatures in today's modern printing presses now come in multiples of eight. If you envision a 32-, 48-, or 96-page paperback, you might fold the appropriate number of pieces of paper into a simulated book format. Then write what will be entered on each page: introduction, table of contents, copyright page, appendix, chapter one, chapter two, and so on. This simulation will discipline and organize your thoughts on paper, and indicate how much of your content will fit into your book, and where. The "dummy" is effective for a visual book, a children's picture book, a novelty book, a parody book, but obviously not for an historical saga or novel. Again, research the bookstores for best-selling formats similar to your own book.

The nonfiction book is easier to outline because it contains factual subject material. It is also similar in form and content to previously published books. Once you have your outline of contents, you can break it down into sequential chapters. When I worked with Paul Posnick and Arkady Leokum to write and publish *Where*

Words Were Born—an entertaining and educational book for children about word origins—we began with a master list of interesting words that we considered candidates for inclusion in our book. When we guesstimated the number of likely book pages, we figured that approximately one definition and one illustration would fill one two-page spread. We allowed room for an introduction, opening title, and copyright information, and then began to write and illustrate our word origins.

Another Pinnacle author, Elaine Partnow, aspired to be an actress and a creative writer. While seeking biographical material on female artists, she was startled to find how few women were repre-

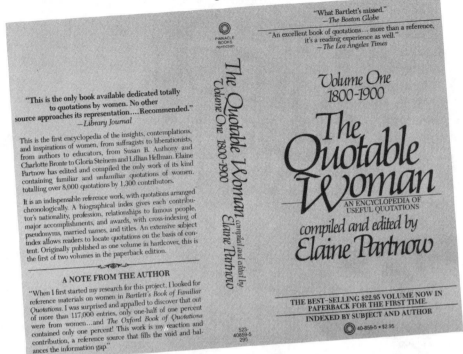

"What Bartlett's missed."
— *The Boston Globe*

"An excellent book of quotations... more than a reference, it's a reading experience as well."
— *The Los Angeles Times*

The Quotable Woman Volume One 1800-1900 compiled and edited by Elaine Partnow

Volume One 1800-1900

The Quotable Woman
AN ENCYCLOPEDIA OF USEFUL QUOTATIONS

compiled and edited by Elaine Partnow

"This is the only book available dedicated totally to quotations by women. No other source approaches its representation....Recommended."
— *Library Journal*

This is the first encyclopedia of the insights, contemplations, and inspirations of women, from suffragists to liberationists, from authors to educators, from Susan B. Anthony and Charlotte Bronte to Gloria Steinem and Lillian Hellman. Elaine Partnow has edited and compiled the only work of its kind containing familiar and unfamiliar quotations of women, totalling over 8,000 quotations by 1,300 contributors.

It is an indispensable reference work, with quotations arranged chronologically. A biographical index gives each contributor's nationality, profession, relationships to famous people, major accomplishments, and awards, with cross-indexing of pseudonyms, married names, and titles. An extensive subject index allows readers to locate quotations on the basis of content. Originally published as one volume in hardcover, this is the first of two volumes in the paperback edition.

A NOTE FROM THE AUTHOR

"When I first started my research for this project, I looked for reference materials on women in *Bartlett's Book of Familiar Quotations*. I was surprised and appalled to discover that out of more than 117,000 entries, only one-half of one percent were from women...and *The Oxford Book of Quotations* contained only one percent! This work is my reaction and contribution, a reference source that fills the void and balances the information gap."

THE BEST-SELLING $22.95 VOLUME NOW IN PAPERBACK FOR THE FIRST TIME.
INDEXED BY SUBJECT AND AUTHOR

40-859-5 • $2.95

523-40859-5 295

sented in anthologies of quotations. She began to record her idea on tape, and researched the market on other books of quotations.

When Elaine brought me her book proposal for *The Quotable Woman,* I found her and her subject stimulating and unusual. Thus began an author-publisher relationship that lasted four years. Elaine never lost her determination to produce one of the most monumental and enduring books of recent years.

She chose her female biographical subjects from the *Encyclopaedia Britannica* and planned her initial outline by writing down the woman's name, her accomplishments, her chronological period in history, and the famous quotations attributed to her. Later, the book was cross-indexed so that a reader could find a famous quotation in the biographical index or in the subject index. Elaine organized her chronology from 1800 to the present, and carefully selected her subjects and their representative quotes. It was a massive piece of research. When *The Quotable Woman* was finally published in 1977 by Corwin Books, it received the critical and commercial success those years of labor deserved. Spend as much time in researching your book as you need to become an expert on

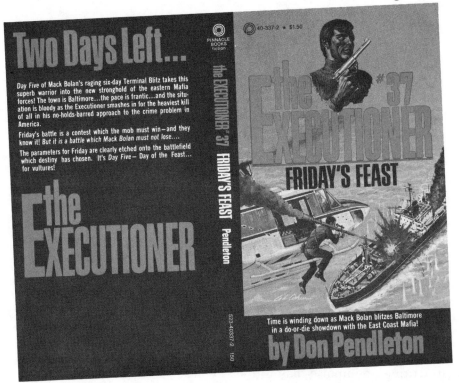

Two Days Left...

Day Five of Mack Bolan's raging six-day Terminal Blitz takes this superb warrior into the new stronghold of the eastern Mafia forces! The town is Baltimore...the pace is frantic...and the situation is bloody as the Executioner smashes in for the heaviest kill of all in his no-holds-barred approach to the crime problem in America.

Friday's battle is a contest which the mob must win—and they know it! But it is a battle which Mack Bolan must not lose....

The parameters for Friday are clearly etched onto the battlefield which destiny has chosen. It's *Day Five*—Day of the Feast... for vultures!

the EXECUTIONER

40-337-2 ★ $1.50
PINNACLE BOOKS fiction

the EXECUTIONER #37 FRIDAY'S FEAST Pendleton

523-40337-2 150

the EXECUTIONER #37

FRIDAY'S FEAST

Time is winding down as Mack Bolan blitzes Baltimore in a do-or-die showdown with the East Coast Mafia!

by Don Pendleton

your subject and to write a significant, definitive, and commercial outline or proposal.

An outline is just as vital in writing a novel. You should also make a separate list of characters, with their personality traits and descriptions. On the outline itself, include a chronology of the plot. If you're writing an historical novel or saga, you prepare a separate list of historical and other events in the period to sustain your story over as many years as you select. This list will suggest significant historical scenes and episodes relevant to your story plot. Before you have begun to write, you will have listed your plot, your characters, and your historical episodes on paper.

After you have prepared an initial outline, a list of events, and a list of characters, you can merge these into *one* outline. At this point you should know your basic plot, your subplots, your main characters, and the chronology of your story. You are ready to write your novel. The master commercial writers of our day—Harold Robbins, Sidney Sheldon, James Michener—use similar outline techniques before they begin to write.

As president of Pinnacle Books, I was fortunate to publish one of the most successful best-selling authors; Don Pendleton, who has written and sold over 30 million copies of his *Executioner* series throughout the world. The new titles in this continuously best-selling series are now published by Harlequin Books.

Since every *Executioner* volume features the supermacho protagonist, Mack Bolan, and a running generic plot of avenging Mafia crimes, Pendleton has adopted a different approach to preparing his popular novels. The special element of each *Executioner* is that each is set in a different locale. Pendleton chooses his setting carefully and spends several weeks there, walking city streets, frequenting neighborhood hangouts, and talking to the inhabitants. Once he has assimilated the mood and pulse of his new setting, characters begin to emerge in his mind—the heroes and the villains. Unlike many authors, he conceives no plot outline in advance, but rather begins to write each new *Executioner* novel after he has done his research. He writes only from past experience, without the help of a formal outline.

Pendleton refers to himself as a "gut writer," more accustomed to writing on impulse than to the structure of an outline. His extraordinary success nullifies any criticism of his personal writing habits.

The novelist Peter DeVries once commented, "I love being a writer. What I can't stand is the paperwork." But the paperwork is essential in preparing your book outline. You must organize your thoughts on paper and focus on the most important topics in your book by writing initial outlines. The reason for outlining both fiction and nonfiction books is to provide you with a clear understanding of what you want to write about. You can then eliminate whatever is superfluous, or perhaps belongs in another book you may write some day.

Let's take a typical example. One of the attendees at my UCLA seminar, "How To Become A Best-Selling Author," was noted Los Angeles pain therapist Dr. Judith Walker, head of the very successful Walker Pain Institute in Westwood (Los Angeles). Subsequently she came to me to discuss the creation of *her* best-seller. We researched the market on pain books and found most of them fairly dull and clinical. The only attractive and commercial pain book was written by an exercise teacher, not a physician.

Then we focused on the kind of book the market needed—a sound, lively, short book written by a medical authority. We chose our title at the outset: *Dr. Walker's 6-Week Permanent Pain Relief Program*. When we had a concept, a workable idea, and a title, I asked her first to do a comparison between her projected book and the competing published books.

Then I told her to list on one piece of paper all the essential topics she wanted her book to contain. This included headaches, backaches, nutrition, stress, muscle spasm, vitamin deficiency, infections, and numerous other subjects. We eliminated extraneous topics and put the remaining topics in a logical order. Then we broke this down into chapters entitled "Painproofing Your Office and Your Life," "Hormonal Factors," "Drugs and Muscle Spasms," and so on until we had prepared a formal chapter outline. We also prepared a section of questions and answers.

I found the title "Painproofing Your Office and Your Life" most interesting, and most suited to excerpting for magazine or newspaper serialization. I asked Dr. Walker to write this as our sample chapter.

I'm pleased to report that on the basis of a definitive outline, a best-selling title, one excellent and commercial chapter, and the author's credentials, we succeeded in signing a publishing contract with a New York publisher.

● ● ●

I'm often asked, "How much do I have to write before I get a contract?"

There is no precise answer. In nonfiction, a sound outline, a strong title and concept, and several chapters could spark a publisher's interest to buy. You will probably not have to write an entire book if the basic idea is salable.

In fiction, the opposite is more often true. Major New York publishers these days want to read finished novels, especially first novels. They maintain that they cannot judge the literary quality or commerciality of a first novel without reading all of it. Still, books have been bought on the basis of reading one chapter, five chapters, an entire manuscript. Primarily, a publisher must be able to make a commercial judgment based on the material submitted.

A word about discipline. I recommend that you adhere to a formal work schedule when writing and preparing your nonfiction book. Allot certain hours each day of the week to researching and outlining. Stay on a specific schedule.

As for fiction, I find it easier to write when my imagination is fertile and I am creatively high. At that point I write as much as I can; then wait for the next creative inspiration. I don't believe you can successfully write a prescribed number of pages of a novel each day. Work on your novel when your imagination is flowing. Don't write when it is not.

After you have completed your definitive outline of everything that will go into your book—whether fiction or nonfiction—you should begin by writing Chapter One and continue to write in chapter order. Sooner or later you will have to *write* that first draft of your book. It is important to get it down on paper, so make that beginning and write it.

Whether you write in longhand or type your first draft, you should type up each chapter triple-spaced after you've written it. This arrangement will allow you to edit your manuscript as you proceed. The complete or partial manuscript that you present to the publisher should be clean and double-spaced, with all pages numbered.

I have often been asked, "At what point should I submit my manuscript?" Very simply, the answer is "When it is ready to be presented." You wouldn't go out to an important dinner or event only partially dressed. Don't submit a manuscript that isn't clean and neat and doesn't represent your best effort. Make the best presentation you can to the publisher you select—a well-organized, well-written, edited, thorough, and neat manuscript.

Only submit your book when *you* are completely satisfied that you have achieved your "best-seller" objectives. Write and revise your initial drafts to improve your book. Then I would advise showing it to at least one intimate "literary" friend for objective criticism before you submit. I am reminded of a budding author who asked his editor friend, "Approximately how many words are there in an average novel?" The editor replied, "Oh, about 60,000 words." "Thank God," the author declared. "I'm finished."

●●●●●●●●●●●●●●●●●●●●●

How and Where Do I Submit My Book?

4. You've now conceived enough of a presentable manuscript to submit to a publisher. If you don't have an agent, lawyer, or manager (see the next chapter if you do), you will need to know where, how, and to whom to submit.

It is important to ask yourself which publishing houses might be interested in *your* manuscript. You must ask yourself again, "Is there a need for this book?" You will certainly have to overcome skeptical reactions if your subject is *another* book on tennis or jogging. A promising author recently submitted a book idea to me on Elvis Presley. The market was inundated with Elvis books, and I expressed strong doubt. "But this one is different," she pleaded. Remember that if a subject is too redundant for the publisher or the market, or if it's limited to a narrow segment of the public, the publisher cannot afford to risk publication.

One of the best places to do research about a likely publisher for your book is the bookstore. The large Dalton and Walden stores in most major malls are probably the best bookstores for research or you may want to talk to the proprietor of your neighborhood mom-and-pop bookstore about market ideas and trends. Assiduous browsing in the store is time well spent and it is absolutely free. You can perceive at a glance the general competition for *your* book, the package it comes in, and the retail price. You can also find out whether too many books on your subject have been published recently. In addition, you can learn which publishing houses are publishing your kind of book. Price/Stern/Sloan and Workman generally feature humor books in trade (large-size) paperback format. MacMillan, Tarcher, and Rawson often feature "how-to," popular psychology, and self-improvement books. Dow Jones/Irwin publishes business books. HP Books specializes in cookbooks; Arco in career guides; Contemporary Books in sports.

When you leave the bookstore, you should have some idea of the most suitable publisher for your book. It could be a large prestigious house or a smaller, specialized publisher. If you think you have found a compatible publisher, a house that might be receptive to your book, go from the bookstore to a library and refer to *Literary Market Place (LMP), Writer's Market, Publishers Weekly,* and the *Publisher's Trade List Annual.* Look up the publisher you have selected. Note their areas of specialization, and record their mailing address and the name of a specific editor in the trade or general editorial department to whom you can submit personally by mail. It may be the editor-in-chief, editorial director, executive editor, or managing editor. In a small house it may be the publisher or president. It is not essential to submit to a particular type of editor as long as you submit to an actual person. A phone call will tell you if that person is still with that company. You are now ready to make contact with "your" editor.

Editors in large publishing houses are swamped with bulky manuscripts, both solicited and unsolicited. These go into a large pile until some reader can glance over them. At best, this waiting period could take months. The manuscript for *Jonathan Livingston Seagull* was submitted to almost twenty publishers over a span of two years before an enterprising editor committed her company to the book. Do not submit your *manuscript* to the editor, unless it is a short humor or novelty book. Your initial solicitation to an editor should take the form of a great query letter asking for interest in your idea or book proposal. If it is short, crisp, and cogent, it will be read quickly and answered.

Your query letter should explain a little about your book idea and the special features that make your book special and commercially feasible. In other words, sell your idea. Make it a pleasant but hard-sell letter. You've got this great subject, it has best-seller potential, and you're offering it to Ms. or Mr. Editor first. Sell your book idea and your premise in your query letter so that the editor will be interested and ask you to submit the sample manuscript. Your query letter is designed to evoke a favorable response to move your manuscript out of the slush pile into an editor's briefcase. In your letter you should also state how your proposed book differs from the competition and what is special about it. Publishers are constantly looking for fresh ideas. If you mention your terrific title, commercial idea, special approach, and understanding of the marketplace in your query letter, you can gain the "best-seller edge" at the publisher's level. If you receive a positive reply, the *next* step is to submit your manuscript.

The query letter should be typewritten and double-spaced on either your personal stationery or on plain white typing paper. The salutation should address the editor by name: Dear Ms. or Mr. _____.

Describe your book in letter form, imagining that you have only thirty seconds on a national talk show to sell it to the American public. The query letter should be no more than a page long. If you have supplementary material relevant to your submission—a recent clipping about you, an article from a newspaper or magazine about your subject—by all means include it with your query.

● ● ●

The book proposal is slightly different from your query. (A sample proposal and query letter can be found in the Appendix.) The proposal includes a cover letter stating what's attached, a table of contents, an introduction, and perhaps a definitive treatment or overview (two to ten pages long) that explains "why this book?" Include visual materials, forewords, quotes, or charts, if relevant.

In both queries and proposals, make sure you emphasize what is special and commercial about your book idea. Your proposal will not evoke a positive reaction if it is "just another proposal." It has to be different—and commercial—to be worthy of publication interest.

If your idea is rejected like Richard Bach's idea for *Jonathan*, don't give up. Go on to the next publisher on your list, or submit to several simultaneously. I would recommend three or four at the most. Submitting to one publisher at a time may involve months of waiting for a response. If one or two rejection letters suggest that your proposal is not a good one, change it before the next submission.

If your prospective book is a gimmick, fad, parody—a "non-book"—your presentation should be designed attractively. A sample cover and sample pages in the style and design of your book would definitely enhance your presentation. They will show an editor or a publisher what your physical book and layout will look like.

When you get a favorable response from an editor, he or she may want to see more material—several chapters, more detailed table of contents, the entire book. Send what you have, when it is good enough to send out. If several publishers have expressed interest, make multiple submissions, but let them know you are doing this.

If you have to write additional material, tell the editor when it will be forthcoming. If you have been rejected and you receive specific criticism, make the corrections and adjustments before submitting to the next publisher.

Don't ever give up. You may find your publisher on the first try or on the twentieth. It has happened often to many a best-seller. Patrick Dennis, the celebrated author of *Auntie Mame*, says of his submission experiences: "It circulated for five years, through the halls of fifteen publishers, and finally ended up with Vanguard Press, which, as you can see, is rather deep into the alphabet."

Do I Need One of Those Agents?

5. When I lecture to would-be authors or meet with writers or writers' groups, someone invariably asks if I think his or her manuscript is publishable and how and when it should be submitted. Inevitably, the next question is: "Do I need an agent?"

I respond with a pat though somewhat facetious answer: "If a manuscript is worthy of commercial publication, it will make no difference whether or not you have an agent. If it is not, it will make no difference whether or not you have an agent."

Like a real estate or insurance agent or a stock broker, if a literary agent is honest, aggressive, and effective, it can be quite advantageous to retain his or her services. If a good publication deal can be made, your agent will be justified in taking ten or fifteen percent of the proceeds off the top. But only you can answer the question: "Is an agent worthy of sharing my publishing income in perpetuity?"

Jack Benny's classic remark, "If you took all the sincerity in Hollywood, it would fill 10 percent of an agent's navel . . ." categorically demeaned Hollywood, the glamour business, and agents in general. Literary agents, perhaps a breed apart, have often been characterized as pretentious, insincere, and unscrupulous. Some are, but most are hard-working, shrewd deal makers with an inimitable ability to find the right editor and the right publisher for the appropriate manuscript. Agents, like other people, come in all genders, all ages, all sizes. Some are highly respected and sought after by the publishers for the properties and authors they represent. Some depend on hype and hustle, and deserve the nefarious reputations they have established. Others are known for creating best-sellers.

I recommend that you appraise your manuscript and your contacts to determine whether you can achieve publication without relying on an agent. If you believe your book is commercial and publishable *and* if you have your own contacts in the publishing world, then you may opt not to retain an agent. You don't inevitably need one. If you feel more optimistic and secure about finding a publisher through an agent, you should conduct your search as if you were choosing a broker or an attorney. Ask friends and publishing acquaintances, published authors, or (again) consult *Literary Market Place* and *Writer's Market* to determine the most authentic working agents who are actively selling manuscripts.

There is no scientific basis for determining whether you should contact a publisher directly or use the services of an agent. This judgment is often based on instinct and common sense and your own feelings about whether an agent can perform for you as well as you can for yourself. Often it is difficult to secure the representation of an agent, but an initial rejection does not mean that your book is not publishable; nor does it mean the agent's acceptance necessarily improves your chances of publication. There are too many variables at work. And remember, finding or not finding an agent should not deter you from creating and writing a best-selling book. That is the essential objective; finding an agent is not.

Although the "New York agent" is the best known, there are effective literary agents on the West Coast and in other regions of the country. A number of agents work in major cities such as San Francisco, Boston, Atlanta, and Minneapolis. Jane Jordan Browne in

Chicago and Margaret McBride in San Diego are two of the better regional agents. They and other agents outside New York and Los Angeles handle books of national bestselling appeal. Although they work primarily with the major New York houses, their clientele is mainly in their particular geographic region. Many of these regional agents have been responsible for some recent national best-sellers; Margaret McBride sold *The One Minute Manager* out of San Diego.

Write to "your" prospective agent to discuss yourself and your manuscript. A friendly positive letter describing your book, much like your query letter to a publisher, will suffice. Proceed as if you were choosing a real estate agent to sell your house. Ask relevant publishing questions that come to mind, including what stable of writers the agent represents and what book properties the agent has sold recently. If possible, corroborate the agent's recent record by making whatever inquiries you can.

Choose an agent you feel is compatible with you and your manuscript. Agents specialize, as do publishers. Some are known for representing literary authors. Others specialize in commercial non-fiction ideas. Like the publishers, they are all looking for best-sellers. If you and your manuscript are comfortable in your new author-agent relationship, that is the major consideration. If Agent A does not match your objectives, go on to Agent B. Some agents work on a 10 percent fee, some on 15 percent, a few on 20 percent. Ask yours to justify the higher percentage in terms of what he or she will do for you. It *may* be worthwhile to pay more to get more. *Remember—an agent only gets paid if he makes a deal.*

The agent will ask you to sign a standard agent's agreement, granting exclusive representation of your manuscript for a specified period of time with an option to represent future books of yours. Do you now need a lawyer to interpret the agent's agreement? It wouldn't be a bad idea if you already have an attorney or know a lawyer familiar with this type of agreement, who could look it over. You want to be sure of what representation you are getting and what you are giving up. The basic agreement should reflect all the salient points you discussed with your new agent and the business terms you agreed upon.

When you reach the contract stage with a publisher, you will be assigning certain subsidiary rights (see Chapter Twenty). It is often customary, however, for you and your agent in tandem to control "live media rights," (usually including motion-picture, TV, dramatic, cable, recording, and other ancillary stage and screen rights). Your agent will make these prospective sales apart from the book rights he sold to the publisher. This should be to your advantage, because your agent should be as well attuned to the rights marketplace as he or she is to the publishers. Subsidiary rights can be very lucrative, so it is important that you and your agent retain as great a percentage of these rights as possible.

The agents who are particularly active in negotiating subsidiary-rights sales generally have experience in representing best-sellers. Film, TV, foreign, and other ancillary sales often portend the best-selling potential of a particular book. Your prospective "best-selling" agent should be knowledgeable about the lucrative rights market and be able to stimulate the publisher to spend promotional and advertising dollars on your forthcoming book.

A major subsidiary sale can often be the catalyst for a larger printing and an increased publicity-advertising budget, and can generate early enthusiasm inside a publishing house. When *Up The Down Staircase* was chosen by Book-of-the-Month Club, it sparked us to start thinking about a possible national best-seller. Your agent can affect your chances for best-sellerdom by negotiating a favorable contract for you, making some significant rights sales, and representing you and your book in the publisher's promotional and marketing decisions.

First and foremost, a good agent will attempt to place your book with the best and most appropriate publisher for you—a publisher that can get you on the best-seller lists.

● ● ●

Often it is not any easier to obtain an agent than a publisher. They are busy; they represent many authors; and they may not feel that your manuscript idea is marketable. Agents must apply the same criteria to manuscript selection as publishers do. An agent will undertake representation of your book only if he or she thinks it can be sold. If you are rejected by an agent, evaluate the reasons why. After you have made the necessary changes, you can resubmit to the same agent, solicit another one, or attempt to go directly to a publisher.

Many beginning authors are fortunate to sell first books on their own; then they seek agent representation. It is, of course, much easier to find an agent after you have achieved success.

The best agents are those who work most effectively for you. On the basis of their track records in creating and marketing best-sellers, I would recommend the following agents or agencies:

NEW YORK

Dominick Abel
Julian Bach
Georges Borchardt
Brandt & Brandt
Curtis Brown
James Brown
Knox Burger
Shirley Burke
Connie Clausen
Collier Associates
Richard Curtis
Anita Diamant
Candida Donadio
Lyle Engel
Jay Garon-Brooke
Sanford J. Greenburger
I.C.M—Monica McCall
       Lynn Nesbit
       Arlene Donovan
Robert Lantz
Sterling Lord
Elaine Markson
Harold Matson
Scott Meredith
William Morris—Owen Laster
Harold Ober
Arthur Pine
Aaron Priest

Paul R. Reynolds
Kathy Robbins
Nat Sobel
Writer's House—Albert Zuckerman

LOS ANGELES

Adams, Ray & Rosenberg
Eisenbach & Greene
Andrew Ettinger
Dorris Halsey
Mike Hamilburg
Candace Lake
Irving Paul Lazar
H.N. Swanson
Ziegler, Diskant

REGIONAL AGENTS

Jane Jordan Browne—Chicago
Margaret McBride—San Diego
Larry Sternig—Milwaukee

A new breed of hyphenate—the *agent-lawyer*—has appeared on the publishing scene in recent years. Since negotiations for major literary properties have become so complicated in a legal sense, it was inevitable that the Sidney Sheldons and Harold Robbinses needed more legal than literary representation. Both needs were ultimately filled by the new agent-lawyer, in a natural extension of the basic agent's role. The most noteworthy of these new hyphenates are Paul Gitlin, Morton Janklow (who represents Judith Krantz), and Charles Rembar on the East Coast, and Don Engel on the West Coast. Let us hope that you will soon have a complicated legal contract to negotiate with your next publisher.

The Top Publishing Houses

6. The following "hot chart" lists my own selections of the best publishing companies in America today. Included are the strengths of each particular house, their key authors, and the personnel who make the publishing and editorial decisions. Several caveats: the lists, particularly of key personnel, are likely to be out of date in another year and will require updating. Also, there is no scientific basis for this selection. It is based solely on my *own* judgments and analyses of the book-publishing industry in this country. The houses I chose have generally achieved their position of dominance by years of performance in publishing and marketing bestsellers and commercial books, by the authors they signed to long-term contracts, and by the addition of personnel who changed the image or the editorial direction of the house. The imprints noted for each house are separate lines, imprimaturs, or colophons that a larger publisher uses as trademarks; Silhouette Books, for example, is the romance line or imprint of Pocket Books. Chapter Ten will discuss the effect of imprints in publishing today.

HARDCOVER HOUSES

ARBOR HOUSE
(Sub. of Hearst Corp.)
300 E. 44th Street
New York, NY 10017
212/687-9855

Best-selling Authors:	Gerald Browne, Irwin Shaw, Cynthia Freeman, Herbert Mitgang, Margaret Truman, Gwen Davis, Sloan Wilson, Ann Pinchot
Recent Best-sellers:	*No Time for Tears; Acceptable Losses; 19 Purchase Street; Murder in the Smithsonian; La Brava*
Key Personnel:	Eden Collinsworth, Arnold Erhlich
Strengths:	Primarily commercial novels; numerous best-selling authors
Titles Annually:	100

CROWN PUBLISHERS, INC.
One Park Avenue
New York, NY 10016
212/532-9200

Imprints:	Harmony; Clarkson Potter; Outlet Book Co.
Best-selling Authors:	Jean Auel, Simon Bond, Judith Krantz, Douglas Adams, Trevanian

Recent Best-sellers:	*Mistral's Daughter; 101 Uses for a Dead Cat; The Valley of Horses; Where Have I Been?; The Summer of Katya; The F-Plan Diet; Shield of Three Lions; Ogilvy on Advertising*
Key Personnel:	Alan Mirken, Nat Wartels, Bruce Harris, Betty Prashker
Strengths:	Novels, juvenile, remainders, gift books, "nothing" books; strong marketing and mail-order operations.
Titles Annually:	600

DOUBLEDAY PUBLISHING CO.
245 Park Avenue
New York, NY 10017
212/953-4561

Imprints:	Anchor; Dolphin; Image Books; Dial Press
Best-selling Authors:	Craig Claiborne, William F. Buckley, Isaac Asimov, Victoria Holt, Leon Uris, Irving Wallace, Stephen King, Wilbur Smith
Recent Best-sellers:	*The Neverending Story; Atlantic High; The Almighty; The Angels Weep; Foundation's Edge; The Foxfire Books; Voice of the Heart; Pet Sematary*

Key Personnel:	Sam Vaughan, Walter Freese, Ted Marci, Loretta Barrett
Strengths:	Book clubs; religious and inspirational books; large editorial list, strong sales staffs, backlist
Titles Annually:	600

E.P. DUTTON, INC.
2 Park Avenue
New York, NY 10016
212/725-1818

Imprints:	Elsevier-Dutton; Everyman's Library; Hawthorn; Foxfire Press; Obelisk
Best-selling Authors:	Joyce Carol Oates, John Irving, Donald Barthelme, Stanley Elkin, Caroline Bird, Cynthia Ozick
Recent Best-sellers:	*A Boy's Own Story; A Different Woman; Lana; Significa; The James Beard Cookbook*
Key Personnel:	Joseph Kanon, Bill Whitehead
Strengths:	Juvenile; high-quality editorial list
Titles Annually:	150

**FARRAR, STRAUS &
GIROUX, INC.**
19 Union Square West
New York, NY 10003
212/741-6900

Imprints:	Hill & Wang; Octagon Books
Best-selling Authors:	Bernard Malamud, Walker Percy, Tom Wolfe, Pablo Neruda, Alexandr Solzhenitsyn, John McPhee, Philip Roth, Isaac Bashevis Singer
Recent Best-sellers:	*The Purple Decades; God's Grace; The Anatomy Lesson; Yentl the Yeshiva Boy*
Key Personnel:	Roger Straus, Michael DiCapua
Strengths:	High-quality literary works, prestigious authors
Titles Annually:	100

HARCOURT BRACE JOVANOVICH, INC.
1250 6th Avenue
San Diego, CA 92101
619/231-6616

Imprints:	Helen and Kurt Wolff
Best-selling Authors:	John Jakes, Helen MacInnes, Irving Howe, Georges Simenon, Mark Helprin
Recent Best-sellers:	*A Margin of Hope; The Day Is Short; Cloak of Darkness; North and South; The Name of the Rose; Winter's Tale*
Key Personnel:	William Jovanovich, Peter

	Jovanovich, Julian P. Muller, Irene Skolnick
Strengths:	Fiction, general books, textbooks, juvenile; diversity of publishing, backlist
Titles Annually:	800

HOLT, RINEHART & WINSTON
(CBS Publishing)
521 Fifth Avenue
New York, NY 10175
212/872-2000

Imprints:	Owl Books; Praeger; W.B. Saunders; Webb and Bower
Best-selling Authors:	Charles Schulz, Leo Buscaglia, Skip Morrow, G.B. Trudeau, Pauline Kael, Dee Brown, John Knowles
Recent Best-sellers:	*The G Spot; The Fall of Freddie the Leaf; The Country Diary of an Edwardian Lady; Living, Loving & Learning; Outrageous Acts and Everyday Rebellions; The Rosenberg File*
Key Personnel:	Richard Seaver, Miriam Chaikin, John Macrae III, Jane Pasanen
Strengths:	Strong humor titles; well-bal-

anced line of fiction and non-fiction

Titles Annually: 500

HOUGHTON MIFFLIN CO.
One Beacon Street
Boston, MA 02107
617/725-5000

Imprints: Clarion; J.P. Tarcher; Ticknor & Fields

Best-selling Authors: Howard Fast, Susan Cheever, Roger Tory Peterson, J.R.R. Tolkien, Judith Rossner, Paul Theroux

Recent Best-sellers: *Christina's World; The Puzzle Palace; Unfinished Tales; August; The Anatomy of Power; Kingdom by the Sea*

Key Personnel: Richard Gladstone, Austin Olney, Nan Talese, Robie Macauley

Strengths: Travel, reference; general quality of list; tradition of publishing best-selling authors

Titles Annually: 350

ALFRED A. KNOPF, INC.
(Sub. of Random House)
201 E. 50th Street
New York, NY 10022
212/751-2600

Best-selling Authors:	John LeCarré, John Updike, William Wharton, Miss Piggy, Len Deighton, John Cheever, Chaim Potok, Anne Tyler, Michael Crichton, Nora Ephron
Recent Best-sellers:	*The Fate of the Earth; Miss Piggy's Guide to Life; Dinner at the Homesick Restaurant; The Path to Power; Edie; Berlin Game; Heartburn; A Private View; The Little Drummer Girl; Hugging the Shore*
Key Personnel:	Robert Gottlieb, Nina Bourne, Ash Green
Strengths:	Literary works, prestigious authors; high-quality production
Titles Annually:	150

LITTLE, BROWN & CO.
34 Beacon Street
Boston, MA 02106
617/227-0730

Imprints:	Atlantic Monthly Press
Best-selling Authors:	Norman Mailer, John Fowles, Evelyn Waugh, William Manchester
Recent Best-sellers:	*Ancient Evenings; Blue Highways; The Last Lion; Bloom County; Family Trade; One Brief Shining Moment; The Auerbach Will*

Key Personnel:	Robert E. Ginna, Jr., Henry O. Houghton, Jr.
Strengths:	Good backlist; prestigious authors
Titles Annually:	300

WILLIAM MORROW & CO., INC.
105 Madison Avenue
New York, NY 10016
212/889-3050

Imprints:	Quill; Lothrop Lee & Shepard; Greenwillow
Best-selling Authors:	Joseph Wambaugh, Sidney Sheldon, Ken Follett, Laurence Peter, Steve Shagan, Temple Fielding, Gail Sheehy, Morris West
Recent Best-sellers:	*On Wings of Eagles; The One Minute Manager; Master of the Game; The Circle; The World is Made of Glass; Who Killed the Robins Family?; Lines and Shadows.*
Key Personnel:	Larry Hughes, Sherry Arden, Jim Landis, Al Marchioni, Pat Golbitz
Strengths:	Best-selling authors; strong promotion and subsidiary rights
Titles Annually:	350

THE PUTNAM PUBLISHING
GROUP
200 Madison Avenue
New York, NY 10016
212/576-8900

Imprints:	G.P. Putnam's Sons; Coward-McCann; Grosset & Dunlap; Quick Fox; Perigee Books
Best-selling Authors:	Frank Herbert, William Kotzwinkle, Art Buchwald, Alexandra Penney, Peter Straub, Lawrence Sanders, Jacqueline Briskin, Judy Blume, Dick Francis
Recent Best-sellers:	*E.T. The Extra-Terrestrial Storybook; The White Plague; Crisis; How to Make Love to Each Other; The Seduction of Peter S.; Godplayer; Everything and More; Icebreaker; Fatal Vision; Dream West;* and *. . . And Ladies of the Club.*
Key Personnel:	Peter Israel, Phyllis Grann, Ellis Amburn, Harriet Blacker
Strengths:	Juvenile, how-to; many best-selling authors; strong parent company (MCA) backing; editorial; diversified imprints
Titles Annually:	300

RANDOM HOUSE, INC.
201 E. 50th Street
New York, NY 10022
212/751-2600

Imprints:	Beginner Books; Vintage; Pantheon; Modern Library; Villard Books
Best-selling Authors:	Robert Ludlum, James Michener, Martin Cruz Smith, Truman Capote, William Styron, Dr. Seuss, Jim Fixx, Norman Mailer
Recent Best-sellers:	*Poland; The Parsifal Mosaic; With Enough Shovels; This Quiet Dust; Return of the Jedi; The Discoverers*
Key Personnel:	Robert Bernstein, Anthony Schulte, Jason Epstein, Mildred Marmur, Marc Jaffe
Strengths:	Vintage paperbacks, juvenile; production and high-quality editorial; numerous best-selling authors; exceptionally diversified editorial list
Titles Annually:	550

SIMON & SCHUSTER, INC.
1230 Avenue of the Americas
New York, NY 10020
212/245-6400

Imprints:	Linden Press; Monarch; Summit; Julian Messner; Wanderer

	Books; Cornerstone Library; Fireside; Frommer; Touchstone
Best-selling Authors:	Jeffrey Archer, Graham Greene, Leo Rosten, Harold Robbins, Elie Wiesel, J.K. Lasser, Mary Higgins Clark, Larry McMurtry, William Peter Blatty, Albert Lowry, Robert Allen
Recent Best-sellers:	*Jane Fonda's Workout Book; Having It All; The Prodigal Daughter; The Warlord; Legion; Creating Wealth; Linda Evans Beauty and Exercise Book; Hollywood Wives; Monimbo; Mayor*
Key Personnel:	Richard Snyder, Dan Green, Michael Korda, Joni Evans, Jim Silberman
Strengths:	Outstanding distribution, editorial, advertising, marketing operations; considerable number of best-selling authors
Titles Annually:	500

ST. MARTIN'S PRESS, INC.
175 Fifth Avenue
New York, NY 10010
212/674-5151

Best-selling Authors:	James Herriot, Russell Baker, Mary Ellen Pinkham, Harry Stein, M.M. Kaye

Recent Best-sellers:	*Growing Up; Isak Dinesen; Dreams Die Hard; Battlefield Earth; Death in Kenya; Golden Boy; The Best of James Herriot*
Key Personnel:	Tom McCormack, Leslie Pockell, Charles Hayward, Richard Marek, Toni Lopopolo
Strengths:	Large title output; strong library sales
Titles Annually:	600

THE VIKING PRESS
40 West 23rd Street
New York, NY 10010
212/807-7300

Imprints:	Penguin; Viking Portable; Studio Books
Best-selling Authors:	Stephen King, Saul Bellow, Frederick Forsythe, D.M. Thomas, Judith Guest, Walter Lord
Recent Best-sellers:	*The White Hotel; Different Seasons; Second Heaven; Christine; Grand Delusions; Unto This Hour; The Tao of Pooh*
Key Personnel:	Peter Mayer, Alan Williams, Constance Sayre, Alan Kellock, Kathryn Court

Strengths: Many best-selling authors;
                                    high-quality production

Titles Annually: 300

PAPERBACK HOUSES

AVON BOOKS
(Sub. of Hearst Corp.)
1790 Broadway
New York, NY 10019
212/399-4500

Imprints: Bard; Camelot; Discus

Best-selling Authors: Rosemary Rogers, Kathleen
                                    Woodiwiss, Colleen McCul-
                                    lough, Richard Bach

Recent Best-sellers: *Items from Our Catalog; A
                                    Rose in Winter; An Indecent
                                    Obsession; The Soul of a New
                                    Machine; The People's Phar-
                                    macy; Acceptable Losses;
                                    Heart of Thunder*

Key Personnel: Walter Meade, Page Cuddy,
                                    Sabra Elliott, Suzanne Jaffe

Strengths: High-quality literary and juve-
                                    nile lines

Titles Annually: 300

BALLANTINE BOOKS, INC.
(Sub. of Random House)
201 East 50th Street
New York, NY 10022
212/751-2600

Imprints:	Fawcett; Gold Medal; Del Rey
Best-selling Authors:	Jim Davis, James Michener, John Updike, Martin Cruz Smith, John MacDonald, Stephen Donaldson
Recent Best-sellers:	*Garfield; 2010: Odyssey Two; Chameleon; Color Me Beautiful; Elfstones of Shannara; Gorky Park; Ride the Wind; Truly Tasteless Jokes; Return of the Jedi; White Gold Wielder; Friday; Space*
Key Personnel:	Susan Petersen, Judy-Lynn Del Rey, Leona Nevler, Robert Wyatt
Strengths:	Original and reprint fiction and nonfiction, trade paperback, humor, science fiction, Garfield; established author list
Titles Annually:	400

BANTAM BOOKS, INC.
666 Fifth Avenue
New York, NY 10103
212/765-6500

Imprints:	Peacock; Perigord Press; Skylark; Windsong
Best-selling Authors:	Barbara Cartland, Louis L'Amour, Jerzy Kozinski, Robert Ludlum, John Saul, Dana Fuller Ross, John LeCarré
Recent Best-sellers:	*Keeping Faith; The 13th Valley; The Umpire Strikes Back; Thin Thighs in 30 Days; Red Dragon; Sophie's Choice; The Lonesome Gods; Out on a Limb; The Valley of Horses*
Key Personnel:	Jack Romanos, Linda Grey, Alun Davies, Ron Buehl, Lou Wolfe
Strengths:	Juvenile, classics, trade paperback, hardcover, reprint and original fiction; excellent backlist, sales, marketing, and promotion
Titles Annually:	600

BERKLEY PUBLISHING CORPORATION
(Sub. of MCA)
200 Madison Avenue
New York, NY 10016
212/686-9820

Imprints:	Jove; Ace; Charter; Playboy; First Chance At Love
Best-selling Authors:	Lawrence Sanders, Frank Her-

bert, Robert Heinlein, Peter Straub

Recent Best-sellers:

E.T.; The Third Deadly Sin; Danse Macabre; The Case Of Lucy Bending; The White Plague; The One Minute Manager; 19 Purchase Street; Wrap Me in Splendor

Key Personnel:

Rena Wolner, Roger Cooper, Nancy Coffey

Strengths:

Romance, science fiction, astrology; numerous imprints

Titles Annually:

600

DELL PUBLISHING CO., INC.
(Sub. of Doubleday)
One Dag Hammarskjold Plaza
New York, NY 10017

Imprints:

Delacorte Press; Yearling; Delta; Laurel Editions; Purse Books

Best-selling Authors:

James Clavell, Judy Blume, Irwin Shaw, Rona Jaffe, Howard Fast, Kurt Vonnegut, Danielle Steel, Thomas Berger

Recent Best-sellers:

Deadeye Dick; Life Sentences; The Legacy; Crossings; Bread Upon the Waters; Palomino; Thurston House; Eden Burning; Changes; Max

Key Personnel:	Carole Baron, Susan Moldow, Nick Ellison
Strengths:	Purse books, crosswords; numerous best-selling authors; Dell Yearling juvenile line; well-diversified list
Titles Annually:	650

THE NEW AMERICAN LIBRARY, INC.
1633 Broadway
New York, NY 10019
212/397-8000

Imprints:	Signet; Mentor; Plume; Meridian; DAW
Best-selling Authors:	Robin Cook, Stephen King, Ken Follett, Erica Jong, Len Deighton
Recent Best-sellers:	*Cujo; Fever; The Man from St. Petersburg; Family Trade; Different Seasons; Touch the Devil; Ellis Island; 1984; Christine*
Key Personnel:	Robert Diforio, Elaine Koster, Maryann Palumbo, Maureen Baron
Strengths:	Reprints, science fiction; backlist and classics; school and library sales
Titles Annually:	400

POCKET BOOKS
(Sub. of Simon & Schuster)
1230 Avenue of the Americas
New York, NY 10020
212/246-2121

Imprints:	Silhouette; Washington Square Press; Archway; Timescape; Long Shadow Books, Poseidon Press
Best-selling Authors:	John Irving, D.M. Thomas, Herman Wouk, V.C. Andrews, Zane Grey, Janet Dailey
Recent Best-sellers:	*Real Men Don't Eat Quiche; The Restaurant at the End of the Universe; The Winds of War; The White Hotel; The Color Purple; Spellbinder; Lace*
Key Personnel:	Ron Busch, Martin Asher, Peter Minichiello, William Grose
Strengths:	Silhouette Romances, reference; outstanding promotion and covers; established backlist; strong original title list
Titles Annually:	400

WARNER BOOKS, INC.
666 Fifth Avenue
New York, NY 10103
212/484-8000

Imprints:	Popular Library

Best-selling Authors:	Richard Simmons, Richard Nixon, Jackie Collins, Jennifer Wilde, Valerie Sherwood, Sidney Sheldon, Theodore H. White
Recent Best-sellers:	*Life Extension; Megatrends; A Few Minutes with Andy Rooney; Chances; Master of the Game; A Whack on the Side of the Head; In Search of Excellence; Men Are Just Desserts*
Key Personnel:	Howard Kaminsky, Dorothy Crouch, Mark Greenberg, Bernard Shir-Cliff, Larry Kirshbaum
Strengths:	Hardcover and trade paperback publishing program; major promotion and advertising; parent company (Warner Communications) media tie-ins
Titles Annually:	400

SMALLER HIGH-QUALITY PUBLISHERS

Publisher:	HARRY ABRAMS
City & State:	New York City
Key Personnel:	Paul Gottlieb
Area of Specialization:	Art
Best-sellers:	*Gnomes*
	Walt Disney's Epcot

Publisher:	ANDREWS & McMEEL
City & State:	Fairway, Kansas
Key Personnel:	John McMeel
Area of Specialization:	Syndicated comic characters
Best-sellers:	*Ziggy*
	Doonesbury

Publisher:	BRADBURY PRESS
City & State:	Scarsdale, New York
Key Personnel:	Robert Verrone
Area of Specialization:	Children's books
Best-sellers:	Judy Blume titles

Publisher:	DODD, MEAD/EVEREST HOUSE
City & State:	New York City
Key Personnel:	Lew Gillenson
	Jerry Gross
Area of Specialization:	Trade, hardcover
Best-sellers:	*Danse Macabre*
	The Peter Pan Syndrome

Publisher:	M. EVANS
City & State:	New York City
Key Personnel:	Herb Katz
Area of Specialization:	Trade, hardcover
Best-seller:	*Aerobics*

Publisher:	H P BOOKS
City & State:	Tucson, Arizona
Key Personnel:	Bill Fisher

Area of Specialization:	Cookery
Best-sellers:	*Crockery Cookbook*
	Microwave Cookbook
Publisher:	THE MAIN STREET PRESS
City & State:	Pittstown, New Jersey
Key Personnel:	Lawrence Grow
	Martin Greif
Area of Specialization:	Calendars, gay publications
Best-seller:	Gay calendars
Publisher:	THE OVERLOOK PRESS
City & State:	New York City
Key Personnel:	Mark Gompertz
Area of Specialization:	Nonfiction
Best-seller:	*The Book of Five Rings*
Publisher:	PRICE/STERN/SLOAN
City & State:	Los Angeles, California
Key Personnel:	Larry Sloan
	Charles Gates
Area of Specialization:	Humor and novelty; children's books
Best-sellers:	*Murphy's Law*
	Mad Libs
Publisher:	STEIN & DAY
City & State:	Briarcliff Manor, New York
Key Personnel:	Sol Stein
	Patricia Day
Area of Specialization:	Fiction
Best-sellers:	Jack Higgins titles
Publisher:	STERLING PUBLISHING CO.
City & State:	New York City
Key Personnel:	Burt Hobson
	Lincoln Boehm
Area of Specialization:	How-to, crafts
Best-seller:	*Guinness Book of World Records*

Publisher:	J.P. TARCHER
City & State:	Los Angeles, California
Key Personnel:	Jeremy Tarcher
Area of Specialization:	Popular psychology
Best-seller:	*Drawing on the Right Side of the Brain*

Publisher:	TEN SPEED PRESS
City & State:	Berkeley, California
Key Personnel:	Philip Wood
Area of Specialization:	Career guides
Best-seller:	*What Color Is Your Parachute?*

Publisher:	FRANKLIN WATTS
City & State:	New York City
Key Personnel:	Jon Gillett
	Jeanne Vestal
Area of Specialization:	Juvenile, nonfiction
Best-sellers:	*How to Win a Pullet Surprise*
	Love, Sex and the Single Man

Publisher:	WILSHIRE BOOK CO.
City & State:	North Hollywood, California
Key Personnel:	Melvin Powers
Area of Specialization:	Self-help
Best-seller:	*The Magic of Thinking Big*

Publisher:	WORKMAN PUBLISHING
City & State:	New York City
Key Personnel:	Peter Workman
	Bert Snyder
Area of Specialization:	Humor
Best-sellers:	*The Official Preppy Handbook*
	Chocolate

Publisher:	THE WORLD ALMANAC
City & State:	New York City
Key Personnel:	Jane Flatt
Area of Specialization:	Reference
Best-seller:	*The World Almanac*

•••••••••••••••••••••

You and Your Publisher—A Marriage

7. You've now been contacted by a reputable (based on your findings in book reviews, bookstores, etc.) publisher to discuss the publication of your book. It is an exciting, gratifying moment—the fulfillment of your efforts to turn your manuscript into a published reality. If it's a new experience, you'll be strongly tempted to accept their offer, but that may not be wise.

Apart from the specific negotiations (see Chapter 9), choosing a publisher is somewhat comparable to selecting a partner for marriage. All publishers are not the same and do not perform the same functions. It is vital to your long-term writing interests to establish a compatible relationship with your publisher at the outset. Like other companies in other businesses, publishers excel in different areas of specialization. You will have to choose wisely; *your* manuscript and *your* future are at stake. Your agent or author or publisher friend may be able to guide your selection. It is important to ascertain what *your* publisher intends to do for you. Most major New

York publishers issue several hundred books a year. Some of the largest, such as Doubleday and St. Martin's Press, publish over 500 titles a year. Without editorial care, sales enthusiasm, or proper promotion or advertising, your first book could easily be lost in the shuffle.

In your initial contact with the publisher you will deal with a specific individual, usually the editor who acquired your manuscript. You may be published under the imprint of a particular publisher and work with an individual imprint editor (see Chapter Ten). It is virtually impossible to deal personally with a Doubleday or a Random House. They are giant publishing monoliths. In time, perhaps after future successes, it will be important for you to meet with the marketing, sales, and promotional personnel of the publishing house. But for now, you will have to confine your judgments and evaluations of your publisher-to-be to their reputation and to your rapport with the editor.

It is essential to gauge the publisher's enthusiasm for your project. One criterion, of course, is the amount of money they will pay you as an advance against royalties. It is generally true that the higher the advance, the greater a publisher's commitment to a book. But there are exceptions. Sometimes an escalated royalty scale (see Chapter Nine) or large promotional or sales commitments can be criteria for signing with a particular house. In addition, the enthusiasm of the editor or other company executives, the special qualities of your manuscript, its marketability, the timing, and other variables can motivate a publisher to strive to create a best-seller. Ask the publisher, tactfully but candidly, how they plan to launch your book. Is their publication campaign similar to other best-sellers they have launched?

When I published Patricia Matthews' first book, we believed in the book from the outset, and were committed to promoting it toward bestsellerdom. We transmitted our enthusiasm to the sales reps and ultimately to the marketplace. Our unflagging faith in the book made a best-seller happen. Everyone in the company read the book and generated our personal enthusiasm along to editorial and sales executives. We were dedicated to launching a best-seller.

Authors with proven successes can dictate contract clauses that guarantee them a promotional allowance and advertising expenditures, but it is highly improbable that a new author will obtain such guarantees. A great deal of the initial relationship is simply predicated on good faith, mutual optimism, and your editor's belief in the book.

The publisher hopes that the manuscript they ultimately receive is similar to the one for which they entered into contract. All too often the publisher's original enthusiasm is dissipated when an anticipated best-seller does not materialize. I've seen many a would-be best-seller get "lost" in a house when the publisher is no longer excited about its potential, generally because the finished manuscript did not live up to original expectations. On other occasions, the publication of similar competing books diluted the best-selling marketplace for the author's book. This problem can be avoided if you communicate regularly with your editor while you're writing the manuscript and if you continue to study the book marketplace for trends and publications on *your* subject. You and the publisher should not be surprised by competing books or market changes.

A book enjoys a rather short market and shelf life, unfortunately, because the "literary" business today is mercurial at best and depends on instant success and a quick return on investment. Since the retailer and the wholesaler buy on consignment, what doesn't sell is returned (almost too soon) to the publisher. To endure in the consumer marketplace, *your* book will require a combination of favorable reviews, word-of-mouth recommendation, author publicity, publisher promotion, and a lot of luck and timing. The "marriage" can last almost forever, or about thirty days (the average shelf life of a mass-market paperback), or about three months, the average display life of a new hardcover publication.

After the publisher has expressed formal interest in your manuscript, follow the same advice I offered for choosing an agent. Check out the publisher's recent best-seller successes and see whether they have any books on the best-seller lists. Ask for their catalogue to ascertain what they have published recently. Look for their books in bookstores. Inquire about their recent best-sellers. Ask approximately when your book will be published (see Chapter Twelve). The exact year and month of publication (generally in the spring or fall of a particular year) will rarely be guaranteed by contract, but the contract should state that after acceptance of your manuscript the publisher must publish your book within 18 months or (at most) 24 months. Otherwise the rights will revert to you. Find out what the publisher expects of *you*, other than delivering a complete manuscript on schedule. Should you be available for publicity appearances? Will you be attending the publisher's sales conference? Are you responsible for prepublication quotes? (See Chapter Thirteen.)

I have often been asked whether the new author should pursue prestige or dollars in choosing a publisher. Can you have both? It is

possible. That's why it is essential to find out all you can about your prospective house. There is no doubt that some of the prominent New York publishers can provide both. Outstanding hardcover firms whose titles regularly appear on the best-seller lists include William Morrow, Random House, Simon & Schuster, Crown, Delacorte, Farrar Straus and Giroux, Viking, Doubleday, Knopf, Putnam, and a few others. The leading paperback publishers are Dell, Bantam, Pocket Books, New American Library, Warner, Avon, Ballantine/Fawcett, and Berkley.

Numerous specialty and regional publishers create best-sellers in particular genres and categories. As I mentioned earlier, these include Price/Stern/Sloan, Workman, and Weatherall in the humor field; Ten Speed Press and Arco for career guides; HP Books for cookbooks; Harlequin for romances; Hearst for automotive and nautical books; and Harry Abrams for art books.

These publishers have enjoyed considerable best-seller successes, but publishing with another house does not necessarily preclude best-seller opportunities. Success depends on the publisher's willingness to make a special effort to launch your book. The end result depends on market and consumer reaction—and some luck.

You must avoid certain publishers, if possible. They maintain a poor cash flow or lack credibility in the marketplace; their lists and publishing reputations have declined in recent years; or they are undergoing major transitions in personnel or publishing programs. Your book might get lost in these transitions. Ask bookstore managers, other authors, librarians, stockbrokers (if the publisher is part of a public company), and those "advisors" with whom you counsel about *your* publisher. If you have already decided to wed the first publisher who asks for your manuscript, I wish you luck and good results. But don't be surprised later about what you can find out now. If you have the choice, *sign with the publisher who is best for you and your book.*

● ● ●

Publishers have particular strengths and weaknesses. The large media conglomerates, such as Doubleday, Harcourt Brace & Jovanovich, and McGraw-Hill, or houses that are owned by giant conglomerates—Simon & Schuster (Gulf and Western), Putnam

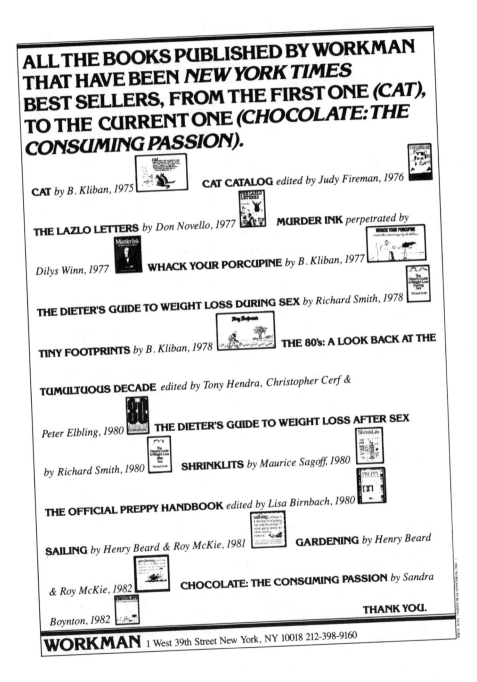

ALL THE BOOKS PUBLISHED BY WORKMAN THAT HAVE BEEN *NEW YORK TIMES* BEST SELLERS, FROM THE FIRST ONE (*CAT*), TO THE CURRENT ONE (*CHOCOLATE: THE CONSUMING PASSION*).

CAT *by B. Kliban, 1975*

CAT CATALOG *edited by Judy Fireman, 1976*

THE LAZLO LETTERS *by Don Novello, 1977*

MURDER INK *perpetrated by Dilys Winn, 1977*

WHACK YOUR PORCUPINE *by B. Kliban, 1977*

THE DIETER'S GUIDE TO WEIGHT LOSS DURING SEX *by Richard Smith, 1978*

TINY FOOTPRINTS *by B. Kliban, 1978*

THE 80's: A LOOK BACK AT THE TUMULTUOUS DECADE *edited by Tony Hendra, Christopher Cerf & Peter Elbling, 1980*

THE DIETER'S GUIDE TO WEIGHT LOSS AFTER SEX *by Richard Smith, 1980*

SHRINKLITS *by Maurice Sagoff, 1980*

THE OFFICIAL PREPPY HANDBOOK *edited by Lisa Birnbach, 1980*

SAILING *by Henry Beard & Roy McKie, 1981*

GARDENING *by Henry Beard & Roy McKie, 1982*

CHOCOLATE: THE CONSUMING PASSION *by Sandra Boynton, 1982*

THANK YOU.

WORKMAN 1 West 39th Street New York, NY 10018 212-398-9160

(MCA), and Bantam (Bertelsmann) generally have greater cash reserves to buy or promote books. They often have ties to other media; Putnam, for example, is in the same conglomerate as Universal Pictures; Simon & Schuster's sister company is Paramount Pictures; Random House, Knopf, and Ballantine are part of the Condé Nast magazine and newspaper chain. Doubleday owns bookstores and book clubs, and Crown has a huge remainder and resale company.

Sometimes smaller or regional publishers can launch and sustain a national best-seller by a skillful or timely advertising or word-of-mouth campaign. This was the case with the perennial best-seller *What Color Is Your Parachute?* published by Ten Speed Press in Berkeley, California; *Drawing on the Right Side of the Brain,* published by Los Angeles-based J.P. Tarcher; and Schocken Books' (once a religious publisher of Judaica) *When Bad Things Happen to Good People.* You may benefit from a publisher's known strength in a particular subject, or your book may introduce a new direction for a publisher who is experimenting in a new area.

Some national best-sellers have originated from university presses. The most celebrated recent examples are *A Confederacy of Dunces* from Louisiana State University Press and the aforementioned . . . *And Ladies of the Club,* from Ohio State University Press.

Specialty and religious publishers often have longrunning best-sellers that do not appear on national lists. Reference books and cookbooks are invariably included in this category of perennial best-sellers.

About twenty-five major publishers (listed in Chapter Five) have had consistent experience in making best-sellers. They have "clout" at the large bookstore chains, in the review media, on the talk shows, at the book clubs, and—not so coincidentally—on the best-seller list. They know how to launch a best-seller campaign and they know what sales, promotional, and marketing strategies to follow. They have done it again and again, and their personnel and sales apparatus is geared to creating best-sellers.

Many authors switch publishers after their initial experiences at one house. Your success or failure with your first book will determine whether you will want to remain with the same company and editor. Or your editor may switch houses, and you may choose to move with him or her to the new company.

Best Sellers

This Week	FICTION	Last Week	Weeks On List
1	THE LITTLE DRUMMER GIRL, by John le Carré. (Knopf, $15.95.) An English girl caught be- tween Israeli intelligence agents and P.L.O. terror- ists.	1	3
2	THE LONESOME GODS, by Louis L'Amour. (Ban- tam, $14.95.) A rugged adventurer stakes his claim in 19th-century southern California.		1
3	THE DELTA STAR, by Joseph Wambaugh. (Mor- row, $15.45.) Los Angeles cops contend with their own city's underworld, some would-be Nobel Prize scientists and an elusive Soviet sub.	6	4
4	VOICE OF THE HEART, by Barbara Taylor Brad- ford. (Doubleday, $17.95.) The friendship of two women survives the strains of 25 years in the worlds of show business, politics and big business.		1
5	MASTER OF THE GAME, by Sidney Sheldon. (Morrow, $15.95.) The hidden truth behind a woman business tycoon's rise to power.	5	31
6	SPACE, by James A. Michener. (Random House, $17.95.) The story of the American space program told through fiction.	3	27
7	BANKER, by Dick Francis. (Putnam, $14.95.) Lon- don bankers gamble on the ability of a hosee breeder to produce a star race horse.		1
8	MISTRAL'S DAUGHTER, by Judith Krantz. (Crown, $15.95.) The art world of the 20's and the fashion industry of the 80's.	2	21
9	ELLIS ISLAND, by Fred Mustard Stewart. (Mor- row, $15.95.) Five young immigrants and the for- tunes that await them in America at the turn of the century.	9	7
10	THE MISTS OF AVALON, by Marion Zimmer Bradley. (Knopf, $16.95.) The Arthurian legend seen through the eyes of four women who played leading roles.	11	7
11	2010: ODYSSEY TWO, by Arthur C. Clarke. (Bal- lantine/Del Rey, $14.95.) A continuation of the tale begun in "2001: A Space Odyssey."	4	21
12	THE VALLEY OF HORSES, by Jean M. Auel. (Crown, $15.95.) A continuation of the saga of human survival at the dawn of civilization begun in "The Clan of the Cave Bear."	10	31
13	FLOATING DRAGON, by Peter Straub. (Putnam, $15.95.) An unspeakable horror invades a suburban commuter town.	8	8
14	FOUNDATION'S EDGE, by Isaac Asimov. (Dou- bleday, $14.95.) The struggle to keep civilization alive in a crumbling empire: science fiction.	7	25
15	E.T. THE EXTRA-TERRESTRIAL STORYBOOK, by William Kotzwinkle. (Putnam, $6.95.) Abridged, profusely illustrated version of the novelization of the film.	13	32

This Week	NONFICTION	Last Week	Weeks On List
1	MEGATRENDS, by John Naisbitt. (Warner, $15.50.) Predictions about America in the next dec- ade based on an analysis of conditions today.	1	21
2	IN SEARCH OF EXCELLENCE, by Thomas J. Peters and Robert H. Waterman Jr. (Harper & Row, $19.95.) Lessons to be learned from well-run American corporations.	2	12
3	THE ONE MINUTE MANAGER, by Kenneth Blan- chard and Spencer Johnson. (Morrow, $15.) How to increase the productivity of those with whom you work as well as your own.	4	27
4	JANE FONDA'S WORKOUT BOOK, by Jane Fonda. (Simon & Schuster, $19.95.) An exercise book for women, seasoned with the film star's phi- losophy of physical well-being.	3	63
5	BLUE HIGHWAYS, by William Least Heat Moon. (Atlantic/Little, Brown, $17.50.) A report on a trip through the back roads of America.	5	7
6	LIVING, LOVING & LEARNING, by Leo Busca- glia. (Holt/Slack, $13.50.) Inspirational talks by a University of Southern California professor.	6	50
7	MARY ELLEN'S HELP YOURSELF DIET PLAN, by Mary Ellen Pinkham. (St.Martin's/Marek, $10.95.) Advice from a veteran dispenser of house- keeping hints.	7	7
8	THE YOUNGEST SCIENCE, by Lewis Thomas. (Viking, $14.75.) The observations of a physician on the changes that have transformed his profession in the last 30 years.	12	4
9	THE FALL OF FREDDIE THE LEAF, by Leo Buscaglia. (Holt/Slack, $7.95.) The seasons of life as experienced by a leaf and its companions: a parable.	13	20
10	AND MORE BY ANDY ROONEY, by Andrew A. Rooney. (Atheneum, $12.95.) A new collection of es- says by the journalist and television commentator.	8	24
11	JANE FONDA'S WORKOUT BOOK FOR PREG- NANCY, BIRTH AND RECOVERY, by Femmy DeLyser. (Simon & Schuster, $16.95.) Advice from a colleague of the film star.	9	22
12	THE F—PLAN DIET, by Audrey Eyton. (Crown, $12.95.) Americanized version of a popular English fiber-based regimen.		1
13	GROWING UP, by Russell Baker. (Congdon & Weed, $15.) The New York Times columnist recalls his boyhood and youth.	14	21
14	THE PARTNERS, by James B. Stewart. (Simon & Schuster, $16.95.) Life inside eight of America's most powerful coporate law firms.		1
15	LIFE EXTENSION, by Durk Pearson and Sandy Shaw. (Warner, $22.50.) Ways to add years to your life and life to your years: a popularly written medical-science book.	10	36

Neophyte authors have achieved best-seller successes with small houses *and* with conglomerates. A potential "best-selling" book with a small publisher can have as good results as with a major house. The results are keyed to timing, luck, and a significant human variable—the public response.

I'm often asked, "Is it better to be the lead book for Oblivion Press, or #47 on the Random House list?" I don't know. I've seen both situations work out favorably *and* disastrously. But it is better to be published *well* than just published. And it is better to be published than not published at all.

Should I Be an Original Hardcover or Paperback?

8. About a decade ago most serious works of fiction and nonfiction were published in hardcover and reprinted later in pocket-size paperback editions. The paperback houses were primarily reprint publishers, and the sale of paperback reprint rights grew into an extraordinarily lucrative business. This process was soon reversed as the paperback houses found it more economical to acquire all publishing rights at the beginning from a best-selling author. Then they licensed the hardcover rights while they retained the mass paperback rights. Irving Wallace, Harold Robbins, Irwin Shaw, James Michener, and Sidney Sheldon all made long-term agreements with major paperback houses as their principal publishers.

In the mid-1960s, an enterprising publisher named Peter Mayer at Avon Books resurrected a long out-of-print book by Henry Roth entitled *Call It Sleep* and published it as an original paperback edition. The nontraditional publication of this dormant literary classic generated unusual excitement. It became the first paperback original to garner front-page recognition in the *New York Times Book Review*. The favorable reception of this innovative republication in paperback marked the beginning of a trend, and the "paperback original" was born.

The paperback publishers discovered that it was cheaper to acquire originals themselves than to depend on the escalating auctions for hardcover books. The stigma of being published in paperback *first* soon disappeared, and book reviewers devoted more attention to the paperback revolution. Best-selling paperback authors who had never been published in hardcover were now gaining reviewer recognition. When the romance genre began to flourish, it spawned soon-to-be household names like Rosemary Rogers, Kathleen Woodiwiss, Janet Dailey, Danielle Steel, Patricia Matthews, and a legendary lady named Barbara Cartland. John Saul, Peter Straub, and V.C. Andrews became mainstays of the occult genre, and the Western was launched by an institution in the person of Louis L'Amour. The original paperback not only became acceptable to the marketplace, but was cheaper and handier to carry around. The paperback had a special quality that appealed particularly to the younger generation. It was instant, fast-paced, casual, and cheaper, much in harmony with the youthful mood of the times.

With the emergence of the oversized trade paperback (generally 5½x8½", 6x9", or 8½x11"), three physical editions of a particular book could be published: hardcover, trade paperback, and mass paperback. Both the hardcover and the paperback houses began to introduce trade paperbacks in the mid-range price category (now approximately $5 to $15). The hardcover houses were able to reproduce their backlists (previously published books) in fresh new trade paperback editions with new covers. The paperback houses could launch new publications in trade paperback before release as mass-market books. Each used the trade paperback edition for different marketing purposes.

Only in recent years has the trade paperback emerged as an accepted best-selling category. The *New York Times* now features a separate trade paperback best-seller list. Such current and perennial best-sellers as *Murphy's Law, What Color Is Your Parachute?, How to Flatten Your Stomach, Fit or Fat, Our Bodies, Ourselves,*

October 9, 1983/The New York Times Book Review

Paperback Best Sellers

MASS MARKET

Mass market paperbacks are soft-cover books sold at newsstands, variety stores and supermarkets, as well as in bookstores. This listing is based on computer-processed reports from bookstores and representative wholesalers with more than 40,000 outlets across the United States.

1 **THE VALLEY OF HORSES**, by Jean M. Auel. (Bantam, $3.95.) A fictional saga of human survival at the dawn of civilization.

2 **MASTER OF THE GAME**, by Sidney Sheldon. (Warner, $3.95.) The secret behind a woman business tycoon's rise to power: fiction.

3 **ACCEPTABLE LOSSES**, by Irwin Shaw. (Avon, $3.95.) A New York literary agent's life is threatened by a mysterious stranger: fiction.

4 **SECOND HEAVEN**, by Judith Guest. (NAL/Signet, $3.95.) Love in various forms heals three battered people: fiction.

5 **TOUCH THE DEVIL**, by Jack Higgins. (NAL/Signet, $3.95.) Tracking down a K.G.B. agent who has stolen NATO secrets: fiction.

6 **DIFFERENT SEASONS**, by Stephen King. (NAL/Signet, $3.95.) Four novellas with mainly nonhorror themes by a modern master of horror.

7 **THE CLAN OF THE CAVE BEAR**, by Jean M. Auel. (Bantam, $3.95.) The beginning of the saga continued in "The Valley of Horses."

8 **MAX**, by Howard Fast. (Dell, $3.95.) The birth of the film industry in New York at the turn of the century: fiction.

9 **THE 13TH VALLEY**, by John M. Del Vecchio. (Bantam, $3.95.) The war in Vietnam: fiction.

10 **DRAGON ON A PEDESTAL**, by Piers Anthony. (Del Rey/Ballantine, $2.95.) Seventh volume of a saga about the fabulous land of Xanth: fiction.

11 **SPELLBINDER**, by Harold Robbins. (Pocket, $3.95.) The rise of a television evangelist: fiction.

12 **A CRY IN THE NIGHT**, by Mary Higgins Clark. (Dell, $3.95.) A newly rewed woman is haunted by her past: fiction.

13 **THE SKULL BENEATH THE SKIN**, by P. D. James. (Warner, $3.95.) The mysterious death of an actress in a castle off the Dorset coast: fiction.

14 **CLOAK OF DARKNESS**, by Helen MacInnes. (Fawcett, $3.95.) A counter-terrorist agent finds himself on an assassination list: fiction.

15 **GOODBYE, MICKEY MOUSE**, by Len Deighton. (Ballantine, $3.95.) Two World War II fighter pilots in love and combat: fiction.

TRADE

Trade paperbacks are soft-cover books usually sold in bookstores and at an average price higher than mass market paperbacks. This listing is based on computer-processed reports from about 2,000 bookstores in every region of the United States.

1 **THE COLOR PURPLE**, by Alice Walker. (Pocket/Washington Square Press, $5.95.) Black men and women in the South: fiction.

2 **THURSTON HOUSE**, by Danielle Steel. (Dell, $7.95.) Three generations of a wealthy San Francisco family: fiction.

3 **LIVING, LOVING & LEARNING**, by Leo F. Buscaglia. (Fawcett, $5.95.) Inspirational talks by a California professor.

4 **COLOR ME BEAUTIFUL**, by Carole Jackson. (Ballantine, $8.95.) Beauty tips for women.

5 **GARFIELD SITS AROUND THE HOUSE**, by Jim Davis. (Ballantine, $4.95.) The further adventures of a fat cat: cartoon humor.

6 **LIFE EXTENSION**, by Durk Pearson and Sandy Shaw. (Warner, $10.95.) How to add years to your life and life to your years.

7 **BLOOM COUNTY**, by Berke Breathed. (Little, Brown, $6.95.) Cartoon strips featuring some very odd characters.

8 **WHAT COLOR IS YOUR PARACHUTE?** by Richard Nelson Bolles. (Ten Speed Press, $7.95.) Guide for job hunters and career changers.

9 **WILD CONCERTO**, by Anne Mather. (Harlequin/World Wide, $4.95.) A brilliant pianist plays the heartstrings of a beautiful English woman: fiction.

10 **MISS MANNERS' GUIDE TO EXCRUCIATINGLY CORRECT BEHAVIOR**, by Judith Martin. (Warner, $10.95.) Etiquette prescribed by an amusingly bossy lady.

11 **LINDA EVANS BEAUTY AND EXERCISE BOOK**, by Linda Evans. (Simon & Schuster/Wallaby, $9.95.) How-to by the television personality.

12 **THE TAO OF POOH**, by Benjamin Hoff. (Penguin, $4.95.) Philosophical humor.

13 **MORE ITEMS FROM OUR CATALOG**, by Alfred Gingold. (Avon, 4.95.) A second spoof of the L. L. Bean catalogue.

14 **THE RAPTURE**, by Hal Lindsey. (Bantam, $6.95.) Predictions about an approaching global event based on an interpretation of the Bible.

15 **FIT OR FAT?** by Covert Bailey. (Houghton Mifflin, $4.50.) Exercises for fitness.

and *Color Me Beautiful* look and feel like trade paperbacks and are packaged and marketed in suitable editions. Other topical trade paperback best-sellers have included such subjects as cubes, preppies, and cats, particularly a cat named Garfield. Trade paperbacks have also been issued on general subjects, including movies, sports, crafts, "how-to," and other nonfiction categories.

The trade paperback differs from the rack-sized paperback not only in size but also in the method of distribution. The bulk of trade paperback sales had always been to bookstores—Dalton, Walden, other chains, and the independent smaller stores. The rack-sized paperbacks continue to be sold to wholesalers or I.D.s (independent distributors) who place the paperbacks in racks at airports, newsstands, and supermarkets. When the trade paperback emerged as a separate best-seller category, the wholesalers began to stock these along with the rack-sized mass paperbacks.

The trade paperback and the mass paperback differ in size and format, method of distribution, and sometimes in type of content. The front cover of the trade paperback retains some of the editorial quality associated with the hardcover book, but also has a flashy commercial appeal similar to mass paperback covers. The trade paperback often has more visual appeal than the hardcover, while retaining the serious image of a hardcover edition. The original intent of the trade paperback was to capture a sales market somewhere between hardcover and mass paperback; in only a few years it has succeeded with extraordinary sales numbers. (The paperback bestseller lists in the "Annual Summary and Highlights" issue of *Publishers Weekly* will give you an excellent idea of the types of books found in Trade and Mass Market editions. This issue is usually in March and covers the previous year.)

● ● ●

All of which leads us back to *your* first book. Should it be an original hardcover or a paperback? What's the difference? Can you have both? How important a consideration is the format in choosing a publisher?

Again, the best place to research the market and evaluate the various types of new editions is your local bookstore. If your work is fiction, the most suitable format is likely to be hardcover or rack-size paperback. It won't matter much in what physical format fiction is published initially. The success of a novel depends more on promotion, publicity, marketing, and ancillary rights (film) than on format. For a first novel, if you have a choice, choose your publisher on the basis of which edition they are most capable of exploiting. Many failed novels were launched either in original paperback or in

hardcover editions; their failure had little to do with format. The major best-seller houses are more likely than another publisher to launch a first novel because they have successful track records. The best-seller lists and the bookstores can help you learn about a publisher's track record in producing best-selling novels.

Nonfiction publication is very much affected by format. Your bookstore or other research will prepare you to ask your prospective publisher intelligently about the most appropriate original edition for your book. Sometimes a book is published simultaneously

in hardcover and in paperback—generally in hardcover and trade paperback editions. The hardcover is often sold as a book-club edition, while the trade paperback is the only edition available to bookstores. Obviously, simultaneous editions are not warranted if they compete and dilute the overall sales that they would have attained in a single edition.

When entertainer Bill Dana and I launched the Dana/Corwin imprint in association with Bantam Books, we created in the trade format a line of humor books by famous celebrities. (*The Unknown Comic's Scrapbag,* by Murray Langston, fit a *small* trade paperback format.) These books were funny and frothy. Later they could enjoy a second publication life in a rack-sized paperback edition. Recent trade paperback best-sellers such as *How to Eat Like a Child, Items from Our Catalog, The Official Preppy Handbook,* and *Real Men Don't Eat Quiche* were packaged in trade paperback formats appropriate to their subject and type of humor.

The larger-sized paperback format (approximately 8½x11"), as evidenced by the successful *Gnomes, The Joy of Sex,* and *The Joy of Photography,* is well suited to this catalog type of book.

When I started my own hardcover imprint, Corwin Books, I was fortunate to publish *The Original Houdini Scrapbook,* very much a trade paperback. Cookbooks, gardening books, art books, books of visual appeal, books on crafts, hobbies, sports, and music are some of the likely candidates for trade format, as well as hardcover. They are generally not suitable for small paperback because the illustrations or line drawings that are likely to be included can be designed more attractively in the larger format.

Ask your prospective publisher whether they contemplate a subsequent publication after the original edition. There may be no contractual guarantees for second publication, but you can check out the likelihood up front. Major houses such as Bantam, Pocket Books, Warner, Random House, and Simon & Schuster are certainly capable of publishing successfully in two editions. Smaller houses may wish to publish a single-format edition geared to their particular sales strengths. If this arrangement severely limits your chances for publication success, I would strongly consider any options you may have for signing with another house. Your decision must be based on your understanding of the marketplace and on indications of how format affected other books similar to your own.

Let me reiterate that it is important to learn from your publisher what edition and format they are planning for your book. This decision will affect your royalty earnings, your sales potential, and the type of market visibility for your book. If you *can* choose your next publisher, their sales and editorial strengths with different types of formats can be crucial to your publishing future. When you first evaluate a specific publishing house, you will benefit if you know something of the publisher's acumen in marketing certain editions and if you have a sense of the size and format that best fit your book. Publishers generally buy all rights for editions of all sizes, but they don't necessarily publish in all editions. They may sell paperback rights to another company, or they may publish only one edition and not publish or sell any other editions in any other formats.

Trade and mass-market paperback editions are more attuned to the trendy, instant pace of our times, but there remains an aura of prestige about being published first in hardcover. A hardcover book seems important, is more likely to be reviewed seriously, and, if successful, is likely to be reissued in a paperback edition. It is unlikely that a reasonably successful paperback will be reissued in hardcover. The hardcover edition also has a more durable quality, physically and editorially. Because it also costs more at the retail level, a major criterion for deciding on hardcover or paperback is the price someone is willing to pay for your book.

The most successful book publication with which I have been involved was *Marilyn* by Norman Mailer. The lavish original edition was believed to be the first hardcover at the coffee-table price of $19.95 ever to appear on the *New York Times* best-seller list. We at Grosset & Dunlap subsequently published a facsimile trade paperback at $9.95; much later, we sold mass paperback rights to Warner Books. These derivative editions were enormously successful in foreign as well as domestic markets. *Marilyn* sold extraordinarily well in every one of its different formats and editions.

Discuss the possible formats for your book when you are choosing a publisher because the ultimate decision regarding the format will be the publisher's. Whether you become successful as a hardcover or as a paperback author will depend on your publisher and on your knowledge of the most appropriate format for your book.

The Publication Contract—When Do I Sign?

9. Your publishers have forwarded their "standard publishing agreement" to you (or to your agent or rep). You may be anxious to execute the contract for your first book, and the terms may appear to represent what you have been offered, but *do not sign it as soon as you receive it.* As with a real-estate deed or any other major transaction, you should understand fully what you are agreeing to. It is strongly advisable to have a lawyer scrutinize and approve a publishing contract. Your attorney should have some expertise in the contractual areas of book publishing, a very specialized field.

It is important that you understand the salient points and intentions of the agreement *before* they are enforced later on. Most publishing agreements feature the same "boilerplate" clauses, the standard ingredients common to all publishing contracts. From time to time these are altered by new phraseology or by additional clauses drawn up by the firm's own attorney. It would also be advisable to compare *your* publishing contract with another firm's, if you can acquire such a contract. You may be able to obtain one from an author or publisher friend or from a lawyer. A sample contract can be found in the Appendix.

All "standard publishing agreements" contain the following basic clauses, which will be explained below:

1. Description of the work
2. Grant of publishing rights
3. Territory
4. Copyright
5. When manuscript will be published
6. Advance and royalties
7. Termination
8. Subsidiary rights
9. Delivery of manuscript
10. Indemnity
11. Agent
12. Option on future works
13. Right to audit; bankruptcy

1. **Description of work.** The first paragraph usually states that this is an agreement between X Publisher and Y Author for a work (and/or book-length manuscript) tentatively entitled _____ and consisting of so many words, plus whatever illustrations or charts or appendices are required.

2. **Grant of publishing rights.** The author will generally grant the publisher the exclusive rights to publish, sell, and license the work in all editions.

3. **Territory.** Generally, the territorial rights granted are either in the English language throughout the world or in all languages throughout the world. Sometimes for beginning authors and almost invariably for proven authors, the foreign-language rights and British rights are controlled by the American agent to license in foreign territories. The U.S. publisher is only granted the right to print, sell, and license English-language editions in North America.

4. **Copyright.** Copyright (see Chapter Eighteen) is taken out in the name of the author or the publisher, usually the author. The

archaic copyright laws allowed your book to fall into the public domain after two 28-year periods, but the law now gives you copyright protection for your life plus fifty years. Insist that the copyright be in *your* name, not the publisher's.

5. **When manuscript will be published.** This clause generally states that if the finished manuscript is delivered on time, the publisher will publish your book within a prescribed time. Twelve months is very reasonable; eighteen months is acceptable. Beyond that point you should question why they need two years or more to publish the book under normal conditions. They *will not* publish the book if it is not editorially acceptable (by their subjective standards) or if it is deemed libelous, obscene, unlawful, or sometimes (in their judgment) unprofitable. I don't know how they can determine profitability beforehand, but sometimes a publisher decides that a market no longer exists for a contracted book, and removes it from its list. A *force majeure* clause is also included, which states that the publisher cannot be responsible for delays in publishing the book caused by wars, civil riots, strikes, fires, governmental restrictions, or conditions beyond its control. The acceptance of your finished manuscript for publication is usually based on your editor's decision and not on any scientific or arbitrary method. If a manuscript is rejected at this stage, the rights should revert to you and you should keep all advance money paid to date.

6. **Advance and royalties.** This is probably the most significant clause in your contract—how much you will be paid up front (the advance) against royalties, generally on an escalated scale of net sales of all editions.

Advances *against* royalties were formerly paid to the beginning author as a loan against projected future earnings, to pay for his typing and research costs in writing the book. Then the advances began to increase, as an upfront reward for obtaining publication rights to potential best-sellers. Advances grew to hundreds of thousands of dollars and even into millions. How big an advance you received swelled your ego and pocketbook, and also committed the publisher to spend promotional dollars to support the investment. The higher the advance, the more likely the publisher's commitment. Or, as Calvin Trillin once proposed, "The advance should be at least as much as the cost of the lunch at which it was discussed."

For a beginning author, the commitment to publish your book by a creditable publisher is usually more important than the size of the advance. The average advance for a first novel will generally range from $1,000 to $5,000. A nonfiction "best-selling" idea may command up to $25,000, but will usually be between $5,000 and $10,000. If you are going to be a *best-selling* author, I would strongly recommend that you ask for an initial advance of at least $5,000. Still, you are only in a position to negotiate advances if you feel that the publisher wants your book badly, or if you anticipate competitive bids from one or more other publishers. Unfortunately, too many new authors only read about the advances received by Judith Krantz and Sidney Sheldon, and not the $1,500 paid to many fledgling authors. Try to get as much of an advance up front as you can.

Yes, a publisher's commitment is determined somewhat by the amount of the advance, but many best-selling books in recent years were created after small advances were paid. Don't lose a good prospect for publication because of an advance. If you have offers from several houses, choose the largest advance only if they fulfill all other criteria as well.

Advances are traditionally paid one-half on signing of the agreement and one-half on delivery of the manuscript, but this traditionally has been altered by the tightness of money. Advances are often paid in thirds these days—one-third on signing, one-third on delivery, and one-third on publication. In another recent arrangement a small amount is paid on signing and additional small amounts are paid step by step as *sections* of the manuscript are accepted. The major publishers no longer want to be out of pocket for manuscripts they have not read and accepted for publication. Advances and advance structures have been changed drastically in recent years to coincide with the economic realities of the time. Be certain that you know when you will be paid your advances, and that you understand what you must produce to receive them.

All advances are paid *against* future royalty earnings or subsidiary-rights income. If your publisher has paid you an advance of $10,000, and subsequent sales of books and/or rights have yet to earn the author's share of income equaling $10,000, you will receive no additional royalty money. Royalties are paid only after all advances have been earned back by the publisher.

At one time there were standard royalty rates, but in recent years publishers have often deviated. Most royalty rates are based on the retail price of the book and are increased after a certain sales plateau. Recently a number of publishers have based royalties on the net price received after the book buyer's discount. A fairly standard hardcover royalty scale is 10 percent of retail price for the first 10,000 copies sold, 12½ percent of the next 10,000 sold, and 15 percent thereafter. The usual royalties for a mass-market paperback book are 8 percent for the first 150,000 copies sold and 10 percent thereafter. Proven and best-selling authors may earn 10 percent initially and later earn as much as 20 percent. For trade paperback books (the newest publishing format) royalties often begin at 7 or 8 percent and rise to 10 percent. Bear in mind that royalties on copies sold refers only to *net* copies sold, after returns come back. The author does not receive royalties on books sold for promotional purposes, copies in the warehouse, and copies returned to the publisher—ONLY ON THE BASIS OF NET SALES.

Many publishers' contracts include a clause that states that an author will receive reduced royalties for copies sold at a discount of 50 percent or higher. This clause is very misleading and potentially dangerous because the large bookstore chains (Dalton and Walden) buy in quantity at a 50 percent discount rate. Since best-selling authors sell in large quantities, almost all your sales could be at a reduced rate. Why should you be punished rather than rewarded for best-seller status? Be very wary of this clause if it appears in *your* publisher's contract.

I can recall several instances where a publisher advertised that a certain book had "sold one million copies." The author was jubilant and fully expected that his next royalty statement would reflect this extraordinary sales figure. It wasn't even close. The publisher advertised "books sold" when "books in print" would have been correct. Actually, 900,000 copies were printed and rounded off to one million. Of the 900,000 printed, approximately 700,000 were shipped and distributed; 200,000 remained unsold in the warehouse. Of the 700,000 shipped, 300,000 were returned unsold, not an unrealistic return on a heavily promoted title. The 400,000 copies of this paperback that were actually sold were reduced by the publisher by 100,000 on the royalty statement as "a reserve against future returns."

The elated author who expected to be paid for "one million copies sold" was paid for 300,000 copies sold, the actual net. The reality of royalty statements and payments is quite a jolt after the hyperbole of publishers' advertising copy.

By contract, royalty statements are generally issued and payments rendered (if they are due) twice a year. They reflect book and rights sales up to the last six-month cut-off period. The statements indicate the number of copies sold at the various royalty rates and the money due after the advance has been earned out.

You should be able to read and understand your royalty statement. If you can't, ask your publisher to interpret it, or consult an accountant or lawyer. The statement should list the number of copies sold at the various royalty rates and the rights sales made. (See sample on next page.) All publishing contracts give the publisher the right to hold a reasonable reserve against returns (copies anticipated to be returned). This has become an area of much discord because "reasonable" is such a vague word. If possible, you or your advisor may want to ask the publisher what they mean by "reasonable reserve" before you sign the contract.

The royalty statement will also list nonbookstore sales made for mail order, premiums, special sales, and other markets, all featuring different royalty rates (see Chapter Seventeen), and will generally hold a reserve against returns.

It is vital to your interests as an author to understand fully how and how much you will be paid in advances and royalties before you sign the publisher's agreement. I have seen too many disillusioned authors who expected to be paid on their "million copies sold." Get the best advance and royalty structure you can negotiate, and then start collecting the money you earned.

7. **Termination or reversion.** The publisher may (and probably will) cease publication and sale of your book if the demand has fallen below normal profit expectations. That is, if they can no longer afford to keep the book in print because it is no longer selling. If and when the publisher informs the author that his or her book is no longer a profitable venture, the publisher will give written notice of

NYT

ROYALTY STATEMENT
#
24469

Stan Corwin Productions, Ltd.
Suite 1850
2029 Century Park East
Los Angeles, CA. 90067

Pub. 9/81

Six-Month Period Ended: October 31, 1981

Retail Price: $12.98

Total Sales to Date: TRADE

Title:

EARNINGS ON SALES

Trade	5000	copies @	1.0384	$ 5192
	2842	@	1.298	3686.32
	including reserve for returns			
Mail Order		copies @		$
Special		copies @		$

TOTAL EARNINGS ON SALES $ 8878.32

OTHER EARNINGS

Cosmopolitan Magazine - 1st Serial	$ 5850.00
Cosmopolitan France - 1st Serial	250.00
	6100.00

TOTAL EARNINGS THIS PERIOD $14978.32

DEDUCTIONS
   Advance $ 12000
   Payments
   Purchases
   Other

TOTAL DEDUCTIONS   12000.00

BALANCE FROM PRIOR PERIOD   -0-

UNEARNED BALANCE $

BALANCE DUE $ 2978.32

Royalty Rates— Trade 10% of invoice price to 5,000; 12.5% on 5,001-10,000; 15% thereafter.
Mail Order ..% of list.

termination. At that time, the author may request that publication rights (except for ongoing and existing licensing contracts) revert to him or her. The plates and physical material for producing the book may be sold to the author at cost. Conversely, if a book is out of print, the author may demand that it go back into print within six months. Otherwise the rights will revert automatically to the author.

8. **Subsidiary rights.** (See Chapter Twenty.) Subsidiary or ancillary rights are those rights licensed to another medium such as print media (magazines and newspapers), book clubs, paperback reprint (if a hardcover publication), movies and TV, cable and new visual media, and foreign publication. For "best-selling" authors and other authors represented by adroit agents, the visual rights and often the foreign rights are controlled by the author, not by the publisher. The primary reason for this is that the publisher's time and expertise in these areas of specialization are limited. It is more beneficial for you to use a knowledgeable agent to sell potentially lucrative rights. The publisher traditionally controls the rights to sell print media, book clubs, and paperback rights (if not an original paperback publication) on a 50/50 percentage split. In cases where the publisher or author controls TV, movie, dramatic, and foreign rights, the split is usually 75 to 90 percent to the author and the remainder to the publisher. The income split is different from the *control* of rights, which belongs to the party who is legally responsible for making the sale. More later on this very lucrative subject.

9. **Delivery of manuscript.** A clause in the contract states when the finished or "final" manuscript shall be delivered to the publisher. In some publishing houses, this due date is followed strictly. Most firms, however, are lax about enforcing this clause, which really means that on or about X date the manuscript is due; if it doesn't make that date, the contract will still be in full force and effect, and the publishing date will be delayed a season. Some publishers enforce this clause rigidly, and many demand return of the advance if the manuscript is not delivered on time. Several autobiographical works, including John Mitchell's Watergate revelations, were never delivered, and the publishers have instituted lawsuits to recover advance payments. Generally, though, the publisher will not require the author to return advances if a due date is not met.

You will be more likely to receive an extension, delaying the publication of the book. If you renege on your obligation in the contract and never deliver a manuscript, then the publisher is legally entitled to repayment of those advances paid to you.

10. **Warranties and indemnity.** This is the most legal of the publishing clauses, which states most specifically (and in similar language in all publishing contracts):

> The Author will hold harmless and indemnify the Publisher from all claims, actions, or demands that constitute a breach of any of the Author's representations or warranties.

The indemnification clause means, in essence, that if there is anything libelous or litigious in the manuscript—the manuscript *you* submitted—you are responsible for any costs and damages incurred as a result, and that the publisher is free from liability.

The most alarming libel case in recent years concerned Bindrim vs. Mitchell. Best-selling author Gwen Davis Mitchell had a contract with major publisher Doubleday to write a novel, based loosely on a nude encounter marathon. In her novel, she depicted the nude guru, Mr. Bindrim, in somewhat demeaning fashion. Unexpectedly, he sued over his resemblance to the character in the novel and, incredible as it was to the literary community, won his case; the first time a major libel suit was granted to the plaintiff in a case involving a work of fiction. Still more unbelievably, Doubleday subsequently sued Gwen Davis Mitchell on the indemnity clause. Watch out! Although your fiction or nonfiction book is clean and nonlibelous, you are indemnifying your publisher against libel, slander, and the like—and you could lose money, reputation, and time. You are agreeing to indemnify and hold harmless your publisher from all damage, costs, and expenses arising by reason of any breach of the author's guarantees.

It is best to consult an attorney regarding this very legal clause. Most publishers, however, will not negotiate their interpretation of this clause. But it can be important, particularly because best-selling authors are sued more often than unprofitable authors. Many major publishers now have libel insurance, which they provide to their authors at no cost.

11. **Agent.** If you have an agent, he or she will be written into the contract to receive all payments, agreements, and correspondence before you do (as your representative), unless you make contractual arrangements for yourself and your agent to be paid separately. Make sure you have a written legal agreement with your agent.

12. **Option.** Often the publishers will add a clause that says they have an option on your next work *on terms to be mutually agreed upon*. Sign it if you wish, or negotiate not to sign it or to limit it to a work in a specific genre or on the subject on which you've just written. If Book Number One becomes a best-seller, you will still be legally free to negotiate for more money for your next work.

13. **Right to audit; bankruptcy.** One clause will give you the right to audit (at your expense) the publisher's accounting statements of your book. The bankruptcy clause states that you may automatically terminate your agreement if the publisher goes into bankruptcy.

These are the *major* clauses of the publisher's contract. Be sure to consult with an attorney who is familiar with publisher's legalese, or a publishing friend or expert. You should learn how to interpret your own contract.

Feel free to discuss and question the substantive and legal points. Publishers will respect you, and will assume that you have solicited legal representation. Alter, delete, negotiate if you must. It is expected of you, and will serve you well in the long run. It will serve as a precedent and a contractual base for your next publishing contract.

Compare and contrast publishing agreements and ask a lot of naive questions. You are, after all, the new author. Then sign the contract and write your best-seller—Rule Number One, Clause Number One.

●●●●●●●●●●●●●●●●●●
My Editor, Myself

10. In the beginning, your relationship with your new publishing house will be confined almost solely to your assigned editor. He or she most likely has had many years of experience editing books similar to yours. The editor-author relationship should be a close one; its prime objective is *to bring to publication the best written, most commercial book possible.* Your editor can be your best friend and your severest critic.

Beginning authors have often asked me about how to handle the editorial relationship. If you have doubts when you begin writing—whether to contact your editor for some guidance or minor inquiry—I would advise you to make that contact. Your editor is there to guide you toward publication. Establish a favorable rapport at the outset and use the relationship. Don't be embarrassed to ask simple questions to which you don't know the answers. The editor may have many more years of experience than you. Also, it would be inappropriate and counterproductive to work with your editor only after you have submitted a finished manuscript. Let him or her guide you in the early stages of manuscript development.

Does gender matter in the assignment of an editor? Sometimes; it depends more on your project than on your gender. When I made a copublishing arrangement with Times Books for Marion Zola's *All the Good Ones Are Married,* the provocative subject matter required working with a bright, fairly *au courant female* editor. It was essential that a woman edit such a topic, which was written from a female point of view.

When Dana/Corwin began our publishing association at Bantam, we switched from a more literary female editor to a more marketing-oriented male editor. The projects we were creating and publishing seemed to warrant an editor with a sales background, and most of the female editors didn't have sales training. It is highly recommended, but not mandatory, that your assigned editor have rapport with your subject and with you. A lack of personal and editorial compatibility in the initial stages could prove detrimental to your book and to future publishing relationships. Choose (if you can, and if one is not assigned to you) an editor with empathy for your subject and with whom you believe you can enjoy creative rapport. Without wishing to sound sexist, I can say that men usually edit sports books and women usually edit beauty books, but in general, your editor's gender is not relevant to your subject matter.

Because you will have to trust your editor's advice and decisions, you should *trust your editor.* Form a relationship in which you both understand what your editorial objective is and what kind of book you hope to publish. You must be writing and editing the same book, the book for which the publisher contracted. Open and early communication will ensure this. Trust your editor's advice, but if you disagree, say so and discuss the disputed points as they surface. It is *your* book, but a knowledgeable and caring editor is invaluable. The legendary and eminent editor Maxwell Perkins served as a friend, confidant, father, mother, and editor to Thomas Wolfe, F. Scott Fitzgerald, Ernest Hemingway, and many other literary figures. The more he coddled and nurtured their creative writing efforts, the more they depended on him. The byproduct of these famous literary associations was more than best-selling books. It was comparable to offspring from a marriage.

It is often lamented that an editor like Perkins does not exist in today's commercial publishing milieu. In general, this is a rare phenomenon, but current editors and publishers like Bob Gottlieb at Knopf, Roger Straus at Farrar, Straus & Giroux, and Simon Michael Bessie at Harper & Row are caring, concerned, skilled editors in the tradition of Maxwell Perkins. Collectively they have produced a significant number of best-selling books, a feat achieved only because of dedicated and personal author-editor relationships and because of the respect the book industry holds for their selection of future best-sellers.

If you are fortunate to be assigned an editor with significant "clout" in his or her publishing house, you will enjoy a greater likelihood of strong marketing and promotional effort on publication. The editors mentioned above have that clout in their respective companies. Other outstanding editors in publishing today include Aaron Asher, Tom Wallace, Gladys Carr, Marc Jaffe, Michael Korda, and those with individual imprints at a specific house: Richard Marek, Helen Wolff, Seymour Lawrence, and Joni Evans. Marek was previously the individual editor/publisher of best-selling author Robert Ludlum. He maintained an obviously close editorial relationship with Ludlum. The resulting book enjoyed his imprint and was jointly published and distributed with a larger company. The imprint relationships afford a highly personal rapport in all phases of the manuscript process. If you have the good fortune to work with a well-known imprint editor, I believe it would increase your chances for bestsellerdom. But understand that a first-time author will rarely be assigned such an editor.

Your editor is likely to be a good, hard-working man or woman who believes in you and your book. The editor should read chapters or sections as you progress, rather than seeing the finished manuscript for the first time. Keep in touch with your editor. Ask for advice. Establish a working rapport, and a personal one, if possible. If you are separated by distance, make one trip to New York or wherever for a personal meeting. *Your editor should know what is happening with your manuscript*—when and what part of it is altered, what new direction or approach you have taken, any new writing style, any major change in characters, plot, subject, content, ending.

The editor is your link to the publisher and your vital connec-

Publishing: Imprints Prosper in Spite of Doubters

By EDWIN McDOWELL

Imprints — those small personal labels within large publishing houses that have been around for more than 20 years — appear to be prospering. Yet editors and publishers are still divided about their value.

This week's fiction and nonfiction best-seller lists in The New York Times Book Review include three books published by imprints, and three other imprint books are cited as being of particular literary, topical or scholarly interest. In addition, one other best seller, although published by a larger commercial publisher, originated with a smaller independent publisher.

Under the typical independent imprint, a larger publishing house provides financial backing to a smaller publishing entity or to an individual publisher or editor in return for a split of profits. And some of the books on the current best-seller list have been profitable indeed: the No. 1 fiction best seller, "The Name of the Rose" by Umberto Eco, originally written in Italian, recently sold for paperback reprint for $550,000, which is thought to be a record for rights to a translation.

"The Name of the Rose" is a Helen & Kurt Wolff/Harcourt Brace Jovanovich book. So are two of the titles the Book Review lists as meriting particular interest: "An African in Greenland" by Tété-Michel Kpomassie and "Bluebeard" by Max Frisch.

The No. 5 nonfiction book this week, "The Price of Power" by Seymour M. Hersh, is published by Summit, a division of Simon & Schuster run by James H. Silberman, its president and editor in chief. Another Summit book, Barbara Woodhouse's "No Bad Dogs," was the seventh-biggest-selling hard-cover book of 1982.

Not All Imprints Succeed

Other current best-selling imprint titles include "White Gold Wielder" by Stephen R. Donaldson (No. 10), a Del Rey/Ballantine book from the highly successful team of Judy-Lynn and Lester del Rey, and "Ascent into Hell" by Andrew M. Greeley (No. 11), a Bernard Geis/Warner Book. Unlike most of the other imprints, Bernard Geis Associates is an independent publisher that works with various bigger houses. But all three of its best-selling Andrew Greeley novels have been published by Warner Books.

Helen Gurley Brown's "Having It All," a best-seller this year, was a Simon & Schuster/Linden Press co-publication. Linden is a Simon & Schuster imprint, and so is Poseidon Press, the hard-cover imprint of Pocket Books. One of the newer imprints, Cornelia & Michael Bessie Books, affiliated with Harper & Row, has published Theodore H. White's "America in Search of Itself" and John K. Fairbank's "Chinabound," and has signed up such authors as Freeman Dyson, Lionel Tiger and Oscar Handlin.

Despite these successes, a number of imprints have fallen by the wayside in recent years, and many others have recently changed addresses. Dial was a small, independent imprint within Doubleday when its editors signed up "Modern Baptists" by James Wilcox, a comic first novel on the current particular-interest list, but Dial has since been absorbed into the overall Doubleday list. Houghton Mifflin and its subsidiary, J.P. Tarcher, recently agreed to go their separate ways.

Within the last year or so, Joan Kahn moved her mystery-book imprint from Ticknor & Fields, another subsidiary of Houghton Mifflin, to E. P. Dutton & Company and then to St. Martin's Press. Truman Talley Books moved from Times Books to Dutton. Seymour Lawrence moved his fiction imprint from Delacorte to Dutton, and his wife, Merloyd, moved her nonfiction imprint from Delacorte to Addison-Wesley. Eleanor Friede, who also had an imprint at Delacorte, took her line of aviation books to Macmillan.

'Ego Trips' and Independence

But not everyone is in favor of imprints. The publisher of one medium-size house summed up a fairly common attitude toward the imprints by saying, "We really should be worrying about how to get books out more effectively than thinking about ego trips for editors."

But for some, if not most, of the editors and publishers of imprints, the reasons have less to do with ego than with the independence and flexibility this method of publishing offers than with substantially less risk than publishing completely on their own. "I can't work with committees," Mr. Lawrence said, "and this way I get to establish my autonomy and exert my own taste."

Roger W. Straus, president of Farrar, Straus & Giroux, said that while the imprint is a "super idea" in the case of Helen Wolff (Kurt Wolff died in an accident 20 years ago, two years after William Jovanovich asked the Wolffs to join Harcourt Brace Jova-novich), in most cases it is not so good. "We've turned down people who have come to us wanting an imprint," he said. "We want the editor working with everybody else in the house, and you basically need the whole house behind you to make a book a success."

Imprint publishers say they sometimes have to fight the corporation for publicity and advertising, and some of them take extra steps on their own to promote their titles. A recent letter to reviewers from Richard Marek, an independent publisher with St. Martin's Press, described his personal enthusiasm for "The Redemption of the Unwanted" by Dr. Abram Sachar, a September book that describes what happened to the survivors of the Holocaust immediately after the liberation of Hitler's death camps.

William Abrahams Books

A new imprint at a major house is William Abrahams Books, associated with Holt, Rinehart & Winston. Mr. Abrahams had been a senior editor at Atlantic Monthly Press before joining Holt in 1977 and he has edited books by Francis Steegmuller, John Knowles, Claire Sterling, Thomas Flanagan, Pauline Kael and Evan Connell. Not incidentally, Holt's publisher, Richard Seaver, and his wife, Jeannette, had their own imprint, Seaver Books, at the Viking Press from 1971 to 1979. (Now an independent publisher, Seaver Books is run by Mrs. Seaver, who is president and editor in chief, and is distributed by Arbor House.)

"Imprints are only successful insofar as they do something the parent publisher can't do as well," Mr. Seaver said. "In the case of Billy Abrahams, having him is a plus for our sales reps because literary fiction is difficult to sell, and reps and booksellers know that an Abrahams book has a special cachet." Moreover, Mr. Seaver said that in order to do justice to good fiction, "the editor who takes it on must do so with a great deal of zeal, and the in-house editor usually doesn't have the time for that with each book."

To Richard Snyder, chairman of Simon & Schuster, whether to have an imprint boils down to: "If you have qualified people, they'll work." That means editors and publishers who are not only talented, he explained, but whose talents are best used outside the structure and strictures of a large organization. "All bulls like a lot of space," he said, "and this way I can have all the bulls in the same china shop."

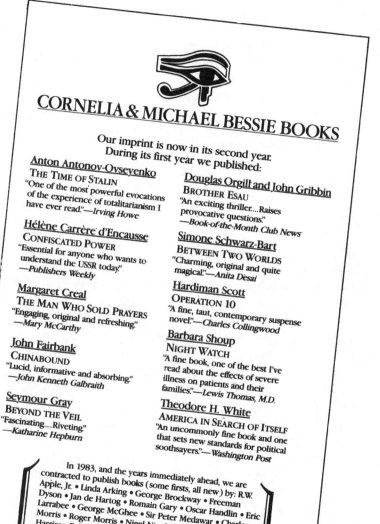

tion to bestsellerdom. The editor is also your link to the other departments in the publishing company, and will communicate with you regarding the publisher's marketing and advertising plans for your book: blurbs, promotional copy, sales leads, and publicity opportunities. In addition, your editor will guide you in the appropriate editorial directions, helping you to improve the slant and coverage of the evolving book, and can also encourage and stimulate you through all phases of writing and revising. The editorial relationship should help you to write a better manuscript and deliver the finished book that the publisher expects to sell, and provide a stimulus for you to produce a *best-selling* book. Like a marriage, the relationship will be as good as you work to make it.

In recent years a kind of combination editor/publisher has emerged in the publishing business. Book producers and book packagers (often synonymous designations) imitate the working relationship that independent film producers have with the major studios finance and distribute their products.

The book producer generally initiates the project, prepares the outline, finds the writer, edits and plans the initial marketing of the book, and arranges a copublishing venture with the publishing company who finances and physically produces the book, and distributes and sells it to the marketplace. Sometimes the producer will deliver a finished book. The producer/packager often has an imprint association with the major house and maintains a close working association in the sales and marketing stages.

This new phenomenon in publishing emerged in the mid-1970s, when larger houses began to merge and assimilate because of economic cutbacks. A former agent/packager, Lyle Kenyon Engel, launched Book Creations, Inc., to produce literary properties for major publishers. His initial successes included the extraordinary Kent family saga by John Jakes and the Windhaven series, which I began at Pinnacle. This venture motivated other "packagers" to develop copublishing relationships with companies. Such former publishers and editors as James Bryans, Bernard Geis, Bill Adler, Richard Gallen, Paul Fargis, and Jeffrey Weiss work full time as book producers. (See Paul Fargis' article in the Appendix for more on the fascinating world of packaging.)

Similarly, when I began Stan Corwin Productions several years

ago, I had the innovative intention of developing literary properties in both book and film versions. My bicoastal existence and visibility would afford me an opportunity to initiate projects in both media and to allow the financing, production, and distribution to be handled by a larger company. I have enjoyed co-venture relationships with such organizations as Dick Clark Cinema Productions, Davis-Panzer Productions, Appledown Films, William Morrow & Co., Ballantine Books, Bantam Books, Putnam, New York Times Books, and Prentice-Hall. The successful book and film projects that have issued from this production company include *The Destroyer* series, *All the Good Ones Are Married* by Marion Zola, *The Laughter Prescription* by Dr. Laurence J. Peter, *Love Is Love but Business Is Business* by Merle Horwitz, *The Red Moon* by Warren Murphy, and . . . *And Ladies of the Club* by Helen Santmyer.

Publishers have generally been receptive to the recent book-packaging phenomenon because it reduces their overhead costs for full-time editorial staff and because it brings fresh new best-selling ideas to the company from outside sources. These new book producers are often former editors or publishers of major houses who have an eye for the best-seller. Recent best-sellers such as *Ascent into Hell* (Geis/Warner); *Items from Our Catalog* (Cloverdale/ Avon); and *How to Satisfy a Woman Every Time* (Bibli O' Phile/ Dutton) were packaged books, produced in association with a major publisher.

Since editors are constantly switching jobs in the trade-book industry, authors work more and more often today with outside editors (hired by the author or the publisher) or with book producers who can coventure with a particular company. It is generally advantageous for a beginning author to work with a book producer/packager if the producer can supplement the publisher's editorial and sales activities and if the producer has the ability to create best-sellers. Otherwise the author is served better by working with an actual publisher and an assigned editor.

In all his editor/agent/publisher roles the producer/packager has become a viable part of the changing publishing industry. Like their precursors in the film industry, books are now written by —, conceived by —, and produced by —.

Of Co-Authors, Ghosts, and Script Doctors

11. The writing and publishing of a first book may be a collaborative effort between two people. Two prospective authors (or sometimes more) create an idea and agree to work together on the manuscript. They may share writing assignments equally, or one may serve as writer, the other as researcher and planner. The criterion for choosing a co-author is this: will the other person's contribution enhance the publication, the sale, and the commercial and literary success of the book? And does this contribution justify sharing half the advance and royalties, or whatever split is arranged between the co-authors? If the answers are affirmative, it is worth involving a co-author.

It is also *fun* to collaborate, and far less lonely. If the relationship is harmonious and productive, working with a co-author can enable you to finish a manuscript more quickly, using another person's insights and creative offerings. Co-authors must share their inspiration, perspiration, and ideas, and their efforts ought to

achieve more lucrative results. Among the most notable author teams are Collins and LaPierre, who have collaborated on such best-sellers as *O' Jerusalem, Is Paris Burning?, Or I'll Dress You in Mourning,* and *The Fifth Horseman;* DeBorchgrave and Moss, who wrote the best-selling novels *The Spike* and *Monimbo;* and Knebel and Bailey, who wrote *Seven Days in May.* Collaborations are generally arranged in one of several ways: one co-author does all the research and the other all the writing; both authors research and write each chapter together; or each author writes certain chapters, which are edited by the other. When I published the best-selling paperback novel *Weather War,* authors Paul Posnick and Leonard Leokum each created ideas and plot, and they researched and wrote the entire book together. Another celebrated partnership that I was privileged to publish at Pinnacle Books consisted of authors Richard Sapir and Warren Murphy; they used still another form of collaboration when they wrote the best-selling *Destroyer* series, "soon to be numerous motion pictures." Murphy described their writing technique in the following manner:

> Dick writes the first half and creates the plot and the characters. I take over in the second half and sex the characters who need sexing, kill off the characters who need to be killed.

A unique writing method. A unique writing team.

Noteworthy nonfiction collaborations include Masters and Johnson, who also merged nuptially after they created their bestseller. Milton and Rose Friedman wrote their recent book *Free to Choose* as a husband-and-wife team. Until their recent deaths, Will and Ariel Durant were celebrated co-authors of major historical works. The phenomenal *In Search of Excellence* was written by Thomas J. Peters and Robert H. Waterman, Jr., and sold over 1 million copies in hardcover.

Still another form of collaboration is that between a celebrity and a writer. Sometimes an expert on some technical subject, such as computers, or aerospace, or a new medical breakthrough, will collaborate with a writer on a potential best-selling book idea. The expert has the credentials and the knowledge, but needs someone to do the actual writing and organizing of the book. *The Doctor's Quick Weight Loss Diet,* which I was instrumental in discovering and publishing, features the medical expertise of Dr. Irwin Stillman and the writing skills of professional writer Samm Sinclair Baker. Nathan Pritikin also used the writing services of a co-author. The authorship is shared, but it is clear that the expert has joined forces with a writer. The contractual arrangement is generally a 50/50 split, unless the "celebrity author" can secure the writer's participation for a smaller percentage share or for an outright fee. The great

actor Henry Fonda shared with his co-author, Howard Teichmann, writing credits and royalties on his autobiography.

Collaborations often involve a published ghost such as Hollis Alpert, who wrote a celebrity autobiography for Lana Turner. Numerous celebrity "co-writers" emerged as well-known biographers and were subsequently credited as co-authors. The most notable are A.E. Hotchner, who has written for Sophia Loren and Doris Day, and Gerold Frank, who has "done" Judy Garland. James Bacon is now "doing" Jackie Gleason, and Doug Warren has just written James Cagney's life.

If the ghostwriter's name does appear, the credit often reads "by—with—." Sometimes, but rarely, it reads, "by—and—." Most of the post-Watergate books were actually written by other people, credited by name or pseudonymously. Many writers have gained enormous fame and considerable profits by writing celebrity memoirs. A lot of dollars have been earned for lesser egos who were willing to write someone else's book.

A popular Hollywood book scenario these days is for an aging, forgotten star to write his or her memoirs and to reveal scandalous secrets from the past. These "kiss 'n' tell" autobiographies are often stale, boring, and replete with innuendoes about celebrities no longer alive. Each of these stars enlisted the services of a ghostwriter. The more people the stars kissed and the more they told to the writer and the public, the more likely their chances of instant best-sellerdom. The celebrity memoir has become such a big business that famous ghosts now hire lesser-known ghosts to work for them. It is the latest thing in Hollywood to ghost for a ghost.

The celebrity "autobiopic" originates when a long-forgotten star wants to do the talk-show circuit and be in the limelight again, or to make a lot of bucks. After all, *So-and-So* did. The star calls Swifty Lazar, or a similar Hollywood agent of considerable clout, and a publishing deal is made on the basis of revelations about their sleeping histories.

A writer with a commercial track record in this genre is chosen to do the actual writing, working in concert with the celeb. The ghost may hire another minor ghost, a researcher, or a tape-recorder decipherer, depending on the dollars allocated to the project. In recent years, the results have been mixed.

Often, books and memoirs are written by a recognizable name, but a writer/editor was hired to make the book literate and coherent. Editor/rewriters or "script doctors" have been retained by *best-selling authors,* first novelists, and name people to make their books read better. It is known within the publishing business that numerous best-selling authors have worked with script doctors, who rewrote most of their manuscripts. Every book can use some kind of rewrite. Major authors and name people can afford these services; beginning authors generally cannot. The alternatives are to engage a friend/editor/rewriter for a modest fee, or to seek at the outset to work with a co-author. (See the collaboration agreement in the Appendix.)

Ghosts and rewriters are effective and sometimes necessary writing partners, if they are experienced in "creating best-sellers." If ghostwriting doesn't enhance the literary or commercial appeal of your book or increase your chances at bestsellerdom, then I would not recommend it.

A not-so-pseudonymous co-author will probably share author credit and talk-show appearances with you. Decide at the start whether this is an advantage or a liability. Will a best-seller by two or more people help you get a best-seller contract for your next book? Although numerous young authors created the clever best-seller *The Official Preppy Handbook,* only one of the authors—Lisa Birnbach—emerged as a talk-show celebrity author and a recognizable best-selling name.

The final criterion, of course, is whether you need a collaborator in the development of your book. Conflicting egos, different editorial philosophies, or incompatible work habits can break up a writing partnership. "I've always believed in writing without a collaborator," said Agatha Christie, "because where two people are writing the same book, each believes he gets all the worries and only half the royalties." Like any marriage, the divorce can be painful and costly. Choose wisely.

Will I Ever Finish My Manuscript?

12. You have a publisher. You've been assigned an editor. You have signed the publishing contract. Next comes book publication, but it doesn't come fast or easily. You suffer a long period of doubt and waiting; a feeling that no one cares about your book, particularly your publisher. And you have your own doubts. Through numerous drafts, revisions, rewrites, you will constantly wonder whether you will ever finish this best-seller.

There is no such thing as a publishable first draft. All manuscripts require revision and editing. Your editor will generally guide you at each stage of manuscript development. Some editors will ask you to submit sections as they are completed; others will want to see the entire manuscript before they begin the editing process. In many instances, publishers are doing little editing these days, or less than in the past. It may be up to you to edit your own book as meticulously as possible.

The type and timing of editing will often depend upon whether

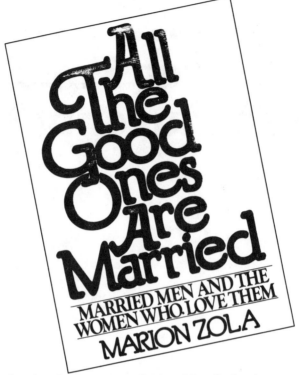

your book is fiction or nonfiction. Nonfiction is generally sectioned into subcategories that can be edited individually, but fiction is easier to edit as a completed manuscript. The complexities of character, plot, and denouement necessitate reading and editing a finished novel.

When I published Marion Zola's nonfiction book *All the Good Ones Are Married* in association with Times Books, Marion wrote the book in three parts, relating to the man, the "other woman," and the wife at home. Because she adhered firmly to this three-part structure, it was easier for me and for her house editor to edit and critique. Years earlier, when I edited Leonard Mosley's Book-of-the-Month Club selection *Hirohito*, I had to edit the entire manuscript, although it was a nonfiction subject. The work included so many people, events, and dates that it required cross-editing and checking between one chapter and another.

Your editor will alter your manuscript to make it better and more commercial. If you strongly disagree with your editor's suggestions about organization and content, say so, and be prepared to defend your objections. You both want a manuscript of the highest quality that is also salable. Work toward that objective. When you are both completely satisfied that what you have written is the very best you can write, the manuscript is ready for copy editing—editing for grammar, spelling, and punctuation.

Even after you submit your final manuscript, you will go through a lengthy transition period in which it seems that no time and effort is being expended on your book. The publishing industry generally has two publishing seasons for hardcover books—spring and the fall pre-Christmas seasons. Everything published from January to July is on the "spring" list. Generally, books published from August on for the fall season are categorized as pre-Christmas releases. Consequently, few books are actually shipped or published in December, since it is generally too late to market them for Christmas shopping.

Mass-market paperbacks are published on a monthly cycle, like magazines. The publishers generally release a specific number of titles each month. At Pinnacle, we published approximately twelve titles a month.

Within normal production schedules, manuscripts delivered in one season are likely to be published in the next. A finished manuscript given to a publisher on September 15th can usually be published by midspring of the following year. It takes approximately six to nine months to prepare a jacket cover and advertising and promotional materials, to print and bind the book, and to send the completed book to reviewers and retailers before actual publication.

This seasonal formula has exceptions. One is the very timely, topical subject that should be printed and published immediately, or the sports or political book related to a particular season or event. When I published Ken Stabler's football autobiography, it was rushed into print soon after he had guided his (then) Oakland Raiders to the Super Bowl championship. At Grosset & Dunlap we published a Hubert Humphrey book simultaneously with his campaign for the Presidency. Bantam Books is best known for publication of instant books on very current subjects, such as the triumphant victory of America's hockey team in the Winter Olympics of 1980. Sometimes a book is rushed to publication to beat the compe-

tition to the market. This situation was exaggerated when a plethora of Elvis Presley and John Lennon books flooded the marketplace after their deaths.

Because some of the larger companies, such as Doubleday, have too many books to publish each season, they often schedule a year in advance. Ask your publisher when they anticipate publication, assuming that you deliver a manuscript on schedule. Smaller companies have fewer bureaucratic problems in printing and publishing a book; you may be in print four or five months after delivery.

The seasonal timing for publishing your book could be significant in achieving success. Sometimes your subject, or the competition, will warrant a specific time for publication. While I was at Prentice-Hall, we published *Up the Down Staircase* in January, enabling us to herald it as the outstanding new book of the season. When it became a national best-seller, it was the first hit of that season. The timing was accidental but fortuitous.

Publishers have generally found that golf and tennis books sell better in the off seasons than when devotees are actively playing those games in spring and summer. Diet and exercise books, however, fare better if they are published in the spring, when everyone is suddenly concerned with his or her appearance in a bathing suit, come summer. Expensive coffee-table books are planned for publication in the pre-Christmas season, when consumers traditionally have extra money for holiday gift giving.

First novels often receive a greater reception in early January or late summer, when they can garner reviewer and public acceptance

James A. Michener

A towering new novel of exhilarating power and depth

A giant, sprawling novel spanning a courageous people's proud history from the Tatar invasions to the present day.

Alive with the color, sweep, and majesty of such earlier Michener best sellers as *Chesapeake, Centennial,* and *The Covenant,* POLAND is James A. Michener's towering saga of a land, and three families— nobility, gentry, and peasants—whose destinies are intertwined with that of their nation, through generations of its history. Combining fact and fiction with the flair and mastery for which he is famous, James A. Michener vividly shows us the Polish people in all their valor and zest for life— their enjoyment of music and feasting, romance and intrigue, and their struggle for freedom through the ages.

• A Literary Guild Selection
• 576 pages
• At all bookstores
• 450,000 COPIES IN PRINT

Photo: John Kings

POLAND
A Novel by
James A. Michener

RANDOM HOUSE

INSTANT BEST SELLER

before their competition comes to the marketplace. Of course, if your publisher is excited about your book and foresees best-seller possibilities, he will rush it to early publication.* Often, only an intuitive guess determines publication of the right book in the right season, unless you are Robert Ludlum or James Michener. In that case, any season of publication will assure the publisher of an immediate best-seller.

● ● ●

Communicate openly and often with your editor and your publisher. Although "nothing" appears to be happening, it can be a propitious time for your publisher to start getting excited about you and your book. I strongly recommend that you visit your publisher at least once while you are writing. You are an essential part of your book. Visit your editor, and also make it a point to meet the sales personnel, the rights director, and the publicity manager. If you are to be sent on a promotion tour or presented on talk shows, discuss this prospect with the promotion and publicity people. Let them know subtly but firmly what you expect of your publisher. If you have an agent, he or she can supplement your efforts in communicating with your publisher. Let your publisher know if anything exceptional happens to you—an award, achievement, other successes; and inform them again of any new sales contacts you may have for bulk sales or rights sales.

Remember that a best-seller can be achieved if you create a rapport that helps bring it about. Like you, the publisher wants to sell as many books as possible. You can fight loneliness during the writing period by reading a great deal, staying current with book-industry trends and the best-seller lists, being familiar with your publisher's current titles, and maintaining liaison with the publisher. And writing the best damn manuscript you can.

Your "high" from having signed a book contract will abate

---

*Samuel Johnson once told an aspiring writer: "Your manuscript is both good and original. Unfortunately, what is good is not very original, and what is original is not very good." If you want to *be* a best-seller, you have to *write* a best-seller.

somewhat during the laborious writing and rewriting stages, but you won't have a book published if you don't finish and deliver it. You must adhere to some kind of disciplinary schedule, writing regularly in an environment conducive to creating ideas. When I was writing this book under a strict publication deadline, I wrote only when I felt like writing, but I made sure I completed two chapters every week to maintain the schedule. You must stay on your schedule and finish your manuscript. The discipline is as important as the writing. (See "Publishing: Dealing with Tardy Authors" in the Appendix for a publisher's-eye view of writers who go off their schedules.)

●●●●●●●●●●●●●●●●●●●●●
Who Loves Ya, Baby?

13. Prepublishing quotes and endorsements are vital in establishing credibility and authenticity for an author, particularly a new one. If you are virtually unknown and if your subject is not obviously commercial, endorsements on book jackets, in advertisements, and in promotional pieces are essential to the launching of your book. The public is highly receptive to recommendations and accolades from people whose names are recognized and credible. Often the endorser's name is featured more prominently on the book jacket than the author's, which nobody ever heard of.

I always advise beginning authors to solicit prominent people and celebrities for endorsements and to get them *before publication,* if possible. A prepublishing quote is extremely valuable in attracting reviewer, bookseller, and ancillary-rights attention. If you are a beginning novelist, a quote from the likes of Norman Mailer, Kurt Vonnegut, John Irving, Irving Wallace, or Wallace Stegner will greatly enhance your chances of being bought and read in the con-

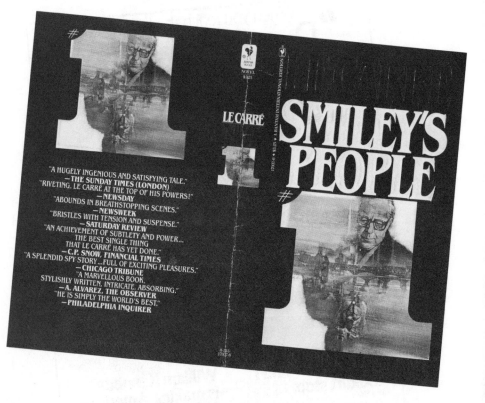

sumer marketplace. *Their* names are significant to book buyers. Their endorsement verifies your talent as a novelist. The public reacts positively to someone notable telling them, "This is good, read it." This is my advice to first-time novelists: try to secure the endorsements of a notable by sending your manuscript to him or her to read, via a friend, relative, or other contact. Lacking a personal contact, I would solicit comments from a name writer. The worst that can occur is a "No" or no response.

With nonfiction, endorsement depends upon your subject. If yours is a medical treatise of some sort, seek a "name" in the medical profession; if it's a baseball book, try for a luminary in that field; you might seek a quote from an executive in an organization if your book is about business or management. It works.

Your audience would be pleased to know and perhaps motivated to buy a book endorsed by a "name" personality in the field or the genre in which you are writing.

Some years ago, a particularly effective advertising campaign was created for the book *How to Be Your Own Best Friend,* by husband-and-wife psychiatrists Newman and Berkowitz. Their patients included Richard Benjamin, Tony Perkins, Paula Prentiss, and numerous others. The patients—all celebrities—endorsed the book in all the ads and promotional copy because they believed so strongly in the authors. The campaign was singularly effective in launching a best-seller.

Get *someone*—the more famous the better—to endorse your book before publication. Be sure to clear the use of his or her name and comments for advertising and public relations by getting written permission. Use the quote on the book and in all copy that sells or hypes the book.

The letter to the prospective endorser should be friendly and enthusiastic, describing why your book is special and why you would be honored if he or she would give you a prepublication comment. Send only a description of your book, not the entire manuscript. Your celebrity can always ask for it later. If it is possible to call or visit in person, this would be quicker than writing a letter.

Often celebrities or prominent individuals are receptive to endorsing first books even if they do not know you, because you are appealing to their egos. It may enhance their images if their name appears on the cover of a book. If a name person is particularly responsive to giving you a quote, you might consider asking for something longer, in the form of a preface or a foreword. Again, you are "flattering" them by asking for their endorsement.

I would not recommend that you *pay* for an endorsement or foreword *unless* you can afford the price quoted, it is a reasonable price, and you feel that the fee is worth this particular endorsement. An initial endorsement is also extremely helpful in soliciting another. If you were asking Norman Mailer for an endorsement, it would be a plus if you could tell him about an earlier endorsement from Saul Bellow. When the authors of *The One Minute Manager* received favorable comments from the vice president of IBM, the chairman of the Joint Chiefs of Staff, and the general manager of Chevron, they used these endorsements to obtain others. Early endorsements can also be effective when you are soliciting a publisher. Publishers are generally impressed with someone else's comments about your book, particularly if it is someone prominent.

Use any connection you have in securing an endorsement. It is a very important potential ingredient in creating *your* best-seller. A friend or contact may know a suitable "name" to solicit for a quote, and you can continue to try for quotes before, during, and after publication. Ask for them! A great quote from a celebrity is always valuable in creating a best-seller. It can go on later editions or on the cover of a subsequent paperback reprint.

When Dana/Corwin Enterprises produced *The Lotus Position*, by rising young comedienne Lotus Weinstock, we got a prepublication quote from Phyllis Diller. The Diller endorsement helped greatly in evoking a market response that we might not have received otherwise.

"The best novel written in America since . . ." can't hurt. Bestsellers thrive on it.

●●●●●●●●●●●●●●●●●●●●●

Looking for Cover

14. In today's publishing marketplace, the jacket or cover is absolutely essential in selling your book to prospective buyers. In the past, when the literary quality of a book was its most marketable component, what was between the covers was more important than the cover itself.

But the marketing and promotional hype of all books—literary and otherwise—soon began to resemble the hard-sell marketing of other mass products: soap, toothpaste, beer, and cigarettes. Jackets on hardcover books, self-printed cloth covers (primarily on children's books) and the covers of paperbacks featured striking typography and eye-catching artwork. Alluring cover blurbs (quotes or "sell the book" copy) were used to sell the product inside. Art directors and jacket designers at major publishing houses were elevated to top executive status and were asked to create best-selling covers for all kinds of books. Cover meetings became part of a publisher's primary work, and included participation by the heads of sales and marketing, promotion, editorial, and subsidiary rights, and often by the publisher or president of the company. The jacket or cover was often the key element in selling the book initially at the retail display level. It was important that the head of a publishing company make the final decision for "the right cover look." Selling and promoting a book by its cover became a vital function of every publisher, and a substantial amount of time was spent on achieving the right cover look and design and capturing the right buzzwords in the blurb.

Freelance artists and designers were commissioned to express visually the appeal of books of every genre. Jacket designs and blurbs had to be approved by all the previously mentioned heads of departments. Sometimes the author, especially if he or she was a best-selling author, was also consulted.

Because the author has usually had only a one-time or infrequent experience with book publication, the final approval of all the "publication specifications"—size, price, cover design, format, and overall concept—rests with the publisher, by contract and by mutual understanding. The publisher, with its collective years of experience, has a broader, keener sense of how a commercial and appealing cover should look. The staff has tested many book covers, and generally has a feel for what covers will or won't work. Most authors have not had any experience in gauging the reactions of the marketplace to covers or jackets.

The only exception is a specific contractual clause that gives the author cover approval. This rarely happens, and is usually a privilege enjoyed only by the best-selling author.

There are some general rules about what will work on book covers. The cover should reflect appropriately what the book is about, and promote its subject and message accurately. It should be faithful to the subject or genre it represents. The typeface (carefully chosen to depict a strong, feminine, light, businesslike, or humorous look, for example), and the artwork should please the eye and evoke an emotional response from the consumer. Thousands of new books appear on shelves and racks each month. Any appealing look that attracts attention is a definite plus factor in selling books. (One paperback publisher recently commented that today's paperback industry has been reduced to "the selling of artwork.")

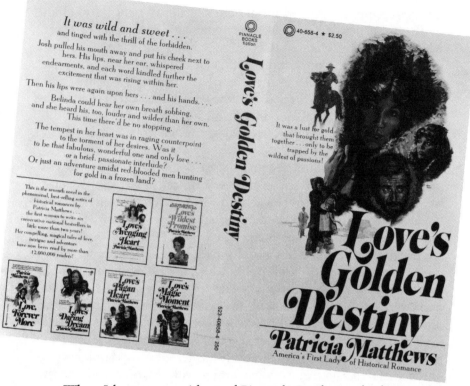

When I became president of Pinnacle Books, and when we became one of the early publishers to succeed in the categories of romance and historical saga, we devoted a great deal of our time and promotional energy to exotic and titillating cover art that depicted the mood of titles like *Love's Avenging Heart, A Fatal Passion,* and *Storm over Windhaven.* The art conveyed the fantasy appeal of the romantic titles, and the public began to buy romances at an increasing rate until the genre became slightly oversaturated. Although we often consulted with the author and the sales staff, I, as head of the company, made the final cover decisions.

Every book should have its own unique cover, but a cover that suggests (subtly) a previous best-seller often achieves commercial results. This practice has been demonstrated most effectively with certain cover looks for books that resemble *Jaws, The Joy of Sex,* and *Thin Thighs in 30 Days.* Similarly, best-sellers such as *Scruples, The Godfather,* all the Ludlum titles, the Patricia Matthews and

Rosemary Rogers sagas, and the Sidney Sheldon-type novels have imitated each other with common jacket concepts and artistic renditions.

Other jackets have succeeded by using type layouts rather than pictures or paintings. A specific typeface is chosen because of its connection with the subject of the book. A masculine, austere typeface is often used for business books; scribbly, lighter type for humor books; and bold, convincing type for "how-to" and inspirational books. Choosing the most effective typeface for a particular book is of major importance to the art director and the publisher in their plans to sell a book. They must also decide whether type, art, or a combination of the two would represent the book most commercially. Nonfiction subjects feature more use of type; fiction uses more artwork, often originating in lavish artists' paintings or sometimes in line drawings or photographs.

Sell copy or cover blurbs should convey the boldest, most commercial message possible in the fewest words. The location of cover copy is important to attract reader attention, and should be integrated into the design. The title is usually set in the biggest type, unless the author's name is made more prominent. (See books by Robert Ludlum, James Michener, James Clavell, and others.) Prominent names are generally followed by "Author of—," their last or most enduring book. That layout leaves little room for a blurb, and a blurb isn't really needed. A new novel "by Irwin Shaw, Author of *Rich Man, Poor Man*" doesn't need much else on the cover. Paperback reprints of previous hardcover best-sellers often feature such blurbs as "No. 1 National Best-Seller List," "30 weeks on the *New York Times* best-seller list," "Coast-to-Coast National Best-Seller," "A Book-of-the-Month Club Selection." The previous success story of a book is the most effective cover blurb. Endorsements or excerpts from reviews, if available and meaningful, are often featured prominently on covers.

If these are lacking, clever copywriters have to manufacture blurbs that sell books. An effective blurb is almost mandatory for first novels and new authors. It will generally be used again in promotional pieces, advertising, sell copy, and—believe it or not—in *review columns* describing the new book. Years ago, when I wrote ad copy for books, I was surprised at how often *my* copy appeared

Three Clavell Masterpieces

Delacorte Press is proud to reissue in hardcover the three great novels by James Clavell which preceded *Noble House* in his Asian saga.

"THE HUMAN STORY, FAR FROM ENDING, HAS ONLY JUST BEGUN."
—ALVIN TOFFLER

Futurist Alvin Toffler believes we are right now in the midst of a sweeping global revolution: The death of industrialism, and the rise of the first truly humane civilization.
THE THIRD WAVE makes sense of the violent changes now battering our world, and predicts how you will live in the new world:
With new forms of marriage and family life · New sex roles · More responsive political and economic structures · New definitions of work, play, love and success.

"A PROVOCATIVE GLIMPSE INTO AN EXCITING FUTURE."
—BUSINESS WEEK

"MAGNIFICENT ...A book that anyone concerned with the future must read."
— THE WASHINGTON POST

STARTLING, BRILLIANT AND PROPHETIC, ALVIN TOFFLER'S THE THIRD WAVE IS A BOLD FORECAST OF A BETTER NEW WORLD.

THE THIRD WAVE
ALVIN TOFFLER

HE ROCKED THE WORLD WITH FUTURE SHOCK
NOW COMES HIS BOOK FOR THE '80s

"A PROVOCATIVE GLIMPSE INTO AN EXCITING FUTURE."

THE THIRD WAVE
ALVIN TOFFLER

verbatim in a reviewer's original critique of a new book.

The perfect integration of cover art with blurb can and will attract attention and sell more copies. Even though unoriginal blurbs and overused buzzwords like the "greatest novel since *Gone With The Wind*" and "the only book that . . ." continue to be written, original covers with original selling phrases are still more effective in the long run.

What can *you*, as a beginning author, do to influence the design of your cover or jacket? Read this chapter, peruse the book racks, and study the jackets of books on subjects similar to yours so that you are familiar with the market. Then you can suggest some designs and layouts and cover copy to your editor (*not* to the art director). Your suggestions will be welcome if they are pertinent. If you were able to solicit a prepublication quote of commercial value, send it to be used on the front or back cover. Ask (and say "please") to see the cover art along with the front and back copy before it is approved and printed.

The design of a cover or jacket is influenced strongly by the physical format of the book. There is obviously more room on an 8½x11" trade paperback cover than on a rack-sized paperback. The cover should be filled only if warranted; sometimes a simple design and less copy are just as effective as a fuller look. What the cover conveys is the essential objective, but to take liberties with the words of the late Marshall McLuhan, the format is often the message. The right size and shape, the appropriate blend of artwork and words, can make a significant difference in achieving a bestseller. *Your* title and *your* cover will be tested and approved in the marketplace long before anyone reads *your* book.

The jacket or cover is a vitally important tool that will sell your book to the publisher's sales staff, to the rights marketplace, to the retailer and the wholesaler, and finally to the consumer. The publisher spends considerable time in achieving the right cover look because the appropriate cover will sell more copies. Because the book buyer and the public visualize what the book is like before they read it, the cover serves as a small, strong, graphic poster. The right blend of vibrant colors, raised or foil-stamped type, cutouts on the front cover, wraparound art, bold type, unusual design, and a powerful message in a few persuasive words can move the consumer to buy this particular book. Just a few seconds in a bookstore may make the difference between the purchase of one book and another.

Jacket copy (which the publisher may sometimes ask you, instead of another person, to write) and author biography are other essential ingredients that sell books at the retail level. Often the copy will have an appealing best-seller aura about it—"If you read only one book this year . . .," "From the moment you start reading this wonderful story . . ." That's why books are bought. That's how books become best-sellers.

When you have ideas about your cover, about a commercial design, about a strong selling blurb, express them in a positive, enthusiastic tone to your editor and publisher. And do it early, before they spend hundreds of dollars on designs or typesetting. Let them know that you, too, want to create a best-seller, and here's how you think it can be done. They may listen to your ideas; they may not. But at least communicate with them to achieve one mutually desirable result—the creation of a cover that looks, feels, and sounds like a best-seller. Nothing less.

The Bottom Line

15. The potential best-selling author must realize that publishing is a *business*. The literary "maven" at all book companies (usually the publisher or editor-in-chief) will generally share with marketing or financial people the responsibility for acquiring new manuscripts. A publication proposal with P&L (profit and loss) guesstimates is the norm, and a rigid financial criterion is established before a book is accepted for publication. Seldom is a book published because one person says, "I want to publish this book." It is essential for the beginning author to understand the financial considerations behind every publisher's editorial decisions.

Financial and P&L variables include amount of advance, royalty percentages, format, size, retail price, estimated net sell, anticipated rights income, manufacturing cost, size of first printing, and whether the cost can be amortized over more than one edition. These days it is not so much a question of whether it is a good book. The primary criterion is "How much money can it earn?" In the past, the president or publisher of a company rose through the editorial ranks, but many publishers of the sixties and seventies were schooled in marketing and subsidiary rights. Today an increasing number of heads of houses are female.

When I became president of Pinnacle Books, I had traveled the training route of rights and marketing. Howard Kaminsky, president of Warner Books, was once the rights director at Random House. Susan Petersen, president of Ballantine-Fawcett, has a marketing background. So has Jack Artenstein, formerly the head of Simon and Schuster's trade paperbacks division. Rena Wolner, publisher of Berkley-Jove, worked for many years as an overall assistant to the publisher of Bantam Books, Oscar Dystel.

Today's breed of publisher grew up in the publishing business, fully aware of the bottom line. It was no longer a gentleman's business, but was now concerned with sizes and formats, innovative merchandising and marketing, computerized analysis, escalated costs and returns, and retail prices. There was no rigid formula; constant marketing, editorial, and financial variations altered publishing decisions and programs. Our generation had to learn "the business" better than our predecessors. And when the conglomerates bought in, they forced editors to apply slide-rule formulas to the way books were bought, sold, and merchandised. The formulas affected best-selling books *and* first novels.

In recent years the publishing industry suffered along with the general economy. Too many books were being published, retail prices accelerated at an inflationary rate, and the costs of doing business rose sharply. Some of the major conglomerates, such as RCA and CBS, became disenchanted with the publishing companies they had bought, and they resold them. Many companies with publishing backgrounds and backlists were assimilated into or sold to larger houses. For all intents and purposes, publishing giants like Grosset & Dunlap, Popular Library, Fawcett, and Dodd, Mead no longer existed. One giant media conglomerate, MCA, owned what had been eight separate publishing companies: Putnam, Coward McCann, Grosset & Dunlap, Ace, Quick Fox, Berkley, Playboy Press, and Jove. These were now imprints of larger companies. Unfortunately, jobs were also eliminated, and there were fewer employment opportunities for experienced publishing personnel. (For more on the economics of publishing see "Can Trade Publishers Ever Make Money?" and "Publish AND Perish" in the Appendix.)

What did this trend mean for the author of a first book? It meant that he or she was dealing not only with Simon & Schuster, Putnam, Morrow, and Random House, but with the corporate structure of their respective parent companies—Gulf and Western, MCA, Hearst, and Condé Nast. It became more important for a book to make money than to receive literary accolades. The successful, profitable houses survived, not necessarily those that published better books. The first-time author had to think commercially, to think of creating a *best-seller*. With the advent of the conglomerates into the publishing business and the demise of many unprofitable publishers, the book industry also demanded the survival of the fittest. You were a successful author, a best-selling author, if your book made a lot of money for you and for your publisher.

No one expected that one day books would be sold by the pound, or that editorial decisions would be made by the firm's chief accountant. A blend of the two might be responsible for publishing decisions. But it was certainly true that in order to survive, publishing would remain a business, run by business people and formulated on business principles. Literary works, both critically acclaimed books and best-sellers, would be welcome as long as they made money on the bottom line. For the publisher, for the book buyer, and for the new author, it was important that everyone understand the bottom line.

There's No Such Thing as Too Much Publicity and Advertising

16. Sidney Sheldon, Irwin Shaw, and the like are generally guaranteed an advertising and publicity budget—a dollar amount that must be spent to promote their forthcoming books. You, as a first novelist or new author, will have no such promotional guarantees. Publicity and advertising expenditures on your book not guaranteed by contract are subject to the mercurial whims of your publisher.

There's no disputing that expenditures for advertising and promotion of books are effective. The public buys best-sellers that are heavily advertised and publicized, just as they buy any product that is made highly visible. A promoted book has a decided advantage over one that nobody has ever heard of. Yet, the publisher's hyping and publicizing of a new book is often directed more to luring lucrative subsidiary rights sales—paperback, book-club, foreign, and serialization—than to selling books. Promotional dollars do attract public and rights market attention to one book rather than another.

Dr. Tessa Albert Warshaw's book, *Winning by Negotiation* (Mc-Graw-Hill), appeared in print simultaneously with *You Can Negotiate Anything,* by Herb Cohen. Cohen's publisher, Lyle Stuart, advertised and promoted his book very heavily. As a result, the Cohen book attracted a larger share of public attention and eventually made the *New York Times* best-seller list. Although I felt that Dr. Warshaw's book was better written and researched, the competing book was better advertised and promoted, and became a bona fide national best-seller. It also commanded a higher offer for paperback reprint rights.

Even if you can't effect a promotional guarantee in your contract, you can aid your publisher in creating your own promotion. One major ingredient is *you*. If you are appealing and attractive (visually or conversationally) and if you can conduct a lively and informative interview about your book, you can gain access to the major talk shows. A personality "shtick" about your book and subject can be very effective in talk-show conversation. Lisa Birnbach and her *Preppy Handbook* demonstrated this point most successfully. The best-known shows include the *Today* show, *Good Morning America*, the *Tonight* show (less likely for authors), *Phil Donahue*, *Merv Griffin*, *20/20*, *Entertainment Tonight*, *Hour Magazine*, *David Letterman*, and *Thicke of the Night*, as well as many regional shows that people watch in their home towns, and the burgeoning cable programs.

A national appearance will definitely generate book sales and rights attention. A regional appearance on *A.M. Los Angeles, Kup's Show* in Chicago, or *The Joe Franklin Show* in New York will affect sales favorably in that particular city.

A publisher generally allocates an overall promotion and publicity budget for the entire season's list of new publications. This budget is based on sales forecasts and expectations of how well each particular book will do. Obviously the anticipated best-selling books and authors will be allocated more money for publicity and author tours. The new author's book will probably get less of the publicity budget. It is essential that you try to find out where your book will fit in a particular season and approximately how much of a budget you can expect to receive for promotional expenditures.

If your publisher's budgets or efforts can't arrange a national talk show, you may consider trying to obtain such appearances on your own and *out of your own pocket*. Your publishers may be on a tight budget or may be allocating the whole season's promotion budget to *their* Sidney Sheldon, and may not be planning to spend *any* money on your book. Try to find this out as early as possible so that you can make your own publicity plans, if necessary.

Nonfiction subjects (a new diet, exercise, sports, cooking, biography, new approach to living, money) will generally appeal more to talk shows than will fiction. These subjects are usually of broader interest and easier for the general public to respond to. If your sub-

About the Authors
Lynette Triere is a practicing divorce counselor on the staff of the San Diego Institute in La Jolla, California. She has served as the director of the Palomar College Women's Center, San Marcos, California. She lives in Leucadia, California.

Richard Peacock is a journalist, screenwriter, and teacher at the Palomar College, San Marcos, California. He is the father of four children. Both authors have been divorced.

$25,000 Advertising and Promotion Campaign
☐ Author tour to 12 cities:

New York · Washington · Boston · Philadelphia · Chicago · Los Angeles
San Francisco · Dallas/Ft. Worth · Atlanta · Minneapolis · Cleveland

☐ 10-copy counter display unit with special riser 12-745-0, retail value $79.50 (In Canada: 12-746-9, $95.00)

☐ National publicity

Learning to Leave: A Woman's Guide
by Lynette Triere with Richard Peacock
37-719-8, $7.95 (In Canada, 37-720-1, $9.50)
5¼ x 8   400 pages   COBE
Shipping July 1
Originally published in hardcover by Contemporary Books

The Best of Trade Paperback Bestsellers

WARNER BOOKS

The Complete Publisher
A Warner Communications Company

"An Indispensable Survival Kit for a Woman Whose Marriage Is on the Rocks"
—Gay Talese

Are you divorced? Divorcing? Thinking of divorce? Here is the help you need when you need it most!

Learning to Leave

"By dispelling guilt, fear and other negative feelings with information, the book provides emotional support needed by women going through divorce and offers nitty-gritty advice..."
—*Detroit Free Press*

A WOMAN'S GUIDE
Lynette Triere with Richard Peacock
Foreword by Gretchen Cryer

ject is truly unusual or of major topical concern, it may be of interest to the national shows, and it just could be the catalyst that generates the best-seller book sales. When I was involved in publishing *My Shadow Ran Fast* (Prentice-Hall), Bill Sands' unorthodox autobiography about his life in and out of prisons, sales were meager—until we were able to book Bill on Johnny Carson's *Tonight* show. He mesmerized the audience in his debut, and was invited back. The two appearances were sensational and far-reaching; his book became a *New York Times* best-seller and then sold for a large paperback advance.

● ● ●

Can you use your own publicist? Yes! If your subject is commercial and interesting, if you are promotionally attractive, and if your book has appeal to a national audience, the media are accessible to you. If your publisher won't spend and if you can afford to, do it. It will not diminish your potential status as a best-selling author if you spend publicity dollars that your publisher won't or can't spend. It can be an effective way to determine your own best-seller destiny. Hire a local publicist. Ask your editor or the publicity director where you can find them. They exist in every major city. Among the best are Irwin Zucker, Mike Daugherty, and Judy Hilsinger in Los Angeles, and Mike Beinner, Mike Levine, Selma Shapiro, Alice Allen Donald, and Betsy Nolan in New York. At approximately $1500-$2000 per month for their services they will get you on significant local talk shows and perhaps some national ones. They have all worked with or created best-sellers.

There is no doubt that appearances on *Good Morning America* and the *Today* show can spark national bestsellerdom. They have worked for Wayne Dyer, Durk Pierson, the Wallace family, Howard Ruff, and others. Talk-show appearances lead to other talk-show appearances.

Once you have had the experience of appearing on a talk show—national or local, radio or TV—you will get a feel for the format and time restrictions of the show and how best to plug your book. If possible, the ideal television appearance will allow you to mention the title of your book, show it to the viewer and studio audiences, and tell where it can be bought. (You may have more time to do this on a local than on a national show.) It is generally best to begin publicity appearances on regional shows to practice, unless you are summoned at the outset by *Good Morning America* or the *Today* show. Do not turn them away—at any time. I believe that publicity can and does sell books. It makes the public *aware* of your book and subject.

I used the PR services of the Edye Rome firm in Los Angeles when I locally published *Love Is Love but Business Is Business* by attorney Merle Horwitz. This appealing trade paperback on cohabitation contracts, which was printed and published privately in Southern California, was aimed more at a mail-order audience than at the consumer retail market.

Through the diligent and creative efforts of Edye Rome and her associate, Mike Daugherty, they were able to book the author on every major radio talk show in Los Angeles and San Diego. Merle was very effective on the airways, and he constantly plugged the book and told where it could be obtained. Subsequent print articles, an Associated Press nationally syndicated story, and a *Money* magazine feature mentioned the book and where it could be bought.

We were inundated with orders and checks from all across America. Again, it was *publicity* that sold books—combined with an appealing subject, an attractive author, and a very efficient PR firm.

When Robert Ringer published Dr. Irene Kassorla's national best-seller, *Nice Girls Do* (Stratford Press), he created a best-seller by running full-page newspaper ads in every major city and following them with author appearances. When the author toured the country and appeared on every talk show, she stimulated attention—and plugged the book right onto the national best-seller lists. Dr. Kassorla was fascinating and highly promotable, and sales followed her appearances.

Insurance promoter Barry Kaye tried to use this publicity-advertising formula when he self-published *How to Make a Fortune on Your Life Insurance*. He spent hundreds of thousands of dollars on his own national tour and on full-page ads throughout the country. Because the subject was specialized and the book was not written well, the book sales didn't justify the cost of investment. But the campaign effectively promoted Kaye himself, and it definitely helped his insurance business.

In contrast, Robert G. Allen has parlayed his master salesmanship techniques into two long-running Simon & Schuster best-sellers, *Nothing Down* and *Creating Wealth*. Both books tell how to make a lot of money through real estate and other financial ventures. The primary reason for the extraordinary successes of the books is probably the author himself. "Robert Allen is a masterful promoter," said the business-book buyer at B. Dalton. "He goes into an area, sets up a seminar, 'A Free Evening With Robert Allen,' and gets people excited about his ideas. He never fails to sell books."

This formula of overhype, as evidenced by the success of such self-promoters as Robert Ringer and Wayne Dyer, works if the subject is broadly appealing. The ad saturation for Judy Mazel's *Beverly Hills Diet* (Macmillan) worked well because the formula and title appeal were reminiscent of *The Scarsdale Diet* success pattern. Heavy ad saturation did not work, however, for Jack Dreyfus' *A Remarkable Medicine Has Been Overlooked* (touting a new medicine) because the subject was obscure and its appeal limited.

The national book market is broken down demographically into approximately fifteen to twenty major metropolitan markets (the largest cities in America) and some fifty bookstores and chains

that report regularly to the best-seller list. By saturating these markets simultaneously with advertising and author publicity, the public is reminded constantly of the new, talked-about book. The stores respond to the media attention by stocking an ample supply of copies and displaying the book prominently.

Generally, the magic formula subjects respond to these extraordinary expenditures of promotional dollars. We're referring again to books that tell you how to make more money, help you improve your looks, health, and image, make you live longer or more happily, or emphasize self-help. It would not be prudent to invest a great

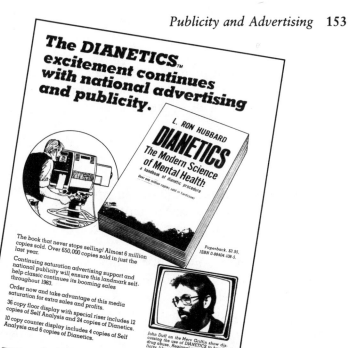

deal of promotional money in a work of fiction. The appeal is often literary and esoteric. Producers of talk shows generally feel that fiction is not topically appealing to their mass audiences. Also, it is difficult to promote a plot and writing style as well as a particular subject. A nonfiction book on a specific subject, such as gardening or tennis, can be advertised to a specific market via newspapers, journals, and magazines that feature those subjects.

A dominant, appealing personality such as Luciano Pavarotti or Shirley MacLaine has immediate access to all national talk shows on radio and TV, and requires less hype and creative publicity. If your budget is limited and your subject difficult to advertise, you can gain more promotional mileage from publicity. National advertising, even a cooperative ad with a national bookstore chain (where the publisher generally spends 75% and the bookstore 25% of the cost of the ad), is expensive, although it is worthwhile to have a Walden or Dalton chain contribute to the advertising of a "bestseller." Publicity appearances are less costly after you pay for a publicist, except for your own time. If you or your book are promotable, many publicity outlets are available in this country to generate public reaction. Remember—there is no such thing as *too much* publicity.

Another effective form of promotion is the lecture circuit. In every major city lecture bureaus will book creditable or famous authors. The lecture circuit affords an author national exposure before large audiences and an opportunity to sell books directly to his or her market. Appearances at national conventions of organizations related to your subject or your area of expertise can also launch a best-seller.

Perhaps the most important authors' convention is the annual American Booksellers' Convention (ABA), which is held in a different American city each year, usually around Memorial Day weekend. You would probably appear at the ABA at your publisher's request—to meet booksellers and the publisher's sales personnel, and to autograph copies if finished books are available. If your book generates favorable advance reactions at the ABA convention, it could be a much-discussed future publication.

At some time in the publication process, your publisher may decide to increase the advertising and promotion budget of your book. The book may have greater sales potential long after you've signed a publication contract. Also, *you* can be aware of the various ways to promote future sales. "Off-the-wall" or creative advertising and publicity is often effective. Years ago, comedian Pat Paulsen decided to run for President, and wrote a book about it. The publishers of *Masquerade* stimulated reader response by offering a hidden treasure that could be found by following the clues in the book. The publishers of *Who Killed the Robins Family?*, by Thomas Chastain and Bill Adler, offer a $10,000 prize to the reader who submits the best answer.

If a special market or audience exists for you and your book idea, suggest to your publisher where to advertise, where to send press releases or advance notices, and where to send free copies. A feature article or ad placed in a trade or local publication can often stimulate sales. An author bio, a press release, or review copies can be very effective best-seller catalysts in the hands of the appropriate influential people.

The obvious media for book advertising are the *New York Times Book Review* and book sections of other regional and local newspapers; national magazines and TV and radio spots (all very expensive); trade and industry journals; community weekly newspapers; *Publishers Weekly* and *Library Journal* for the book trade; cable TV; billboards (for big best-sellers); and in-store flyers and bookmarks. Although TV and radio ads reach more people, they are also prohibitively expensive compared to selective print advertising. If you are spending your own money on advertising, be very sure of the market you are reaching and the cost-effectiveness of such an expenditure. Evaluate ads for previous best-sellers as models for promoting your own book.

On the publicity circuit, an author tour can "make" a best-seller if all the right and necessary ingredients coincide. These include appearing on the important talk shows in the major cities; appearing on as many shows as possible in a two- to three-day period; setting up author autograph sessions in several key downtown or mall bookstores; having your books well stocked in the stores in that city at the time of your appearances; and arranging the advertising or publicity articles to run simultaneously. One city can launch a best-seller. It can happen to a best-selling author at any time.

Delivering the Mail Order

17. Mail-order advertising has been effective for selling everything from records and knives on late-night TV to all the gadgets and gimmicks imaginable via the print media. Mail order is not the same as "direct mail," which elicits response from advertising sales letters mailed directly to prospective buyers.

Selling books through mail-order coupon ads has been a viable alternative to retail sales ever since the advent of book clubs in the United States. The Literary Guild and the Book-of-the-Month Club have sold millions of books through mail-order ads, mostly in the *New York Times Book Review, TV Guide,* and numerous monthly magazines and Sunday newspapers. Their initial offers of "Any 4 Books for $1" to join the club (the Book-of-the-Month Club now offers "Any 4 Books for $2" as a result of inflation) have attracted an extraordinary number of new members who buy best-sellers through the mail rather than purchasing them at a bookstore.

Generally, the book subjects that are commercially best suited to mail order are those "how-to" categories that often occupy the nonfiction best-seller lists. Except for book club ads, novels are rarely solicited through coupon advertising. The categories of sex, diet, health, longevity, pop psychology, making money, or learning how to do or get something specific for $9.95 or $14.95 are essential ingredients for book mail order. It costs an appreciable amount for a book publisher or for you to buy space for mail order advertising. Therefore, it is essential that the book advertised be *needed* by someone, that the ad copy be alluring and evocative, and that the appropriate advertising medium be selected at the outset. If a full-page ad in a national newspaper or magazine costs $5000 and your book product retails at $10.00, you would have to sell five hundred books to break even on your investment (after the costs of writing and preparing the ad). It is generally only profitable to sell a book by mail order for $10.00 or more.

Self-publishers are very cost-conscious, and are cautious in selecting media. The larger New York publishers generally run their mail-order ads in Sunday newspaper book-review sections, particularly *The New York Times*. This placement serves two purposes: the ad is seen by book devotees who purchase at retail outlets; and it provides a coupon for consumers to purchase by mail. The latest diet or "how-to" book is often the subject for this ad.

When I was a beginning publisher at Prentice-Hall, we initially offered Dr. Stillman's *The Doctor's Quick Weight Loss Diet* through bookstores with no appreciable results. Only several months later, when a mail-order company acquired the rights to run coupon ads, did sales begin to increase to best-seller proportions. The impetus for this extraordinary multimillion-copy best-seller came from mail order. The title and subject lent itself to that kind of campaign, and the ad appealed to the purchaser's personal needs. Dr. Atkins' diet books were also sparked by initial mail-order ads.

Years ago in New York, I met an enterprising young man named Eric Weber. He was a successful advertising copywriter who self-published a book entitled *How to Pick Up Girls* and sold it through small coupon ads in magazines. Weber shipped the books and ran his sideline business out of his home.

This tiny shoestring business soon grew into an extraordinarily successful and lucrative mail-order book enterprise. Books fol-

lowed successful books, all adhering to a specific formula. Cassettes and seminars followed the books, and the operation thrived as Symphony Press, one of the most successful mail-order merchandisers in America today. Presently, Eric Weber and Symphony Press run a number of full-page coupon ads every month in national magazines such as *Esquire* and *Psychology Today*. The product line has expanded to the Encyclopedia of Picking Up Women at $49.95, and includes numerous books on this subject, including the original *How to Pick Up Girls*.

My close friend Melvin Powers, president of Wilshire Book Company in Los Angeles, has successfully launched and sold many best-sellers through mail order for over 25 years. His own book, *How to Get Rich in Mail Order*, is the best book written on the subject, and has been sold by mail order with great success. His mail-order campaigns and techniques for *Psycho-Cybernetics* and *The Magic of Thinking Big* are unprecedented in the publishing industry.

Mel Powers' formula for mail-order success is based on a best-seller copycat technique. He and other mail-order entrepreneurs co-pycatted the proven formula of Joe Karbo *(The Lazy Man's Way to Riches)* and Mark Haroldsen *(How to Wake Up the Financial Genius inside You)*. Karbo's and Haroldson's coupon ads are almost classic for evoking a "best-seller" response. The ad copy is appealing and hard-selling, and the basic message is ". . . Here is a proven formula for making money and for only $10 . . . $15 . . . you can have it too . . . Otherwise you can have your money back in 30 days . . . 90 days . . ."

In the ad, the publisher has created a bandwagon effect: people are buying this book and it's working for *them*. Now, here's *your* opportunity. For only . . . The mail-order technique thrives on the message that *you need this book*. It's not something to read casually. You need it. It will change your life.

The product is needed, the ad copy is compelling and appeals to that need, and the coupon tells just what to do. Mail $— to —. Add $— for postage and handling. Tell how many copies you want and provide your name and address. Generally allow about three weeks for delivery. It's that simple.

Through the years, mail order has sold a lot of books, including

many recent best-sellers that generated national retail sales *after* coupon ads appeared in print. Selling books through the mail is invariably more profitable for the publisher because there are no wholesaler or retailer discounts off the list price, no returns (all sales are final after thirty to sixty days), and no sales commissions; only the cost and preparation of the ad and shipping and handling (fulfillment). At its best, mail-order book advertising has launched many a best-seller. Even at its worst, it can be a profitable adjunct to a promotion and advertising campaign to sell a particular title to the public.

If your book lends itself to mail order, you may want to meet with the sales and advertising personnel at your publisher to discuss such a campaign. You may have some leads and ideas for mail order to which your publisher will be receptive. You may also be able to retain mail-order rights, either exclusive or nonexclusive, and pursue this market yourself. When we sold *Love Is Love but Business is Business* to William Morrow, we retained the exclusive mail-order rights and continued to sell books through that market. Since the ads invariably provide more detail about a book, retail sales are also generated if the book is available in bookstores simultaneously with the ads.

A variation of mail order is "direct-mail" advertising, which consists of mailing a flyer or brochure about a book to persons on a specific list of consumers who are likely to be responsive to that subject. At Grosset & Dunlap, for example, we sent direct-mail flyers on Hubert Humphrey's pictorial autobiography to members of the National Democratic Party. Direct mail can be effective if you present the right book to the right mailing list: flying books to aviators, golf books to golfers. Ask yourself and your publisher whether your book should be aimed at a selected audience.

Premiums

Another way to augment retail book sales is through premiums and special sales. Premiums are products created to promote and sell other products. They can be the World Series booklets that came with Gillette razor blades, the toasters and calculators received when you open a savings account, or the secret rings and ce-

lebrity posters you sent away for with cereal boxtops. Either the actual book or an abbreviated portion of a book is offered in a special premium edition.

When I was a marketing VP at Grosset & Dunlap, we were the publishers of the well-known children's series, *The Hardy Boys* and *Nancy Drew*. A close friend of mine had started his own premium company, and through his contact at General Foods, we were able to make a premium offering of special editions on twenty million boxes of Post Raisin Bran cereal. Over a million Nancy Drew and Hardy Boys titles were sold through this premium outlet, and additional retail sales were generated through this extraordinary point-of-purchase advertising. We repeated this successful offering with Nestle's Quik. The net income to the publisher was about ten cents per book, which was split with the author.

Books have been sold effectively as premiums, and such enterprises as The Benjamin Company achieved significant sales exclusively in book premiums. All the major paperback houses now have

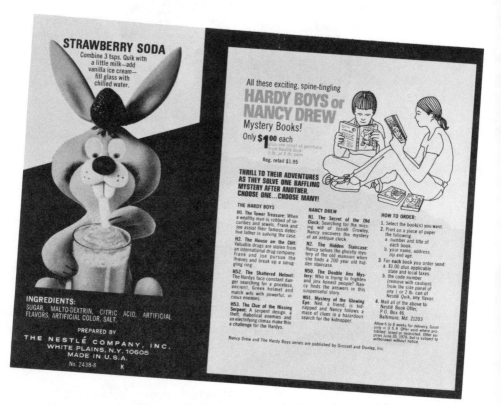

thriving premium departments, and such perennial titles as *The Guinness Book of World Records* (Bantam Books) and *How to Flatten Your Stomach* (Price/Stern/Sloan) enjoy considerable annual premium sales.

Premiums can earn large book revenues because of the quantity produced. Because they are extra sales, they generate additional advertising and promotion, and the sales are nonreturnable. Nonfiction titles are useful premiums in selling higher-priced products, such as cookbooks with kitchenware. Often a book is condensed in a special paperback format, and a company edition is produced with a special imprint. *The Betty Crocker Cookbook, The Joy of Cooking,* and the Ortho gardening books have been offered by banks and other companies as premiums.

"Special sales" are bulk sales of an existing book to a specific company, generally at a reduced price. When we published Captain Eddie Rickenbacker's autobiography at Prentice-Hall, we prepared and sold a special imprinted edition of 15,000 copies to Eastern Airlines. At Pinnacle, we sold large quantities of the *Baskin-Robbins Ice Cream Book* to that sponsoring company, all nonreturnable.

Special and premium sales are ways to sell quantities of a title other than through the regular book market, but matching the right title to the right potential market calls for creative selling and planning. The appropriate product must be offered to the appropriate market at the ideal time. If *you* have some specific ideas regarding possible premium markets or premium packaging for your book, inform your publisher. Premiums can bring additional income in the making of a best-seller.

Can I Publish My Own Book?

18. With the proliferation of regional publishing during the past five years, the decreasing number of major publishing houses, and the emergence of national bookstore chains, it was inevitable that self-publishing would become an economic alternative in America's book business.

When such individual entrepreneurs as Moody (*Life After Life*), Vicki Lansky of Meadowbrook Press (*The Taming of the Candy Monster*), and Robert Ringer (*Winning Through Intimidation*) successfully self-published their own books, many prospective authors were encouraged to follow suit. Bill Montapert's *The Omega Strategy*, self-published in California, was bought by Warner Books for $100,000. If one had a commercial project and some capital to invest, why bother finding an agent, submitting manuscripts to unknown New York publishing houses, and worrying about advances, royalties, contracts, and returns of books? Why not invest in yourself and become a self-publisher? There are financial rewards, certain advantages of control, and entrepreneurial pride. But there is a risk . . . and a lot of work involved.

Many self-publishers have emerged in recent years, predominantly in California, New England, the Midwest, and Texas. Often the success of an individual book has enabled the self-publisher to publish additional titles and become a bona fide publisher. This was the case for Meadowbrook Press, Ten Speed Press in California, and H P Books in Arizona. They all followed a specific formula for success, based on their best-selling experiences, and began to publish more books and maintain a backlist.

If you are planning to self-publish, the publishing and editorial guidelines used in submitting a manuscript to a publishing house still apply. Since it will be necessary for you to complete a content-edited, copy-edited manuscript, ready for production, either you or someone you retain will have to serve as editor. Freelance editors, copy editors, and designers for the jacket and the text are available in most major cities. They generally charge by the hour. Inquire about them through the publishing and literary societies in your area.

An initial marketing plan will have to be devised and a budget of anticipated cash outflow and inflow will have to be prepared. From the beginning, you will have to focus on all aspects of the publishing process: editorial preparation, production, marketing and promoting, distribution, financing. You will be doing as an individual what Doubleday or Simon & Schuster do as companies for their hundreds of annual publications.

After your manuscript has been prepared editorially for production, and when all necessary graphics, illustrations, indices, and similar materials are ready to be reproduced, it is time to choose a printer. The printer should be in your immediate vicinity and should be a specialist in book printing and binding. Meet with several printers and compare design and format, estimates, and costs. Also determine up front how many copies you will print (5,000 copies is a generally acceptable and economical first printing) and at what retail cost, based on estimates from author and publishing friends, the printer, and the retail price of similar books on the market. You must also decide where you will warehouse the books. Often, printers can store books for you at their plant. The self-publisher may also warehouse at home, in a garage or an attic. You will also have to determine whether your book will be printed as a hardcover or a paperback.

When the books are off press, secure the copyright immediately. Write to the copyright office of the Library of Congress (Washington, D.C. 20559) for an application for copyright. Fill it out and send it back with two copies of the book and a check for $10.00. At the same time you can also obtain an International Standard Book Number (ISBN) for library orders by writing to R.R. Bowker, 1180 Avenue of the Americas, New York NY 10036.

While you are planning the printing, you will have to devise a marketing method to sell your self-published book. Write a one-page brochure or flier that lists all the important features of your book. Purchase a copy of *LMP (Literary Market Place)* from the Bowker Company (address above). This will provide you with names of review media, sales markets, and retail bookstore and library outlets. Then send a mailing to these sales and review markets.

If you are selling your book primarily by mail order, you will have to target your sales copy to the particular medium and obtain rates for various sizes of ad displays. When several associates and I self-published *Love Is Love but Business Is Business,* we initially targeted the *Los Angeles Times, Intro* magazine, and several weekly "singles" newspapers for multiple ad insertions. These ads did not justify our dollar investments; we subsequently found that radio interviews that included a mention of where to buy the book were more effective.

If you plan to sell to retail outlets, keep in mind that approximately 75 percent of the retail book business in America today is dominated by a few large chains and jobbers—Walden, Dalton, Crown Books, Doubleday, Ingram, and Baker and Taylor. If your book is salable and topically appealing, you will achieve considerable national exposure and representation if you sell to these accounts. You can sell either directly, through a commission sales rep, through a regional or national distributor listed in *LMP,* or by writing to the American Booksellers' Association in New York. Bowker also publishes *The American Book Trade Directory,* which lists all independent stores, chains, and jobbers in the U.S. You can sell your book by mailing your flier, with attached order card, to these book markets.

Whether you are selling in person, by mail, or by phone, you will probably have to ship sample copies to these accounts. Hopefully, when the books are ordered, you will make bulk shipments. Consult your local post office about special shipping and postal rates for books.

You will have to establish a very orderly system to record costs, number of copies shipped, to what account, and at what discount, and to keep track of each book sent out. After all, it's your business, not Doubleday's or Viking's. And remember, books are almost always bought on consignment, so instead of getting paid, you may receive your book back. Set up a billing procedure for retail accounts. A rule of thumb for discounts is generally based on quantities shipped:

1 to 5 books	25% discount
6 to 25	40%
26 +	45-46%

For larger quantities (to a Dalton or Walden chain on a national order), up to 50% discount.

Terms are usually sixty days, and you pay the freight costs. Don't be surprised, however, if you are paid later than sixty days after shipment because you are a small self-publisher and the major conglomerate publishers have to be paid first. And remember, the account has full return privileges.

If you are selling by direct mail (through a specific list), or by mail order (with a coupon in a newspaper or magazine), ask for cash up front plus postage and handling (approximately fifteen percent of your suggested retail price). This arrangement can be extremely lucrative when you are shipping a product that you've already been paid for, but remember that you have already spent considerable money for the ads and mailings that induced the respondent to buy.

Self-publishing can be an exciting venture because physically creating your own best-seller is a very rewarding experience. Oftentimes the self-publishing experiment may lead to a contract with a major national publisher. This was the case with Robert Ringer's *Winning Through Intimidation,* for which Fawcett acquired national publication rights after his considerable self-publishing success, and *The One Minute Manager* by Johnson and Blanchard, published nationally by William Morrow. Coach Jim Everroad's *How to Flatten Your Stomach* was purchased by Price/Stern/Sloan after it was successfully self-published.

Why sell these rights if the self-publishing formula is working? Because in most cases, the authors just didn't have the manpower, the time, or the financial resources to sustain the sales efforts. The greater the self-publishing success, the more work and cost involved. Considerable dedication, time, and money are required to be an effective self-publisher. You must initially choose the right book to market. As in the cases above, the book should be nonfiction, topical, "how-to," on a generally popular or appealing subject, and should provide something the public wants. The mini-books of *Quit* (stop smoking) and *Diet* were attractively marketed and contained subject matter that appealed to everybody. It is very unlikely that a first novel or an esoteric book can be self-published successfully.

A considerable number of self-published books have been best-sellers in recent years. It is because of the few bookstore chains that have emerged to dominate the market; because some of the best-sellers mentioned above have been successful; and because self-publishing has an entrepreneurial appeal. If your book is not bought by Random House, Harper & Row, or the like, you should consider self-publishing *if* your idea has best-seller potential. To go this route, you will have to learn the publishing business and have a considerable amount of time and patience, as well as sufficient capital. The monetary investment will probably be at least $10,000.

If you can meet all the above criteria and if you can adhere to the best-seller formula prescribed in other chapters, self-publication could reap you faster, richer rewards than a recognized publishing company. Remember that *you* are likely to be the sales, rights, publicity, and advertising managers of your company, and you will have to plan your best-seller campaign very assiduously and very aggressively. You will, of course, need the right subject (see Chapter One) and the right title (see Chapter Two), and you will need a great deal of luck and timing as well.

● ● ●

When a self-published or regional best-seller goes national—
that is, when it is bought for publication by a Warner or a Bantam—
the major house often has enough impetus to create or sustain a true
national best-seller. Warner accomplished this on a number of occasions with such books as *Learning to Leave, A Whack on the Side
of the Head,* and *The Omega Strategy: How to Be Rich by 1986.* It
is rare that a national publisher does not promote a bigger best-seller out of a self-published best-seller. Consequently all major New
York trade publishers—particularly the aggressive paperback
houses—are constantly combing the country for undiscovered or
potential local best-sellers that are self-published. (For more detailed information on the self-publishing process see "The Self-
Published Bookshelf" in the Appendix.)

If you choose to self-publish, remember that you are adhering to
the same guidelines for editing and marketing that any publishing
house must follow, but on an individual basis. Again, consult the
various chapters in this book on all aspects of publishing. The major difference in the self-publishing process is that *you,* not Doubleday, will print, warehouse, ship, bill, and act as sole agent and
publisher in every aspect of publication. It's risky. It's costly. It's
time-consuming. But when it works, when you've created your own
best-selling book, it's very rewarding, financially and personally.

I would advise you to stay away from "vanity" or "subsidy"
publishers. They are not legitimate publishing companies. They are
businesses that appeal to your vanity. For a considerable fee, such
houses will "edit" and prepare your manuscript for "publication."
They will print and bind finished editions of your book *at your expense,* and attempt to market the book to retail and rights outlets.
You have no guarantee that any results will follow your printing
bill. In fact, all major media—reviewers, bookstores, and book
clubs—generally stay clear of books published by the vanity presses. You can accomplish the same goals with self-publication and
achieve a greater acceptance from review media and rights markets.

In my opinion, vanity publishing is a costly, precarious, and unorthodox business. Numerous companies solicit vanity-press business with national ads in major magazines. They appeal to your literary frustrations and aim for your pocketbook. Stay away!

● ● ● ● ● ● ● ● ● ● ● ● ● ● ● ● ● ● ●

Your Neighborhood Bookstore

19. Once upon a time in America, there were a lot of neighborhood bookstores where you could browse for hours, discuss the latest best-sellers with the proprietor, and buy one or two of the latest novels by your favorite authors. You could find this ambience in your local bookseller, in *your* town, in *your* city. It was the "mom-and-pop" bookstore. Campbell's in Westwood, California, was such a place. So was the legendary Pickwick's in Hollywood. And so were countless other stores throughout America. These independent bookstores served a need and a purpose, and they helped shape and reflect what America was reading.

No more. Sadly, they have been replaced. In the 1970s, the rapid pace of inflation and the frenetic fast-food, fast-merchandise syndrome reached the publishing industry. The dedicated mom-and-pop book lovers could not comprehend a new business world of simultaneous mass discounts and returns, special deals and innovative merchandising, and the emergence of instant counter best-

Leading United States Bookstore Chains, 1981-82

Rank	Stores	'81 Revenues (millions)	'80 Revenues (millions)	'82 Revenues (millions)	# of Stores, 5/82	# of Stores, 5/81	Proj. # of Stores, end '82
1	B. Dalton Bookseller (parent: Dayton Hudson Corp.)	$319.3	$255.6	—	595	526	689
2	Waldenbooks (parent: Carter Hawley Hale Stores Inc.)	$310-$315[1]	$255-$260[1]	—	748	704	822
3	Barnes & Noble	$96.0	$100.0	—	62	52	69
4	Crown Books	$40-$45[1]	$15-$20[1]	—	81	33	100
5	Kroch's & Brentano's	$36.0	$32.0	$37.5	18	18	18
6	Bro-Dart Industries	$34.7[2]	$5.0[2]	$44.0[2]	46	44	51
7	Brentano's[3]	$22.0	$18-$23	—	28	31	16-18
8	Zondervan	$21.8	$18.4	—	70	57	75
9	Coles (U.S.)[4] (parent: Southam Inc.)	$15.6 (Can.)	$11.8 (Can.)	$19.5 (Can.)	62	60	63
10	Doubleday	$15-20[1]	$15-$20[1]		25	26	28
11	Cokesbury	$14.0	$13.0	$15.6	37	34	39
	Total	$924-$939	$739-$759		1772	1585	1970-1972

[1] Estimates.
[2] Includes revenues from 40 J.K. Gill stores, 35 of which sell office, art and engineering supplies in addition to books; five Gill stores do not sell books.
[3] Brentano's has filed for protection from its creditors under Chapter 11 while it develops a reorganization plan.
[4] Figure includes U.S. outlets only; 171 Canadian outlets brought in revenues of $57.2 million (Canadian) in the year ended Oct. 31, 1981.
© 1982 Knowledge Industry Publications, Inc.

sellers and packaged books in all sizes, formats, and genres. It was suddenly overwhelming. The business needed new sophisticated microfiched and computerized technology to list every title and author on a machine that told you how many copies were in stock and where you could get more. The "old" stores generally couldn't afford to buy or adapt to a computer. The publishing business in America had become technocratized, bureaucratized, and impersonalized. The distribution conglomerates had taken over.!

Campbell's was bought by Brentanos; Pickwick's was purchased by B. Dalton; and independent Martindale's in Beverly Hills was acquired by Doubleday. Throughout the country, small bookstores owned by individual book lovers were assimilated into giant chains. The business was changing.

In the 1970s the large national retail chain, Dayton Hudson, spawned the B. Dalton chain of bookstores. Simultaneously, the Broadway-Hale retail combine launched Walden Books. With the proliferation of shopping malls and giant suburban galleries, the bookstore that opened in each new mall was invariably a Dalton or a Walden. "Mall publishing" had arrived. Mass discount chains like Barnes and Noble in New York and New Jersey flourished and began to offer items from the best-seller list at 35 percent off retail price. An enterprising young man named Robert Haft, whose father was chairman of Thrifty Drug, the parent company, opened the Crown Book discount stores in Washington, D.C. to great public response. He repeated his success formula in the Los Angeles area, and at last notice was opening Crown stores in Chicago and San Diego. It was only a matter of time before he reached New York and other cities.

The marketing concept was simple and beneficial to the consumer. All *New York Times* best-sellers were 35 percent off retail price; everything else in the store, including magazines, was 20 percent off. This arrangement was both a boon and a detriment to the book-publishing industry in America. The buying public reaped the rewards of hefty consumer discounts and modern merchandising techniques that featured "sale" books, posters, window displays, autographings, and floor dumps (displays that held about 36 paperback books and featured an eye-catching header ad) to catch the consumer's eye. The discount chain had replaced the old neighbor-

hood bookstore. As one elder publishing salesman said at a recent convention, "Ultimately, the retail book business in America will be two national chains (Walden and Dalton) and a discount store (Crown)."

The bad news was that Crown Books and its imitators featured only best-sellers and established, perennial backlist titles. If you were looking for an obscure Naipaul title, the poems of Neruda, or the works of Hannah Arendt, you would not be likely to find it in a Crown bookstore. You would have to go a library or to a "real" bookstore like Scribner's on Fifth Avenue in New York or Krochs and Brentanos in Chicago. Publishers lamented that literary works, belles-lettres, and middle-list books (books that were neither best-sellers, classics, backlist titles, nor series, but somewhere in the middle) were not being bought for publication and were not selling because everybody wanted *best-sellers*. It became a self-fulfilling prophecy. The more Crowns, the more merchandising of best-sellers, the less room in the marketplace for middle-list books and the more publishers looked only for the *big* books that would become best-sellers.

The mom-and-pop stores often carried a greater breadth of titles and catered to the individual tastes of a loyal clientele. The modern chain and mall stores devote more of their inventory and space to titles that will turn over quickly. Thus they stock fewer speciality and backlist titles than the old stores. The new merchandising also tries to show as many books as possible face out, and makes appropriate use of floor, window, and counter displays to evoke consumer reaction. They emphasize the best-seller list over and over again. "That's what is selling; that's what you should buy," they say to the customer. And it works. It is essential for *your* best-seller that your book have visible display in the store, preferably up front or on the counter, or better yet . . . on the list.

The merchandising displays of the large chains and discounters feature numerous tables of "sale" or "remainder" books, usually the hardcover editions of previous best-sellers that are now mass paperbacks, and coffee-table books reduced from $24.95 to "only $9.95." Up front, floor and counter dumps display recent and new best-sellers in trade and mass paperback editions. Along the walls are the various categories of health, psychology, business, and computers. One curious category is usually referred to as "fiction and literature." In this bizarre grouping of titles, Kafka is next to Judith Krantz; Shakespeare shares a wall with Sidney Sheldon, best-sellers from then and now. An author's first book has to compete with fiction, literature, and proven best-sellers.

The Walden and Dalton chains have flourished. So have Crown Books and Barnes and Noble. Brentanos experienced management and inventory problems and filed for Chapter XI under the Bankrupty Act, and subsequently closed down a large portion of their stores. Doubleday continued as an independent chain of stores, but did not compete with Walden and Dalton for new shopping-mall space. Ingram out of Nashville, Tennessee, Bro Dart in Pennsylvania, and Baker and Taylor in New York and New Jersey functioned well as book jobbers (suppliers and middle sales operations) to independent stores, schools, and libraries. The book retail business became very centralized and today approximately ten

bookstore companies control over 75 percent of the business in America. It has become easier to call on them to solicit new book ideas and titles for sale. A new publisher or a self-publisher with a single book idea can test the national market by visiting Walden in Stamford, Connecticut, which operates almost 1,000 stores in the U.S., and Dalton in Minneapolis, which has over 800 stores. This development has fostered the growth of the many self-published best-sellers noted in the previous chapter. Walden and Dalton are receptive to potential bestsellers, whether published by Random House or published by you.

The chain stores can afford to sell at large savings to the consumer because they buy in bulk at large discounts. Dalton, Walden, and other chains buy for *all* stores at discounts up to 50 percent off the publisher's suggested retail price, and they buy on consignment. All books are returnable. If you're going to launch a national best-

Don't miss **Victoria Holt's** other great bestsellers!

MASK OF THE ENCHANTRESS

LORD OF THE FAR ISLAND

HOUSE OF THE THOUSAND LANTERNS

SPRING OF THE TIGER

DEVIL ON HORSEBACK

Waldenbooks

seller, it will be hard to do this without an order from Dalton and Walden. They buy thousands of copies for computerized distribution to their stores throughout the country. The other jobbers and discount stores also buy in bulk quantities at discounts ranging from 45 to 50 percent.

The mass-market paperback publishers sell to Dalton, Walden (called Direct Accounts), and the others, but most of their distribution and sales are to I.D.s—independent wholesalers who distribute magazines, periodicals, and paperbacks throughout the country. Charles Levy in Chicago is the largest individual wholesaler in the

U.S. ARA Services, located in about twenty different cities, is the largest chain of wholesalers.

The I.D.s buy at 50 percent off, and also receive special rack, display, and shipping allowances. Since they are mass distributors to retail accounts, airports, supermarkets, and the like, their returns run high; but they also force out a large distribution of titles. The average net sale throughout the paperback industry is only about 55 percent, which means that approximately 45 percent of all paperbacks are returned unsold. The book itself is not returned for full credit, only the cover which is stripped from the book. The rest is shredded by machine.

Hardcovers and trade paperbacks are generally returned as full books for credit. The current hardcover net sale percentage runs anywhere between 60 and 75 percent, depending on the type of book and the publisher involved. Major houses, which publish more best-sellers and distribute books in greater volume, generally have more clout in selling greater quantities and minimizing returns. Often a long-running best-seller ends up with sizable remainder numbers because there were more copies in the pipeline. When the book appears in paperback, approximately a year later, great quantities of the hardcover are available for sale as "remainders" at discount.

The new-age bookstores are all computerized and microfiched to trace orders, reorder, and keep track of the sales history of each title. These stores are also creative merchandisers, constantly featuring author appearances, in-store displays (floor and counter dump displays and special racks), and more promotion and special sale offers than in the past. Books are being sold and merchandised like other mass products.

It is sad that the traditional mom-and-pop bookstores are fading into memory, but the outlook for the new type of retail book business in America is quite hopeful economically. A different, modern bookstore system has emerged to fit this computer age. Conversely, it is heartening to know that in every large or small city in America, you can still find at least one good old bookstore, where you can browse for hours and talk about books with the shopkeeper. He or she has probably never returned a Dreiser or a Thomas Wolfe or a Nathanael West, with or without the cover.

• • • • • • • • • • • • • • • • •
From Writes to Rights

20. Around 1964, I became the subsidiary rights director (a relatively unknown industry title at that time) at Prentice-Hall, where I was responsible for trying to generate ancillary income from the licensing of book *rights* as opposed to the direct sale of books.

A first novel had crossed the desk of a brilliant young editor named Gladys Carr. It was written by Bel Kaufman, granddaughter of the renowned storyteller Sholom Aleichem. Her book, *Notes From A Teacher's Wastebasket,* was a collection of poignant, humorous anecdotes about the New York City school system. *Notes* became *Up the Down Staircase,* one of the most heralded bestsellers of our time.

It wasn't so at the beginning. Almost in opposition to skeptical company management and an uncertain marketplace, four enthusiastic publishing young 'uns created the number-one *New York Times* best-seller out of *Staircase.*

I conducted the paperback reprint auction. It was before the days of *Princess Daisy* and *Shogun,* and exaggerated wild bidding. Ultimately I sold *Staircase* to Avon Books for $152,000 and an initial 16 percent royalty rate with escalations, an unprecedented offer for a first novel back in the mid-sixties. This lucrative rights sale served to raise the bidding for additional book rights. The $150,000 + advance was a record in 1965; a pittance in light of the 1980 reprint purchase of *Princess Daisy* by Bantam Books for $3.2 million.

In the mid-sixties, when I first entered the exciting world of trade book publishing, book sales to bookstores were the predominant source of publishing revenue. Income from subsidiary rights was an occasionally lucrative adjunct to sales.

Over the following decade, though, ancillary dollars became a publisher's main source of profit. The major book clubs—Book-of-the-Month and Literary Guild—competed intensely for future bestsellers. Foreign and domestic serial markets competed avidly for the "big books." Film and paperback producers began to bid astronomical prices for book properties (which rarely earned back their initial guarantees). The *rights* hysteria swept New York publishing enclaves, and advances escalated far beyond the estimated worth of the books. *The Rise and Fall of the Third Reich* was sold to Fawcett paperback for $400,000, and *I'm OK, You're OK* for over $1 million. The bidding wars had begun.

More recently, *Red Dragon* was sold to paperback for almost $2 million, and John Irving's book, *The Hotel New Hampshire,* for over $2 million. Warner Books purchased paperback rights to Judith Rossner's best-seller, *August,* for over $1 million, a high figure in today's less hysterical bidding climate.

Authors, both established and new, began to earn considerably more money from the sales of subsidiary rights than from the sale of books. In many instances, the hardcover publisher would hype, promote, and advertise a book to attract rights buyers. After a successful rights sale, the publisher would pocket his profit and limit any further expenditures for promotion. The rights profit went directly to the bottom line. Because they were now bringing in a considerable amount of new publishing revenue, the major best-selling authors and their agents and lawyers negotiated new contracts to

The book that took America by storm arrives in Britain this Spring!

A run-away bestseller in the States last autumn, *The One Minute Manager* is a revolutionary book which teaches the quickest way to increase productivity, profits, job satisfaction and personal prosperity.

The text is brief, the language is simple – and the method works!

"This is a remarkable book about management. It takes very little time to read its powerful recipe for getting very big results from people – in very little time."
Robert Heller
Management Today.

Increase Productivity, Profits, and Your Own Prosperity

The **One Minute Manager**

Kenneth Blanchard, Ph.D.
Spencer Johnson, M.D.

A GEM –
SMALL,
EXPENSIVE
AND
INVALUABLE

* full media promotion
* specialist advertising
112pp   210 x 145 mm
0 00 218061 8
£6.95   March 24

COLLINS
WILLOW

The New York Times
Book Review
October 17 1982

provide the author with a better share of rights income and payment when money was received, not at the traditional twice-yearly royalty payment.

When I became rights and international director at Grosset & Dunlap, we had successfully published a perennially selling juvenile series by Arkady Leokum entitled *Tell Me Why*, which had steady, decent sales. I explored the rights-market potential of this series and licensed rights to approximately ten foreign countries and four U.S. book clubs. A "backlist" book and series became enormously profitable through the rights marketplace.

Foreign rights are generally sold by language rather than by territory. Spanish rights usually encompass Mexico, Spain, and South and Latin America. Portuguese rights cover Portugal and Brazil; and the British Commonwealth market invariably includes England, Scotland, Ireland, Australia, New Zealand, South Africa, and many "publishing colonies" no longer under actual British control.

The major markets for licensing and sales revenues are the Brit-

You will find these and other prominent international names on our list:

André Brink   Margaret Atwood
Agatha Christie
Toni Morrison
Han Suyin   Italo Calvino
Czeslaw Milosz
Isaac Bashevis Singer   Pavel Kohout
Elie Wiesel   William Golding
Saul Bellow   Siegfried Lenz
John Fowles
Salman Rushdie   Marilyn French

Leading publisher of Norwegian and foreign fiction and non-fiction, childrens books and text books.

Aschehoug   Norway

ish Commonwealth, France, Germany, and Japan because they are large, populous, and generally attuned to American tastes and trends. For internationally marketable literary properties, considerable income can be earned from both book and serialization sales. Outstanding and experienced agents like Evelyne Duval, June Hall, and Ed Victor in England; Michelle LaPorte in France; Carmen Balcells in Spain; and Ib Lauretzen in the Scandinavian countries represent both best-selling authors and American publishers in auctions and licensing sales in these major countries. Foreign-rights activities often begin and culminate at the Frankfurt International Book Fair, held every fall in Germany.

In smaller territories, it is generally necessary to use the services of an agent or representative to make foreign sales. Countries like Finland, Turkey, and Italy require specialized solicitations. The foreign agents usually receive a 10 percent commission off the gross sale.

Foreign licensing and licensing of serial rights to magazines, newspaper syndicates, and newspapers have proliferated in recent years. An excerpt sale helps to generate reader interest through magazines and newspapers. One of my first copublications, *All the Good Ones Are Married,* drew its first market response from serialization in both *Cosmopolitan* and *New Woman* magazines. The millions of people who first read the book as a serial in the magazines helped to make it a national best-seller.

The rights market became lucrative, necessary, and a major catalyst in hyping book sales for the book buyer *and* the consumer. Authors and their agent-lawyer hyphenates negotiated fiercely for a greater piece of the profits. Traditional contracts still granted book-club and serial rights to the publisher at a 50/50 percentage share, but paperback reprint rights were often split 60/40 in favor of the "best-selling" author; foreign rights were often divided 75/25 in the author's favor, and live media rights (movie, TV, dramatic, cable) were retained 100 percent by the author.

Probably the most exciting publication event in which I have ever been involved was *Marilyn* by Norman Mailer, which became a landmark book for Grosset & Dunlap in1973-74. The book had become an international *cause célèbre* long before actual publication because of the unprecedented array of Marilyn photos and because Norman Mailer was the author. Before publication, I negotiated deals with the Book-of-the-Month Club to offer it as a book-club selection and with *Ladies' Home Journal* for the first serialization. I traveled throughout Europe and made some extraordinary rights sales to print media and major foreign publishers. Every major foreign market and language purchased the book for considerable advance guarantees. Before it was published in America, *Marilyn* had garnered several million dollars in rights commitments and was destined to become an international best-seller.

Major works of fiction and nonfiction can generate considerable revenue from film, foreign, book-club, paperback, and serial

markets. On many occasions, rights income is substantially greater than cumulative book sales. This is because rights income is net income and book sales are determined by *net sales* after returns. The most advantageous contracts allow the author to receive immediate payment of his or her share after the initial publication advance has been earned out, rather than waiting for the normal royalty period.

The moral is to aim for the rights market; exploit and cultivate this market early in the publication process. It can serve a twofold purpose: to earn lucrative licensing dollars and to provide further impetus in creating a best-seller in the retail marketplace. Make your chapters and chapter titles attractive and commercial, and, if possible, write your best-seller with enough original elements to elicit serialization and book-club and foreign-rights response.

The more attention a prepublished book receives in the rights markets, the more likely it is that the public has heard of it and has been hyped to buy it at the time of publication. Major magazines and book clubs reach an enormous early audience, who are thus motivated to buy the next best-seller that all America will be talking about. When Erich Segal's *Love Story* was excerpted in *The Ladies' Home Journal* before publication, readers reacted with unprecedented enthusiasm.

Fewer magazines are serializing fiction these days. They are more likely to excerpt the unique and commercial nonfiction subjects that can become best-sellers. If you feel that your book subject is particularly suitable for a certain type of magazine, newspaper, or special publication, keep your editor informed about such potential serial markets, as well as any personal contacts you may have. Don't hesitate to use them, and tell any print media editors you know that you have a book coming out. A particular chapter or segment of your forthcoming book might be appropriate for excerpt in just the right publication.

In most cases, the publisher will control the sale of subsidiary rights, except for film and TV (see previous chapters on contracts and agents for splits of income). Generally, pre- or post-publication serialization sales will earn a gross income of a few hundred to a few thousand dollars. Book-club income for a beginning author may bring in five to ten thousand dollars; proceeds from paperback reprints (sold after publication) are unlimited and depend on hardcover success. Rights sales are vitally important, both on the bottom line and in the early creation of a best-seller.

Soon to Be a Major Motion Picture

21. "You've read the book, now see the film," is the hype that often launches a new film. Almost all best-selling novels have been brought to the screen; some have resulted in classic and memorable films, such as *Gone with the Wind, The Grapes of Wrath,* and *The Sun Also Rises.* Others have become classic flops, including *The Great Gatsby* and recent remakes of *Mutiny on the Bounty* and *The Postman Always Rings Twice.* In the last few years, such best-selling blockbusters as *Rich Man, Poor Man, Shogun, The Thorn Birds,* and *The Winds of War* have been transformed into TV mini-series that usually run from two to seven nights, comprise some twelve to twenty hours of film footage, and are watched by over 50 million people at each showing.

The traditional book-to-film sale evolves early for anticipated best-sellers and after publication for more obscure titles. Advance manuscripts or printed pages or galleys of potential or obvious blockbusters are smuggled somehow out of publishers' and agents'

offices to the film moguls who acquire these properties.

It is generally known that publishing "spies" are unofficially paid to get these advance copies away from hungry competitors and into the appropriate Hollywood hands. (For a blow-by-blow account of the NY to LA travels of one book see "The Making of a Bestseller—Hollywood Style" in the Appendix.) "Hot" books like *Gorky Park, Sophie's Choice,* and *The Little Drummer Girl* are purchased before publication for considerable amounts. Other lit-

July 21, 1961...
When the
future began.

On this day,
Virgil "Gus" Grissom
became America's
second astronaut
to achieve suborbital
flight in space.

Fred Ward as Gus Grissom.

THE
RIGHT
STUFF

"THE RIGHT STUFF"
Produced by
IRWIN WINKLER
and ROBERT CHARTOFF
Written for the Screen
and Directed by
PHILIP KAUFMAN
Based on the Book by
TOM WOLFE

A LADD COMPANY RELEASE
THRU WARNER BROS.
A WARNER COMMUNICATIONS COMPANY

erary properties, such as *One Flew over the Cuckoo's Nest* and *Cannery Row,* were purchased many years ago but remained dormant projects long after their intial publication. Many major studios and independent film producers acquire a current popular book for the screen and then shelve it indefinitely because they quickly lose interest in the project or are not sure how to convert it into a film. Recent examples include *Thy Neighbor's Wife, The Ninja,* and *Fear of Flying.*

Often, nonfiction titles are acquired for feature films and television because of their success as books or because a title has generated national familiarity. Screenplays were manufactured out of *Sex and the Single Girl, How to Succeed in Business Without Really Trying,* and *Everything You Always Wanted to Know About Sex.* I enjoyed similar successes when I published *All the Good Ones Are Married* and *Love and the Single Man* which are currently being converted into two-hour Movies of the Week (MOWs) for television.

The major studios—MGM, Warner, 20th Century-Fox, Disney, Universal, Columbia, Paramount—all maintain story departments on both coasts to scout for books to be acquired for film. Numerous independent producers, such as Lorimar, MTM, Aaron Spelling, Orion, Ladd, Melvin Simon, Zanuck-Brown, Jaffe-Lansing, Keith Barish, Neufeld-Davis, and Tandem, as well as many individual producers, are constantly in search of movie properties that might originate from books. The three TV networks—ABC, NBC, and CBS—and HBO and the emerging cable companies are all potential buyers of books and "software." HBO, owned by Time, Inc., and its principal competitor, an amalgam of The Movie Channel and Showtime, are now producing original material for mini-series and TV movies that will be featured exclusively on their cable networks.

It is anticipated that the cable revolution will provide an outlet for all kinds of nonfiction and informational book ideas. In the future, many book subjects will be distilled for cable TV programming and videodisc rebroadcasting.

A film sale usually entails an option payment (from ninety days to six months to a year) against a purchase price, and *points,* or a percentage of net revenues of the movie or TV program. A Hollywood-proven screenwriter is assigned to the writing unless the

book author happens to be qualified in the medium. Authors such as William Goldman, James Clavell, John Gregory Dunne, and, recently, Herman Wouk have adapted their own books for film.

When I was involved in producing the feature film of *The Destroyer* series, we originally commissioned the authors to write the screenplay. Although they were inexperienced as screenwriters, their distinctive style and wit had inspired an avid book readership that we thought could be transferred to the film version. But because the visual medium is so different from books, we later hired former James Bond screenwriter Chris Wood to do the screenplay. Film writing must be tighter and more graphic with certain time restrictions. The rule of thumb is that each page of a screenplay should result in one minute of viewing time on the screen.

A more recent phenomenon in the symbiotic book/film relationship has been the novelization of "soon-to-be major motion pictures." These included the original films *Rocky, Return of the Jedi, Raiders of the Lost Ark,* and *E.T.* (E.T. simultaneously became a hardcover best-seller as well, because of its unprecedented appeal.) As a result, previously published books such as *Ordinary People, Gorky Park, Sophie's Choice, The Right Stuff,* and . . . *Garp* became best-sellers a second time around after the film's release, regardless of the success of the movie. Book/movie tie-ins are an effective advertising tool for each medium, and can generate extraordinary rights income. If a movie is comedic or generally devoid of plot, however, it may not translate into a commercial book.

Book/film tie-ins these days often involve the *creation* of a "best-seller" turned into a film. This is part of the bicoastal media operation of Stan Corwin Productions. An idea conceived by a producer/packager like myself, or by a film production company, is transformed into a commercial plot in a ten- to fifteen-page treatment. The project is subsequently *packaged* with a book writer who is attached to the property. A deal is made with a major New York publisher, often supported by the film producer's promotional expenditures on the book and by the prospect that the book will eventually come to the screen. The original conceivers of the idea hold the copyright. A split-income formula is devised on both the book and the film to include the author, the packager, and the producer. The film company has the advantage of basing its forthcoming film

29

on the book that *they* created. It is a far more beneficial way to "acquire" a book for film than purchasing a best-seller for $1 million. The publisher and the film producer benefit at the outset from their collaborative partnership.

Recently I was able to create such a best-seller with Davis-Panzer Productions on *The Red Moon* by Warren Murphy, now pending as a TV mini-series. This joint production process originated about a decade ago with the creation of such best-sellers as *Love Story* and *Summer of '42* as simultaneously successful books and films. Books that are made into movies have the advantage of a large readership, who eagerly look forward to the film.

The new author can think cinematically while writing the potential best-selling novel. If the book is well plotted and well structured, contains two or three memorable characters, has commercial appeal, and doesn't involve too many locations or too many special effects (both expensive), you and your agent or publisher can start to consider film possibilities in the early stages of manuscript development.

Since you should own the film rights and the larger percentage of the movie revenues to your book (see Chapter Nine), you or your agent can begin to solicit some early film interest *before* the book is published. There are many powerful, creditable film agents and agencies on the West Coast, who can reach the right buyers if your property is filmable. They include ICM, Creative Artists, William Morris, H.N. Swanson, Ziegler-Diskant, Adams-Ray and Rosenberg, and many others. If your publishers control the film rights, they can retain one of these agents to make a film sale.

If a film sale is made—optioned or bought outright—you will probably not be asked to write the screenplay, nor will you have editorial control over the final script. But you *will* enjoy full author credit on the screen, and that is a wonderful feeling for a beginning author.

The synergy of books and movies, and the emerging TV and cable possibilities, afford a new author a great opportunity to benefit from ancillary-rights revenues far beyond book sales. The movie starring—, directed by—, based on the book—, and costing—million dollars, may never materialize, but it is still thrilling to imagine your book "soon becoming a major motion picture."

How Do You Get on the Best-Seller List?

22. There are three national best-seller lists. The most powerful and prestigious list is published by *The New York Times Book Review*. The *Time* magazine list commands a national readership, and *Publishers Weekly* features the list read by the industry. The Walden and Dalton bookstore chains also maintain weekly best-seller lists, which they post in their stores. All are fairly accurate indicators of which books America is reading and buying most avidly.

Once a book hits the lists, it automatically generates national reaction. Everyone wants to read the latest best-seller, the book other people are talking about. Publishers concentrate their ad and publicity budgets on books on the list; rights and film markets are attuned to the best-seller list; bookstores feature the best-sellers. This self-perpetuating sales enthusiasm and hype for a listed book generally assures a book a position on the list for a long time. It's almost difficult to get off the list, once you've been there for three or four weeks.

April 22, 1984

THE NEW YORK TIMES BOOK REVIEW

Best Sellers

Fiction

This Week		Last Week	Weeks On List
1	**THE AQUITAINE PROGRESSION,** by Robert Ludlum. (Random House, $17.95.) A lawyer is caught in a conspiracy to seize the Western world.	1	7
2	**THE BUTTER BATTLE BOOK,** by Dr. Seuss. (Random House, $6.95.) A warning about the nuclear arms race in words and pictures.	2	6
3	**THE HAJ,** by Leon Uris. (Doubleday, $17.95.) One man's experience in the bloody wars of the Holy Land.	11	2
3	**HERETICS OF DUNE,** by Frank Herbert. (Putnam, $16.95.) The fifth volume of a series about life on a faraway planet.	6	3
5	**THE DANGER,** by Dick Francis. (Putnam, $15.95.) A kidnapper at large in the horse racing world.	6	4
6	**LORD OF THE DANCE,** by Andrew M. Greeley. (Bernard Geis/Warner, $17.50.) In seeking her long-lost cousin, a teen-ager probes the mysteries of life and death.	9	7
7	**SMART WOMEN,** by Judy Blume. (Putnam, $15.95.) Three divorcees, their love affairs and their kids in trendy Boulder, Colo.	4	11
8	**PET SEMATARY,** by Stephen King. (Doubleday, $15.95.) The new family in town discovers the horrors that lie in a neighboring cemetery.	3	25
9	**ONE MORE SUNDAY,** by John D. MacDonald. (Knopf, $15.95.) Behind the scenes with a charismatic television preacher.	14	4
10	**WHO KILLED THE ROBINS FAMILY?** created by Bill Adler and written by Thomas Chastain. (Morrow, $9.95.) The publisher offers a $10,000 prize to the reader who submits the best answer.	5	34
11	**ALMOST PARADISE,** by Susan Isaacs. (Harper & Row, $16.95.) Three generations of show-biz people play out their destinies on two continents.	8	11
12	**POLAND,** by James A. Michener. (Random House, $17.95.) Seven centuries of history in fictional form.	10	34
13	**UNTO THIS HOUR,** by Tom Wicker. (Viking, $19.95.) Three days in August, 1862, when a battle was fought at Manassas, Va.		5
14	**THE NAME OF THE ROSE,** by Umberto Eco. (Helen & Kurt Wolff/Harcourt Brace Jovanovich, $15.95.) Unraveling the mystery of a murder in a 14th-century Italian monastery.	12	44
15	**FLOODGATE,** by Alistair MacLean. (Doubleday, $15.95.) Terrorists threaten to flood the Netherlands unless Britain leaves Northern Ireland.		1

Nonfiction

This Week		Last Week	Weeks On List
1	**MAYOR,** by Edward I. Koch with William Rauch. (Simon & Schuster, $17.95.) New York's mayor's opinions about his job, his city and the world.	1	10
2	**THE MARCH OF FOLLY,** by Barbara W. Tuchman. (Knopf, $18.95.) The blunders of government in four periods, from Troy to Vietnam.	2	6
3	**ONE WRITER'S BEGINNINGS,** by Eudora Welty. (Harvard University Press, $10.) The novelist recalls her childhood in Mississippi.	6	
4	**MOTHERHOOD: The Second Oldest Profession,** by Erma Bombeck. (McGraw-Hill, $12.95.) A humorous look at the biggest on-the-job training program ever.	3	31
5	**TOUGH TIMES NEVER LAST, BUT TOUGH PEOPLE DO!** by Robert H. Schuller. (Thomas Nelson, $12.95.) Inspiration from a California preacher.	4	25
6	**MAFIA PRINCESS,** by Antoinette Giancana and Thomas C. Renner. (Morrow, $15.95.) Growing up in the family of the mobster Sam Giancana.	14	4
7	**LINES AND SHADOWS,** by Joseph Wambaugh. (Perigord/Morrow, $15.95.) Adventures of the San Diego police force that stalks bandits along the Mexican border.	5	9
8	**ON WINGS OF EAGLES,** by Ken Follett. (Morrow, $17.95.) The rescue of two Americans from an Iranian prison.	7	34
9	**FURTHER UP THE ORGANIZATION,** by Robert Townsend. (Knopf, $15.95.) Business strategies for the 1980's.		2
9	**IN SEARCH OF EXCELLENCE,** by Thomas J. Peters and Robert H. Waterman Jr. (Harper & Row, $19.95.) Lessons to be learned from well-run American corporations.	13	67
11	**THE DISCOVERERS,** by Daniel J. Boorstin. (Random House, $25.) Man's search to know himself and the world over the centuries.	8	16
11	**PEOPLE OF THE LIE,** by M. Scott Peck. (Simon & Schuster, $15.95.) A psychiatrist's prescription for "healing human evil."	10	11
13	**TOUGH-MINDED FAITH FOR TENDERHEARTED PEOPLE,** by Robert H. Schuller. (Thomas Nelson, $14.95.) More inspiration from a California preacher.	9	10
14	**THE BEST OF JAMES HERRIOT.** (St. Martin's, $19.95.) Selections from the writings of the Yorkshire veterinarian.	15	32
15	**A LIGHT IN THE ATTIC,** by Shel Silverstein. (Harper & Row, $12.45.) Light verse and drawings by the author.	11	83

And Bear in Mind

(Editors' choices of other recent books of particular interest)

ALEXANDER FLEMING: The Man and the Myth, by Gwen Macfarlane. (Harvard University Press, $20.) This biography of the scientist who discovered penicillin in 1928 seeks to explain why it took more than a decade for it to be put to use.

CHILDHOOD, by Nathalie Sarraute. (Braziller, $14.95.) One of the great women of French letters, now in her 80's, recounts her life up to World War I, her purpose to seek out the most delicate of impressions that lie in the unnamed corners of consciousness.

D. W. GRIFFITH: An American Life, by Richard Schickel. (Simon & Schuster, $24.95.) The definitive biography of the pioneering director who transformed movies from a crude novelty into the most influential art form in history.

EDISTO, by Padgett Powell. (Farrar, Straus & Giroux, $11.95.) A first novel in which the narrator-hero, age 12, has lots of questions about the life to come — values, politics, economics, race relations, sex. A sparkling read.

THE LADY FROM PLAINS, by Rosalynn Carter. (Houghton Mifflin, $17.95.) The former First Lady has written what turns out to be the best human account of the Carter Presidency we are likely to get.

SLOW LEARNER: Early Stories, by Thomas Pynchon. (Little, Brown, $14.95.) A writer who has been hiding away for years paints himself back into the public view with this extremely good collection of five early works.

WEAPONS AND HOPE, by Freeman Dyson. (A Cornelia & Michael Bessie Book/Harper & Row, $17.95.) A noted physicist and advocate of nuclear disarmament provides an excellent layman's guide to that most misunderstood problem, arms races.

Advice, How-to and Miscellaneous

This Week		Last Week	Weeks On List
1	**EAT TO WIN,** by Robert Haas. (Rawson, $14.95.) A regimen for participants in sports and fitness activities.	1	4
2	**NOTHING DOWN,** by Robert G. Allen. (Simon & Schuster, $16.95.) How to buy real estate with little or no money.	5	71
3	**THE JAMES COCO DIET,** by James Coco and Marion Paone. (Bantam, $13.95.) A regimen based on nutritional education, menu planning and behavior modification.	2	10
4	**PUTTING THE ONE MINUTE MANAGER TO WORK,** by Kenneth Blanchard and Robert Lorber. (Morrow, $15.) Increasing your productivity and that of those with whom you work.	4	5
5	**THE LIFE EXTENSION COMPANION,** by Durk Pearson and Sandy Shaw. (Warner, $17.50.) Advice about improving your health and lengthening your life.		1

The listings above are based on computer-processed sales figures from over 2,000 bookstores in every region of the United States, statistically adjusted to represent sales in all bookstores. In Advice and How-to, five titles are listed because, beyond that point, sales in this category are not generally large enough to make a longer list statistically reliable.

America feels secure of the musical records on the charts and the books on the best-seller list. Everybody else is buying the latest hit, so it must be good. Some list candidates are almost automatic best-sellers. They are written by best-selling authors, "brand names" who have been there before. Clavell, Michener, Robbins, Krantz, Sheldon, Rosemary Rogers, Robin Cook, John Jakes, Stephen King, Irwin Shaw, Mary Stewart, Ken Follett, Janet Dailey, and many others always make the lists. Their public expects them to write best-sellers continuously, and the bookstores display their latest books prominently.

Once in a while, a sleeper best-seller emerges from an unknown author. The word-of-mouth and reviewer reaction is so strong that a best-seller materializes. Often it is not the author's first book, as in the case of *The World According to Garp, Gorky Park* by Martin Cruz Smith, and *The Color Purple* by Alice Walker. Occasionally, however, first novels such as *Lace* by Shirley Conran and *Scruples* by Judith Krantz break onto the list immediately. A recent number-one best-seller is a novel translated from Italian, entitled *The Name of the Rose.*

In the nonfiction category, surprise best-sellers like *When Bad Things Happen to Good People, How to Make Love to a Man,* and *The Peter Pan Syndrome* made the list as the result of widespread word-of-mouth publicity. The hardcover list, primarily the *New York Times* list, generally includes known authors on the fiction side and, in recent years, "non-books," and "how-to" books, and humor or parody subjects in nonfiction. In past years important works by the likes of William Shirer, John Toland, Barbara Tuchman, and William Manchester made up the nonfiction list, but recently the self-help titles have dominated this category. Examples of this emerging and popular genre are *Creating Wealth, You Can Negotiate Anything, Working Out,* and many similar titles.

The mass-market paperback list generally reflects the previous year's hardcover best-sellers, but original fiction by John Jakes and the romance writers—Kathleen Woodiwiss, Danielle Steel, and Valerie Sherwood—debuted as original paperback best-sellers. So did fad and gimmick books that reflect the times: *The Simple Solution to Rubik's Cube, How to Win at Pac-Man, Real Men Don't Eat Quiche, Thin Thighs in 30 Days, The Valley Girl's Guide to Life*

PW PAPERBACK BESTSELLERS

Compiled from data from independent and chain bookstores, book wholesalers and independent distributors nationwide

April 13, 1984

Mass Market

1. **Seeds of Yesterday.** V. C. Andrews. Pocket Books, $3.95
2. **Crossings.** Danielle Steel. Dell, $3.95
3. **The Little Drummer Girl.** John le Carré. Bantam, $4.50. This new mass market bestseller, published April 1, has 1,915,000 copies in print after two printings.
4. **Megatrends: Ten New Directions Transforming Our Lives.** John Naisbitt. Warner, $3.95
5. **Voice of the Heart.** Barbara Taylor Bradford. Bantam, $4.50
6. **The Michael Jackson Story.** Nelson George. Dell, $2.95
7. **White Gold Wielder: Book Three of the Second Chronicles of Thomas Covenant.** Stephen R. Donaldson. Ballantine/Del Rey, $3.95. Published April, this second new mass market bestseller has an 840,000-copy first printing.
8. **Banker.** Dick Francis. Fawcett Crest, $3.95
9. **Ascent into Hell.** Andrew M. Greeley. Warner/Bernard Geis Associates, $3.95
10. **Blue Highways: A Journey into America.** William Least Heat Moon. Fawcett Crest, $3.95
11. **Michael!** Mark Bego. Pinnacle, $2.95. Total copies in print after seven trips to press: 1,100,000.
12. **Lace.** Shirley Conran. Pocket Books, $3.95
13. **Battlefield Earth.** L. Ron Hubbard. Bridge Publications, $4.95
14. **Floating Dragon.** Peter Straub. Berkley, $3.95
15. **Carioca Fletch.** Gregory McDonald. Warner, $3.50

Trade

1. **In Search of Excellence: Lessons from America's Best-Run Companies.** Thomas J. Peters and Robert H. Waterman, Jr. Warner, $8.95
2. **The One Minute Manager.** Kenneth Blanchard and Spencer Johnson. Berkley, $6.95
3. **Garfield Tips the Scales.** Jim Davis. Ballantine, $4.95
4. **The Color Purple.** Alice Walker. Washington Square Press, $5.95
5. **Color Me Beautiful.** Carole Jackson. Ballantine, $8.95
6. **Jane Fonda's Workout Book.** Jane Fonda. Simon & Schuster, $9.95
7. **The Magic of Michael Jackson.** Sharon Publications (dist. by NAL/Signet), $4.95
8. **Living, Loving and Learning.** Leo Buscaglia. Fawcett/Columbine, $5.95
9. **J. K. Lasser's Your Income Tax.** J. K. Lasser Institute. Simon & Schuster, $6.95
10. **Growing Up.** Russell Baker. NAL/Plume, $6.95

Mass Market Candidates

Heartburn. Nora Ephron. Pocket Books, $3.50. Published April, this new mass market candidate has 971,600 copies in print.

Men Are Just Desserts. Sonya Friedman. Warner, $3.95

Dr. Abravanel's Body Type Diet and Lifetime Nutrition Plan. Elliott D. Abravanel, M.D. Bantam, $3.95

and *Items from Our Catalog.*

In recent years, *The New York Times* and *Publishers Weekly* instituted a trade paperback list in recognition of this popular format. It has become a special novelty list that indicates trends. Not too long ago, nine out of the fifteen trade paperbacks on the *New York Times* list featured cubes, cats, or preppies. Five of the catbooks were about the same feline hero—Garfield. Other trade paperbacks were perennial best-sellers like *The Joy of Sex* and *What Color Is Your Parachute?* which continued to sell every year in best-selling quantities.

I've often been asked in public and in private, "How do you get on the list?" No one knows for sure, but I can give hints for the various methods of getting on and staying on.

To begin with, approximately thirty major cities or geographical locales, encompassing approximately 1000 bookstores and fifty paperback distributors, are canvassed by telephone each week for best-seller reports. Major bookstores, chains, wholesalers, and department stores in each area are called. In Los Angeles, for instance, this group includes B. Dalton, Hunter's, and Crown Books in Westwood; Pickwick's in Hollywood; Hunter's, Brentanos, and Doubleday in Beverly Hills, and such department stores as Robinson's and The Broadway.

In New York, the group polled includes Barnes and Noble, Doubleday, B. Dalton, Scribner's, Classics, Open Book in Grand Central Station, Macy's, Bloomingdale's, and Gimbels. These stores (or rather the clerk or manager who answers the phone) report any of three best-selling trends:

1. Books that are selling the most copies (the truest indicator);
2. Books that the dealers think should be selling the most (the latest Updike or Bellow);
3. Books that they have the most of in the store. (They've overordered and would love to get them on a list to move the stock.)

The list, when published, is generally two to three weeks out of date. Besides, many stores do not report cetain categories, such as

PW HARDCOVER BESTSELLERS

Compiled from data from large-city bookstores, bookstore chains and local bestseller lists across the U.S.

April 13, 1984

Fiction

1. **The Aquitaine Progression.** Robert Ludlum. Random House, $17.95. ISBN 0-394-53674-6
2. **Who Killed the Robins Family?** Bill Adler and Thomas Chastain. Morrow, $9.95. ISBN 0-688-02524-2
3. **Smart Women.** Judy Blume. Putnam, $15.95. ISBN 0-399-12840-9
4. **The Danger.** Dick Francis. Putnam, $15.95. ISBN 0-399-12890-5
5. **Pet Sematary.** Stephen King. Doubleday, $15.95. ISBN 0-385-18244-9
6. **Lord of the Dance.** Andrew M. Greeley. Warner Books/Bernard Geis Associates, $17.50. ISBN 0-446-51292-3
7. **The Butter Battle Book.** Dr. Seuss. Random House, $6.95. ISBN 0-394-86580-4
8. **Heretics of Dune.** Frank Herbert. Putnam, $16.95. ISBN 0-399-12898-0. This new fiction bestseller, the fifth novel in the Dune series, has an April 16 pub date and a 180,000-copy first printing.
9. **Poland.** James A. Michener. Random House, $17.95. ISBN 0-394-53189-2
10. **One More Sunday.** John D. MacDonald. Knopf, $15.95. ISBN 0-394-53673-8
11. **Almost Paradise.** Susan Isaacs. Harper & Row, $16.95. ISBN 0-06-015236-2
12. **The Name of the Rose.** Umberto Eco. A Helen & Kurt Wolff Book/Harcourt Brace Jovanovich, $15.95. ISBN 0-15-144647-4
13. **Floodgate.** Alistair MacLean. Doubleday, $15.95. ISBN 0-385-18263-5
14. **Unto This Hour.** Tom Wicker. Viking, $19.95. ISBN 0-670-42193-0
15. **The Story of Henri Tod.** William F. Buckley, Jr. Doubleday, $14.95. ISBN 0-385-14234-5

Nonfiction

1. **The March of Folly: From Troy to Vietnam.** Barbara W. Tuchman. Knopf, $18.95. ISBN 0-394-52777-1
2. **Motherhood: The Second Oldest Profession.** Erma Bombeck. McGraw-Hill, $12.95. ISBN 0-07-006454-7
3. **Mayor: An Autobiography.** Edward I. Koch. Simon & Schuster, $17.95. ISBN 0-671-49536-4
4. **The James Coco Diet.** James Coco and Marion Paone. Bantam, $13.95. ISBN 0-553-05024-9
5. **Lines and Shadows.** Joseph Wambaugh. Morrow, $15.95. ISBN 0-688-02619-2
6. **Tough Times Never Last but Tough People Do.** Robert H. Schuller. Thomas Nelson, $12.95. ISBN 0-8407-5287-3
7. **Eat to Win: The Sports Nutrition Bible.** Dr. Robert Haas. Rawson Associates (dist. by Scribners), $14.95. ISBN 0-892-56228-5
8. **Putting the One Minute Manager to Work.** Kenneth Blanchard and Robert Lorber. Morrow, $15. ISBN 0-688-02632-X
9. **Nothing Down.** Robert Allen. Simon & Schuster, $16.95. ISBN 0-671-24748-4
10. **Weight Watchers Fast and Fabulous Cookbook.** Weight Watchers. NAL Books, $15.50. ISBN 0-453-01008-3
11. **On Wings of Eagles.** Ken Follett. Morrow, $16.95. ISBN 0-688-02371-1
12. **One Writer's Beginnings.** Eudora Welty. Harvard University Press, $10. ISBN 0-674-63925-1
13. **The Discoverers.** Daniel J. Boorstin. Random House, $25. ISBN 0-394-40229-4
14. **Creating Wealth.** Robert Allen. Simon & Schuster, $14.95. ISBN 0-671-44281-3
15. **In Search of Excellence: Lessons from America's Best-Run Companies.** Thomas J. Peters and Robert H. Waterman, Jr. Harper & Row, $19.95. ISBN 0-06-015042-4. A 50th printing of 10,000 makes 1,390,000 copies in print.

religion or cookery.

Movie companies, publishers, and individuals have often *purchased* books in these "best-selling" stores to get on the list, and it has often worked. You can buy your way onto the lists if you've got the right product, get up-front display space, run cooperative ads with the key stores, and surreptitiously purchase copies all around town. If one of these ingredients is missing, the chances of a new, unknown book getting on the lists are extremely slim. The Robert Ringer approach, blitzing one city at a time to create a national snowball effect, can work if a great deal of money is spent. Regional books do sell beyond their own regions, and often break out nationally—particularly diet and lifestyle books from elegant places. *Brisk sales in key stores in key cities make best-sellers.*

Once you get on a national list, you are entitled to the use of the blurb. On the cover of the hardcover or softcover, or in the ads, you can feature the words: "National Best-seller," "—Weeks on the *New York Times* Best-seller List," and similar promotion copy. It works. Remember that your publisher's sales rep usually has several hundred or more books a year to worry about. Go into the key stores in your home city. Ask the owner if you can arrange a display of your book, autograph those books, run an ad, tell them what shows you'll be appearing on, and have your books bought at a steady rate. Get on a list in your home city. Then try to "go national."

A word or two about reviewers who create best-sellers—they generally don't anymore. Since books are packaged and hyped like movies and other entertainment products, they are less dependent on reviewers' raves or critical comments. Even so, favorable quotes by reviewers—on the books or in ads—are valuable endorsements. Noteworthy major reviewers such as Christopher Lehmann-Haupt and Anatole Broyard of *The New York Times;* Peter S. Prescott of *Newsweek; Kirkus Reviews;* John Barkham of the *Saturday Review* Syndicate; and Eliot Fremont-Smith of *The Village Voice* are still read and respected by literary readers. Critical praise for literary works, such as *The White Hotel* by D.M. Thomas and *August* by Judith Rossner, and for literary authors like Bellow and Marquez contribute to getting on the best-seller lists. But reviews and critiques of the spate of nonbooks have no bearing whatever on their

commercial results. Since more books are now of the packaged and created nonbook variety, reviewers have less critical influence than they enjoyed in the past. But their favorable reviews still generate library sales.

In the exploding paperback marketplace, reviewers' attention has no measurable effect on the sales of a new book. Because *The New York Times, Time* magazine, and *Publishers Weekly* are all high-quality publications, they review critically important works and authors whenever possible, regardless of the original format.

Reviews are meaningful and prestigious, but they don't have a noticeable effect on book sales. When a review appears, a quote is invariably lifted out of context to become the tagline for the book. But the words "one of the best books ever written on this subject" will never be as effective as "10 weeks on *The New York Times* bestseller list."

●●●●●●●●●●●●●●●●●●●●●
The Making of a Best-Seller

23. All my adult life I have been a serious book publisher, or tried to be, or was regarded as such. Then one day, perhaps by chance or by inspiration, I conceived a best-selling idea that I had never anticipated. I followed a formula and created a commercial success. The moral of this brief revelation is that *I did it* . . . and you can, too.

Several years ago, the number-one trade paperback best-seller and novelty fad book was *How to Flatten Your Stomach*. It was approaching the million-copy sales mark, and had become a much talked-about and catchy title.

During lunch with my friend and publisher, Melvin Powers, I expressed my desire to do a parody of this best-seller. Mel asked what I had in mind. *How to Flatten Your Tush* was my idea, a parody trade paperback similar in design and format to *How to Flatten Your Stomach*.

"Let's try it," Mel responded enthusiastically.

The rest became pseudonymous publishing history and an experience of creating a national best-seller. After conception, I wrote *Tush* over three weekends, working hard and following a formula. The book featured a *Tush* diet and bibliography, and was sprinkled with models doing fictitious exercises. It was fun, it was instant, and it was a parody of a proven best-seller. The design and package were intentionally just like *How to Flatten Your Stomach*. The "author" of the book was "Coach Marge Reardon."

Mel and I produced this book in less than a month. The initial printing was 5,000 copies, and we pitched our idea to the Dalton and Walden chains. The response was overwhelming and the timing was perfect. On August 24, 1979, *How to Flatten Your Tush* by Coach Marge Reardon appeared on the B. Dalton best-seller list for the first time.

This event gave me a curious satisfaction. I had always been a working publisher, consciously striving to create best-sellers. Now, in a frivolous moment, I had conceived and written a national best-selling book, and I had done it pseudonymously. No one would know who Coach Marge Reardon really was.

That was a problem. After the overwhelming response, talk shows began to call and ask for appearances by Coach Marge. But there was no coach, no real author. So Mel and I began to interview to find the perfect Marge Reardon to represent "her" book on television. We selected a young lady who caught the "tongue-in-cheek" spirit of *Tush* and faithfully sold "her" book on major shows. She even became a judge in the annual Miss Tush Contest in Redondo Beach, and asked me constantly, "Where was I born?" "What does my father do?" Obviously I hadn't gotten that far in my creative endeavors.

Overnight we had created a national best-seller. It was a parody of a known book and subject, and it also parodied the business and hype of best-sellers. Even the front cover featured the ultimate parody blurb: "Soon to be a major motion picture."

Tush remained on the Dalton best-seller list for six weeks. It generated extensive national publicity and sold over 75,000 copies. *The New York Times* called *How to Flatten Your Tush* one of the funniest lampoons of the year. It had hit at the right time.

It was a clean, fun book, published at the right moment for a receptive market, and it succeeded far beyond my expectations. I had made the best-seller list—not as Stan Corwin but as Coach Marge Reardon. I had followed the best-seller "formula," and it worked. It was very rewarding, and even if it didn't bring me fame and immortality, it certainly provided great peace of tush.

B. Dalton BESTSELLERS

Trade Paperback

August 24, 1979

NO.	TITLE	AUTHOR	PUBLISHER	LAST WEEK	RETAIL
1.	MARY ELLEN'S BEST OF HELPFUL	Pinkham	Warner		3.95
2.	HOW TO FLATTEN YOUR STOMACH	Everroad	Price Stern		1.75
3.	RAND MCNALLY ROAD ATLAS		Rand McNally	2	3.95
4.	JOY OF SEX	Comfort	Simon/Schuster	1	7.95
5.	IN SEARCH OF HISTORY	White		3	8.95
6.	MURPHYS LAW	Bloch	Warner	5	2.50
7.	HOW TO TRIM/HIPS/SHAPE/THIGHS	Everroad	Price S	4	5.95
8.	FREE STUFF FOR KIDS	Blakely	Wald	6	1.75
9.	SACAJAWEA				2.95
10.	WHAT COLOR IS YOUR PARACHUTE				8.95
11.	I, CLAUDIUS				5.95
12.	WOMAN'S DRESS FOR SU...				3.95
13.	DIETERS GDE/WE...				2.95
14.	HOW TO SU...				1.95
15.	DO ...				1.50
16					7.95
					3.00
					1.95
					6.95
					6.95
					1.95
					.00
					.95
					95
					95

THE NEW YORK TIMES BOOK REVIEW
Paperback Best Sellers

April 22, 1984

Fiction

1 **THE LITTLE DRUMMER GIRL**, by John le Carré. (Bantam, $3.95.) A young Englishwoman caught between Israeli and P.L.O. agents.

2 **SEEDS OF YESTERDAY**, by V. C. Andrews. (Pocket, $3.95.) Concluding volume of a horror series about the Dollanganger family.

3 **CROSSINGS**, by Danielle Steel. (Dell, $3.95.) A clandestine trans-Atlantic romance survives the stresses of World War II.

4 **HEARTBURN**, by Nora Ephron. (Pocket, $3.50.) A roman à clef about a marriage breaking up.

5 **WHITE GOLD WIELDER**, by Stephen R. Donaldson. (Del Rey/Ballantine, $3.95.) Book Three in "The Second Chronicles of Thomas Covenant," a fantasy saga.

6 **VOICE OF THE HEART**, by Barbara Taylor Bradford. (Bantam, $4.50.) An actress's return home upsets the lives of her family and friends.

7 **SON OF A WANTED MAN**, by Louis L'Amour. (Bantam, $2.95.) A young man inherits his father's place as head of a gang of Western outlaws.

8 **BANKER**, by Dick Francis. (Fawcett, $3.95.) Placing odds on the ability of a horse breeder to produce a star race horse.

9 **LIGHT A PENNY CANDLE**, by Maeve Binchy. (Dell, $3.95.) A crisis threatens the close relationship of two sisters.

10 **ASCENT INTO HELL**, by Andrew M. Greeley. (Bernard Geis/Warner, $3.95.) A priest quits the clergy for the pleasures of secular life.

11 **FLOATING DRAGON**, by Peter Straub. (Berkley, $3.95.) An unspeakable horror invades a suburb.

12 **DOMINA**, by Barbara Wood. (NAL/Signet, $3.95.) A 19th-century woman's aspirations to become a doctor encounter prejudice.

13 **BATTLEFIELD EARTH**, by L. Ron Hubbard. (Bridge, $4.95.) A saga of the year 3000.

14 **THE COLOR PURPLE**, by Alice Walker. (Pocket/Washington Square Press, $5.95.) Black women and their families in the South.

14 **NIGHT SHIFT**, by Stephen King. (NAL/Signet, $3.50.) Tales of horror, one of which is the basis of the film "Children of the Corn."

Nonfiction

General

1 **OUT ON A LIMB**, by Shirley MacLaine. (Bantam, $3.95.) The film star's autobiography.

2 **IN SEARCH OF EXCELLENCE**, by Thomas J. Peters and Robert H. Waterman Jr. (Warner, $8.95.) Lessons to be learned from well-run American corporations.

3 **MEGATRENDS**, by John Naisbitt. (Warner, $3.95.) Predictions about America in the next decade.

4 **THE SHOEMAKER**, by Flora Rheta Schreiber. (NAL/Signet, $3.95.) The true story of a psychotic killer and his son.

5 **BLUE HIGHWAYS**, by William Least Heat Moon. (Fawcett Crest, $3.95.) A trip through the back roads of America.

6 **THE MICHAEL JACKSON STORY**, by Nelson George. (Dell, $2.95.) A life of the popular singer.

7 **THE MAGIC OF MICHAEL JACKSON.** (Starbook/NAL/Signet, $4.95.) Photographs of the singer and appreciations by a half-dozen associates.

8 **THE ROAD LESS TRAVELED**, by M. Scott Peck. (S&S/Touchstone, $8.95.) Psychological and spiritual inspiration by a psychiatrist.

9 **MICHAEL JACKSON THRILL**, by Caroline Latham. (Zebra, $2.95.) Another biography.

Advice, How-to and Miscellaneous

1 **THE ONE MINUTE MANAGER**, by Kenneth Blanchard and Spencer Johnson. (Berkley, $6.95.) How to increase your productivity.

2 **GARFIELD TIPS THE SCALE**, by Jim Davis. (Ballantine, $4.95.) Cartoon humor.

3 **'TOONS FOR OUR TIMES**, by Berke Breathed. (Little, Brown, $6.95.) Cartoons from the comic strip "Bloom County."

4 **J. K. LASSER'S YOUR INCOME TAX**, by the J. K. Lasser Tax Institute. (Simon & Schuster, $6.95.) Latest edition of a standard do-it-yourself guide.

5 **COLOR ME BEAUTIFUL**, by Carole Jackson. (Ballantine, $8.95.) Beauty tips for women.

6 **RAND MCNALLY ROAD ATLAS: United States, Canada, Mexico.** (Rand McNally, $5.95.) For 1984.

The listings above are based on computer-processed sales figures from 2,000 bookstores and from representative wholesalers with more than 40,000 retail outlets, including newsstands, variety stores, supermarkets and bookstores.

These figures are statistically adjusted to represent sales in all such outlets across the United States. The number of titles within the two subdivisions of nonfiction can change from week to week, reflecting changes in book buying.

The End

24. If you followed the rules and if you enjoyed a certain amount of luck and timing, you may have become a best-selling author, and you are probably comtemplating your *next* book. Even if your first "best-seller" didn't sell, it may happen for Book Two or Book Three. Don't give up! Do you repeat the same formula for future books? Not necessarily. You've learned a great deal about the workings of the book-publishing industry, and you should benefit from the insights and mistakes of your first book experience. The second time around for publication, ask yourself the following twenty questions:

1. Were my subject and title right for the marketplace?

2. Was the book properly prepared and edited?

3. Do I stay with the same publisher?

4. Do I now need an agent or lawyer? Do I retain the one I used for my first book?

5. What are the appropriate edition and retail price for my second book?

6. Do I want to work with the same editor as before? If not, what kind of editor do I need?

7. What aspects of the publication contract would I change?

8. What am I asking in advances and royalties?

9. What endorsements or accolades can I use for my next book?

10. What kind of package (cover, design, size) do I envision for Book Number Two?

11. How effective were my publicity and advertising? What can be done differently and what control can I have over it?

12. What subsidiary-rights markets would be receptive to the second book?

13. Does the new book have film, TV, or cable possibilities?

14. Should I consider self-publishing?

15. How did my retail sales end up (after returns)?

16. What didn't work out the way I wanted it to?

17. What new markets can I sell to?

18. What was the initial catalyst for my best-selling book?

19. When should I publish Best-seller Number Two?

20. How can I repeat this formula?

After you've answered the above questions to your complete satisfaction, begin to write your *next* best-seller.

Write to me and let me know how you're doing.

> *Stan Corwin*
> *2029 Century Park East, Suite 1850*
> *Los Angeles, California 90067*

Good luck! I'll be looking for *you* on the best-seller lists.

●●●●●●●●●●●●●●●●●●
Appendix

How Novels Get Titles

by Robert F. Moss

"My mind running, like high seas, on names," Charles Dickens wrote his friend John Forster in the midst of an anguished quest for a title for "David Copperfield." He went on to subject Forster to a blizzard of possibilities, including "The Copperfield Disclosures," "The Copperfield Survey of the World as It Rolled" and "Copperfield, Complete."

Many 20th-century writers have found choosing a title equally vexing. Before they received the names by which we know them, James Joyce's "A Portrait of the Artist as a Young Man" was "Chapters in the Life of a Young Man," Somerset Maugham's "Of Human Bondage" was "Beauty and Ashes," D. H. Lawrence's "Lady Chatterley's Lover" was "John Thomas and Lady Jane," and John Steinbeck's "East of Eden" was "Cain Mark." The most famous—and awful—of all working titles belongs to F. Scott Fitzgerald, who originally called his masterpiece not "The Great Gatsby" but "Trimalchio in West Egg."

To get a contemporary perspective on the elusive art of titling, a dozen or so contemporary writers were canvassed. Although the responses were as varied as the individual personalities, there were some points of agreement—about the proper esthetic goal of a title, for instance. As Walker Percy put it, "A good title should be like a good metaphor: It should intrigue without being too baffling or too obvious." Similarly, Joyce Carol Oates felt a title "should have a mystery to it. It can't explain everything." Several writers used the word "mystery," while Maya Angelou expressed the same idea from the other direction: "What I want the title to convey is a sense of familiarity, so the reader recognizes something and says, 'Oh yes,' but doesn't know exactly what it is."

"I'm terrible about titles," Eudora Welty confessed. "I don't know how I come up with them. They're the one thing in the story I'm really uncertain about." Thomas Berger was only a little more specific when he identified his own source of titles as "the same never-never land from which my characters emigrate without warning." When Dickens was mentioned, practically everyone expressed great affection for his novels and at the same time less kinship with his reliance on friends as arbiters of titles. Editors, however, are often consulted. "Sometimes I show a title to my editor and let him give a vote," Miss Welty said. When Anne Tyler originally turned in the manuscript of "Searching for Caleb," it was called "Hunting Caleb," but, as she tells it, "the editor felt it would sound like James Dickey's 'Deliverance.' He took the word 'hunting' literally. Where I was raised [North Carolina] you could say, 'Go hunt your brother for supper.' It just meant you were going to find him."

Many editors have a fight on their hands when they come between an author and his title. "On my first book we had problems," William Styron recalled, referring to "Lie Down in Darkness," which borrows its sonorous name from Sir Thomas Browne's 17th-century meditation on mortality, "Hydriotaphia, or Urn Burial." Unfortunately, another novelist had already been smitten by the line. "My editor, Hiram Haydn, said it had been used five years before on a mystery novel by H. R. Hays," Mr. Styron explained. "That threw me into a tailspin. But I stuck to my guns because you can't copyright a title, and the other book was out of print." Later, though, Mr. Haydn evened the score by having his way in another title dispute. Mr. Styron's second book, first published in magazine form as "Long March," was put out in hardcover by Mr. Haydn but only after the editor had convinced Mr. Styron that the title was "too abrupt" without the definite article. It is now officially "The Long March."

Trivial? Perhaps, but Mr. Styron's fellow Southerner, Mr. Percy, said, "My editor at Knopf changed the title of my first novel, 'The Moviegoer,' from my title, 'The Confessions of a Moviegoer.' Maybe he was right. A French structuralist critic once wrote a paper on the significance of the 'the' in 'The Moviegoer.'" "The" can also be the only titular difference between one well-known work and another, as with H. G. Wells's "The Invisible Man" and Ralph Ellison's "Invisible Man."

If writers will occasionally let editors influence their choice of titles, they'll certainly also accept help from stray geniuses who happen to be on hand. John Updike reported that at one time "Couples" was called "Couples and Houses and Days." "I asked Marianne Moore about it one noon when I found myself seated beside her at the Academy of Arts and Letters," Mr. Updike explained, "and she promptly, in her tiny old lady's voice, said, ' "Couples." It's more mysterious.' "

Norman Mailer, a man with a commitment to provocative titles, said he wanted the title taken care of first: "If you have to pick it after the book is done, it's like trying to buy the right wedding ring." When a work becomes a classic, however, its title develops its own eternal flame. Consider Sinclair Lewis's perfectly humdrum "Main Street." Then too, people change their minds about titles, just as they do about everything else. " 'The Naked and the Dead' was taken by Rinehart & Co. in 1946," Mr. Mailer said. "When my editor presented the book at the sales conference, Stanley Rinehart, the publisher, exclaimed, 'Oh, what a dreadful title!' Of course, I in my turn, sending a blurb to Burroughs Mitchell at Scribners on 'From Here to Eternity,' wrote in passing, 'bad title.' I confess that over the years I've come to think it's a very good title indeed. Maybe Stanley Rinehart could have said the same."

The tersest explanation of how a title is conceived came from Robert Penn Warren, whose sole comment was "Sometimes people give them to me, and sometimes I see them on a billboard." Actually, in the case of his novels, neither billboards nor friends have been as fertile a source as previous writers and poets, from whom he has gathered the names for five of his ten works. An apt quotation often comes with its own built-in music, as in the mournful tones of Mr. Styron's forthcoming collection of essays, "This Quiet Dust," a phrase from an Emily Dickinson poem. Miss Oates, who "may spend weeks trying to think" of a title, found some of hers in the Bible or other religious writings: "I love the resonance of biblical language. 'Son of the Morning' is a biblical reference—'O Lucifer, son of the morning!' "

But maybe all a writer needs to do is prick up his ears around his fellow citizens. Mr. Berger is indebted to a man in his native Cincinnati for the name of his first novel, "Crazy in Berlin." After rejecting "several pompous titles," he said, "I remembered the words furnished me by an Ohio bricklayer, *Du bist verrückt, mein Kind/Du musst nach Berlin*' [You are crazy, my child; you must go to Berlin]."

Surprisingly, in view of the notebooks full of random jottings that most writers accumulate, few authors said they had a good title stashed away but no book to go with it. Miss Angelou thought she might use "Spectator at the Feast" sometime, and Mr. Mailer still hopes to find a novel that fits "The Saint and the Psychopath," his working title for "The Executioner's Song." But only Miss Tyler seems to have actually given birth to a title first and then written a novel for it. "I always loved the phrase 'celestial navigation,' " she said. "I even had a cat by that name." At last in 1974 the cat became a novel.

When the writers were asked what titles of other people's books they especially liked or disliked, Mr. Berger reached all the way back to Balzac for one of his favorites, "Spendeurs et Misères des Courtisanes." "The titles of the various translations of that book," Mr. Berger said, "never quite make it, for my money: 'A Harlot's Progress,' 'A Harlot High and Low.' " Miss Oates, although a great admirer of James Joyce, had doubts about "Ulysses." "Today in 1982," she said, "it seems too programmatic." Mr. Percy shrinks from titles that are "too antic" and cited one called "I Love You Now, I Think."

Faulkner and Hemingway, so often mentioned in one breath, wound up at opposite ends of the scale when their titles were assessed, with Faulkner being consistently praised and Hemingway almost as consistently panned. " 'The Sun Also Rises' is part of the canon," Mr. Styron said. "It's unbudgeable. But I think that if I were a contemporary of Hemingway's, I'd probably say, 'Ernest, I think that title is just a little too highfalutin.' "

Robert F. Moss, *whose most recent book is* Rudyard Kipling and the Fiction of Adolescence, *teaches at Hunter College.*

HOW TO MAKE IT IN HOLLYWOOD

An Insider's Secrets
To A Successful
Movie Career

INTRODUCTION

Since the beginning of motion pictures when actors
and actresses fell into movies from vaudeville acts and live
stage shows, the lure of being "a movie star" has captured
the fascination of millions of actors. Each year thousands
of "would-bes" pound the pavements in Hollywood hoping,
praying that they will be miraculously discovered. Some are
so desperate they will try any unique approach to getting
noticed. I saw one actor walk up and down the boulevard
outside a studio spouting Shakespeare in a loud, thundering
voice hoping someone, anyone would hear him. Some come to
Los Angeles penniless; some come with money and hope but
no idea of how to begin, who to meet and how to make each
contact, performance and chance catapult them forward in a
business crowded with talents. Strangely enough in this day
of deflation and recession, the chances of one actor making
it over another are entirely geared to HOW they go about
packaging themselves to agents and casting directors. No
studio these days can be bothered. A plan of action and a
definite way to follow through with it are the criteria
for one actor making a living from what he does as opposed
to another barely eeking out one job a year while waiting
tables to pay the rent. The point of all "hustling" these
days is GET ON THAT FILM! Once there, you can make friends
and acquaintances who will help you parley your work to other

prospective employers. Most actors coming to Hollywood
today have no definite plan and in fact don't even know how
to begin their climb up. the artistic ladder. It took me
ten years of trial and error just to figure out which moves
came first and which could wait until I'd gained some sort
of a name. Many books, magazines, articles, courses and
guidance counselors give advice, but the real course of action
must be told by someone who's lived it. Does sleeping around
really help you "reach the top", can you be discovered
"sitting at Schwabs" and how much training do you need and
with whom? A young actor came up to me at Universal as
I waited to read for a role and begged me to tell him exactly
how I'd managed to win the reading! I took the time out of
practicing to explain the ins and outs of professional actor's
etiquette and then realized that many good, but naive actors
needed the same advice. Only a seasoned professional can
whisper the secrets in a would-be's ears and hopefully this
book, covering exact plans of action, true stories and helpful
suggestions will enable brilliant, untapped talent NOT to
despair, but to make the moves, cover the territory and forge
ahead to give the world talent. I hope I can save them
time, money and pain. If I'd had a book like this to follow
when I first began, I would have forged a different, faster
path to working steadily in Hollywood, a position I am
grateful I now hold.

HOW TO MAKE IT IN HOLLYWOOD

An Insider's Secrets
To A Successful
Movie Career

TABLE OF CONTENTS

Introduction

CHAPTERS

September 15, 1983

Mr. Stanley J. Corwin
Stan Corwin Productions
2029 Century Park East
Los Angeles, CA   90067

Dear Mr. Corwin:

I am enclosing the Table of Contents and two
sample chapters of my manuscript FOR BETTER
OR FOR WORSE - The State of Marriage in America
Today. This book is a compilation of the find-
ings of hundreds of interviews with men and
women (both married and single) all across
America today. Some of the topics it covers
are: The Myth vs. The Reality; Sex; Money;
Growing Together and Apart; What Works and
What Doesn't.

Since marriage is always a topical and commercial
subject, I hope this project will be of interest
to you. I've enclosed SASE. Thanks for your
consideration.

Sincerely,

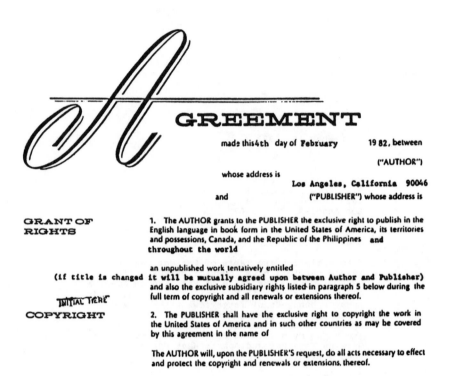

GREEMENT

made this 4th day of **February**   19 82, between

("AUTHOR")

whose address is

Los Angeles, California   90046

and   ("PUBLISHER") whose address is

GRANT OF
RIGHTS

1.   The AUTHOR grants to the PUBLISHER the exclusive right to publish in the English language in book form in the United States of America, its territories and possessions, Canada, and the Republic of the Philippines   **and throughout the world**

an unpublished work tentatively entitled

(if title is changed **it will be mutually agreed upon between Author and Publisher)** and also the exclusive subsidiary rights listed in paragraph 5 below during the full term of copyright and all renewals or extensions thereof.

INITIAL HERE

COPYRIGHT

2.   The PUBLISHER shall have the exclusive right to copyright the work in the United States of America and in such other countries as may be covered by this agreement in the name of

The AUTHOR will, upon the PUBLISHER'S request, do all acts necessary to effect and protect the copyright and renewals or extensions, thereof.

MANUSCRIPT

3. The manuscript, containing about   25,000   words or their equivalent, will be delivered in duplicate by the AUTHOR to the PUBLISHER in final form and content acceptable to the PUBLISHER by   March 30   1982 A third copy will be retained by the AUTHOR.

BOOK
ROYALTIES

4. When the manuscript has been accepted and approved for publication by the PUBLISHER and is ready for publication, it will be published at the PUBLISHER'S own expense. The PUBLISHER will pay the AUTHOR royalties from its sale of the published work, said royalties to be computed and shown separately, as follows:

(1) on copies of the regular trade edition (other than sales falling within (2) through (8) below),   10% for the first 10,000 copies sold, 12½% for the second 10,000 copies sold, and 15% for all copies sold over 20,000 copies of actual cash received.

INITIAL HERE

(2) on copies sold in the book trade at a discount of fifty per cent or higher from the list price of the regular trade edition, 10% of actual cash received for first 10,000 copies sold, 12½% for next 10,000 sold and 15% thereafter.

(3) on copies sold outside the book trade at a discount of fifty per cent or higher from the list price of the regular trade edition, 10% of actual cash received by the PUBLISHER.

INITIAL HERE

(4) on books and sheets for export outside the United States, 10% of actual cash received by the PUBLISHER.

(5) on copies sold by the PUBLISHER direct to the consumer through coupon advertising, radio or television advertising, direct-by-mail circularization, house-to-house solicitation, through any of the PUBLISHER'S book club divisions or institutes, or by the PUBLISHER'S sales representative, 5% of the actual cash received by the PUBLISHER.

(6) on copies of a simultaneous paperback or paperback reprint issued by the PUBLISHER at a retail price of two-thirds or less of the most recent retail price, 10% of the actual cash received by the PUBLISHER.

(7) on copies sold as overstock at a reduced price, 10% of the actual cash received by the PUBLISHER after deducting all manufacturing costs.

(8) on copies produced for Premium distribution, 5% of actual cash received by the PUBLISHER.

OTHER RIGHTS

5.   The exclusive subsidiary rights referred to in paragraph 1 are hereby defined to include the rights enumerated below and the proceeds from the sale or license thereof are to be shared by the AUTHOR and PUBLISHER in the percentages indicated:

	To Author	To Publisher
(1) Digest, abridgment, condensation, anthology, selection, or novelty use	50%	50%
(2) Second serialization and syndication (including reproduction in compilations—magazines, newspapers, or books)	50%	50%
(3) Book clubs or similar organizations	50%	50%
(4) Reprint (including microfilm) edition through another publisher	50%	50%
(5) First serialization in North America (prior to the Publisher's official publication date)	80%	20%
(6) The right to sell or license throughout the world:		
(a) Motion Picture	% of Net	% of Net
(b) Dramatization	% of Net	% of Net
(c) Radio	% of Net	% of Net
(d) Television	% of Net	% of Net
(7) The right to sell or license Mechanical Rendition and/or Recording	% of Net	% of Net
(8) The right to sell or license translation and foreign language publication	80% of Net	20% of Net
(9) The right to sell or license publication rights in:		
(a) United Kingdom—Book Rights	80% of Net	20% of Net
First Serialization	80% of Net	20% of Net
(b) British Commonwealth (exclusive of Canada)—Book Rights	80% of Net	20% of Net
First Serialization	80% of Net	20% of Net

INITIAL THERE

(c) Other foreign countries (in English)—
Book Rights	80% of Net	20% of Net
* ҳѻѻҳ҅ӈҩѻҳҟӽҳҳѻҳ (8)	ҳҳӫӈѻѻҍҍӽҷ	ҳҳӫѻҩӽѻӽҳҳ

*If foreign translation and British rights are not licensed by the Publisher after one year from U.S. publication, these rights shall revert to the Author.

The use of the words "of Net" in **1** through (9) means that it may be necessary to employ agents to make certain of these sales, and that commissions paid to such agents shall be deducted first before the proceeds are divided between the PUBLISHER and the AUTHOR. but not to exceed 10% agent's commission.

PAYMENTS

6. The PUBLISHER will render semiannual reports of the sale of the work during March and September of each year, covering the six-months period ending the prior December 31 and June 30th, respectively, of each year, and at the time of rendering such statement will make settlement for any balance shown to be due. With respect to monies due the AUTHOR as book royalties, the PUBLISHER may determine and withhold a reasonable reserve against returns, but such right to withhold shall terminate with respect to the period ending December 31 of the year following the year of publication.

INITIAL HERE

The Publisher agrees to make an initial payment to the Author as an advance against royalties of $5,000, payable as follows: $2,500 on signing, and $2,500 on receipt of complete manuscript and all artwork in the form acceptable to Publisher, provided, however, the Publisher may retain for its own account the first $5,000 otherwise due the Author under the terms of this Agreement. The terms of this paragraph shall not apply to revised editions of the work.

INITIAL HERE

AUTHOR'S CHANGES

7. The manuscript in duplicate to be delivered by the AUTHOR to the PUBLISHER shall be typewritten in proper form for use as copy for the printer and shall be in such form and content as the AUTHOR and PUBLISHER are willing to have appear in print. The AUTHOR agrees to read, if or when submitted, and within fourteen (14) days of the receipt thereof to return to the PUBLISHER the proofs of the work. If the AUTHOR fails to return the proofs within the period aforesaid, the PUBLISHER shall have the right to publish the

INITIAL HERE

**MATTER
SUPPLIED BY
AUTHOR**

INITIAL HERE

**AUTHOR'S
WARRANTY**

shall
work as submitted. ~~The AUTHOR shall pay, at~~ The PUBLISHER's ~~option have~~ charged against the AUTHOR, the amount of expense incurred by the PUBLISHER because of changes and/or additions other than corrections of printer's errors made in and to the text by the AUTHOR in excess of ten per cent (10%) of the original cost of composition; and the AUTHOR shall pay in full for any corrections in the plates which he requires or which are necessary for the correction of the AUTHOR'S actual errors (excluding printer's errors) after the plates have been made in conformity with the last proofs as corrected by the AUTHOR.

8.   The AUTHOR will supply with the manuscript a preface or foreword, if any; table of contents; and when requested by the PUBLISHER all photographs, drawings, art work, ~~chart, book~~, diagrams, forms and illustrations; if the AUTHOR shall fail to do so, the PUBLISHER shall have the right to supply said photographs, drawings, art work, charts, index, diagrams, forms and illustrations and charge the cost thereof against any sums that may accrue to the AUTHOR under the terms of this agreement.

9.   The AUTHOR represents and warrants that he is the sole AUTHOR of the work and the sole owner of the rights granted to the PUBLISHER hereunder; that he has full power and full authority to copyright the work and to make this agreement; that the work does not infringe any copyright, violate any personal property or other right, or contain any scandalous, libelous or other unlawful matter. The AUTHOR will indemnify, and hold harmless the PUBLISHER against all claims, demands, suits, actions, losses, costs, damages, attorneys' fees, including those attributed to, and computed in accordance with outside counsel rates then prevailing, attorneys in the employ of PUBLISHER when acting as attorney of record and/or associate counsel for PUBLISHER in litigated matters, and expenses that the PUBLISHER may sustain or incur by reason of any breach or alleged breach of any of the foregoing representations and warranties, and until such claim, demand or suit has been settled or withdrawn, the PUBLISHER may withhold any sums due the AUTHOR under this agreement. The provisions of this paragraph shall survive the termination of this agreement.

DELIVERY

10. The AUTHOR agrees that the manuscript of the work shall be delivered to the PUBLISHER by the date provided in Paragraph 3; if by reason of the AUTHOR's death or otherwise the manuscript in final form and content acceptable to the PUBLISHER shall not have been delivered within ninety (90) days after said date, the PUBLISHER may terminate this agreement and thereupon all monies paid to the AUTHOR pursuant to this agreement shall be repaid to the PUBLISHER. In the event that the AUTHOR fails to repay the PUBLISHER in full all monies owing to the PUBLISHER pursuant to this agreement, the PUBLISHER shall retain for its own account monies due the AUTHOR under the terms of all other publishing agreements between the AUTHOR and PUBLISHER until the amount so retained equals the amount owing to the PUBLISHER under this agreement.

COPYRIGHTED
MATERIAL

11. The work shall contain no material from other copyrighted works without the written consent of the owner of such copyrighted material. Such written consent shall be obtained by the AUTHOR and filed with the PUBLISHER.

PUBLISHING
DETAILS
*and will publish the
book no later than 18
months following
delivery and acceptance
of the manuscript.

* 12. The PUBLISHER shall have the right: (1) to publish the work in such style as it deems best suited to the sale of the work; (2) to fix or alter the prices at which the work shall be sold; (3) to determine the method and means of advertising, publicizing, and selling the work, the number and destination of free copies, and all other publishing details, including the number of copies to be printed, if from plates or type or by other process, date of publishing, form, style, size, type, paper to be used, and like details. The AUTHOR agrees that the PUBLISHER may use the AUTHOR'S name and likeness or photograph in connection with the advertising and promotion of the work.

INITIAL HERE
FREE COPIES

13. The PUBLISHER will furnish XXX copies of the published work to the AUTHOR without charge. Should the AUTHOR desire additional copies for his own use, they shall be supplied at a 40% discount from the retail trade price.

INITIAL HERE
TERMINATION
AND
REVERSION
OF RIGHTS

14. If the work shall go out of print and off sale for six (6) months in all editions, including reprints, whether under the imprint of the PUBLISHER or another imprint, and if thereafter, after written notification from the AUTHOR, the PUBLISHER shall fail to place the work in print and on sale within six (6) months No "remainder" sales will be made until one year from publication.

INITIAL HERE

After reversion the Publisher will provide Author with copies of all licensing agreements and the Author will continue to receive any royalty payments due.

INITIAL HERE

COMPETING WORK

INITIAL HERE

OPTION

INITIAL HERE

from the date of receipt of such notification (unless such failure is due to circumstances beyond the control of the PUBLISHER), then this agreement shall terminate and all of the rights granted to the PUBLISHER hereunder shall revert to the AUTHOR. The AUTHOR shall have the right for thirty (30) days after such termination to purchase the plates, if any, of the work at one-half the original cost of composition and plating, and any remaining copies or sheets of the work at the manufacturing cost, all F.O.B. point of shipment. If the AUTHOR fails to purchase, as aforesaid, the PUBLISHER may dispose of all such plates, copies and sheets without further liability for royalties.

15.   The AUTHOR agrees, during the term of this agreement, not to contract to publish or furnish to any other publisher for sale or trade, or otherwise, any work ████████████████ that shall conflict with the sale of the work herein specified.

16.   The AUTHOR grants the PUBLISHER the option to publish the AUTHOR'S next two works of   upon the same terms as those contained in this agreement. The option, however, will not apply to the second of such two works if not exercised by the PUBLISHER with respect to the first. The options may be exercised by the PUBLISHER by written notice to the AUTHOR of its election to publish, given within 60 days after receipt of the complete and final manuscripts of such works. If any such work is less than 50,000 words, however, the PUBLISHER may reject such work without forfeiting any of its options hereunder.

AGENT

INITIAL HERE

~~The AUTHOR hereby authorizes the AUTHOR'S agent,~~
~~to collect and receive all sums of money payable to the AUTHOR under the terms of this agreement and declares that the receipt by the said agent shall be a good and valid discharge in respect thereof, and the said agent is hereby empowered to act on behalf of the AUTHOR in all matters arising out of this agreement; said authorization shall continue in effect unless and until the PUBLISHER shall be otherwise instructed in writing by the AUTHOR.~~

CHANGES

18. This agreement shall not be subject to change, modification or discharge in whole or in part except by written instrument signed by the AUTHOR and an officer of the PUBLISHER.

CONSTRUCTION, HEIRS

19. This Agreement shall be construed, interpreted and governed according to the laws of the State of New York and the parties agree that in any action or proceeding arising under or relating to this agreement, they shall be subject to the exclusive jurisdiction of the courts of the State of New York. The PUBLISHER may assign or otherwise transfer this Agreement in whole or in part. The AUTHOR may assign only the right to receive any amounts which may be payable to the AUTHOR after receipt by the PUBLISHER of written notice of such assignment. This Agreement shall be binding upon the heirs, successors, personal representatives and the foregoing respective assigns of the PUBLISHER and AUTHOR; and references to the PUBLISHER and AUTHOR shall include such heirs, successors, personal representatives and such assigns.

INITIAL HERE

20. The Publisher will print the following on the title page or copyright page: "Published in association with Stan Corwin Productions Ltd."

21. The Publisher grants to the Author non-exclusive mail order rights and will allow the Author to purchase copies for this purpose at 50% off the retail price.

INITIAL HERE

_____   _____
Author
U.S. Taxpayer Identification No. _____

By   _____

9.8/21772-6/79

What Successful Book Packagers Are and How They Create Successful Sellers
by Paul Fargis

If a blurb is the sound made by a publisher, then pizzazz is probably the noise that comes from a book producer. Pizzazz describes the peculiar combination of enterprise, orchestration, imagination, and enthusiasm essential for the producer of books—a person who is at once developer, editor, financier, and promoter.

There seems to be a number of different notions and a good deal of misinformation in publishing about what a packager is and what a packager does. The first thing one ought to know about packagers is that many prefer to be called "book producers," the label adopted by the four-year-old American Book Producers Association. (The terms are used interchangeably in this article.) And the second thing to know is that there are currently so many variations on the theme that a definition has to be written in general terms.

Until the early 1970s most packagers were firms (often British) that delivered either mechanicals or bound books at a fixed price per copy. Often these books were heavily illustrated, and their texts sometimes lacked depth. With only a few exceptions a packager created books that would have international print runs. Paul Steiner of Chanticleer Press claims to have brought the concept to the United States around 1950. He was followed by Ridge Press and Rutledge and others that basically emulated the British model.

Today a book packager is any individual (or firm) who has an idea for a book, finds and aids the people who write and develop it and sells the project in virtually any stage from finished manuscript to finished book to a publisher or other source of distribution.

A number of the new trade book producers have come out of publishing backgrounds. Their firms were created to provide editorial and production services to publishing houses that were trying to maintain high volume with inflation-reduced staffs. Such packagers as Jim Charlton, Stuart Daniels, Bernard Geis, Philip Lief, David Cohn, James Mann, Regina Ryan, Sandra Choron, Suzanne Meyer, and Marsha Melnick of Roundtable have had extensive in-house publishing experience, as have others. These trade producers have a combination of editorial and marketing abilities (or access to them) that are not common today in many publishing houses, where most editors' time and talent are spent on acquisition and editing and—if one believes their secretaries—meetings, not on in-depth development. Therefore, as Judy Linden, editor-in-chief of Perigee Books, says, "I'm very receptive to packagers for Perigee and like dealing with them because they save so much editorial time."

The new crop of book producers are generally tiny companies, and they operate out of small quarters with overhead and productivity that would be the envy of any cost accountant in corporate publishing. More than half the twenty-five current members of ABPA have fewer than three employees. As a rule, the newer packagers are more oriented toward editorial than marketing skills, in that more editorial effort and know-how goes into creating the physical book than in selling it to a publisher. However, there are also a good number of producers who have publicity and promotion capabilities or the special marketing savvy to get their books sold in all kinds of nontraditional outlets.

Bill Adler and Bernard Geis not only have and shape good ideas but also have trade records for best-sellers: "The I Love New York Diet" and "The Cardinal Sins" are prime recent examples. Danceways has been able to sell its books in stores that handle ballet clothing; Tree Communications sells books in gift stores; the Stonesong Press (this writer's company) works in mail order; the Benjamin Company in premium sales; and James Wagonvoord sells large numbers of books to book fairs. Art Watkins specializes in books on homes and housing and sells his packaged books and others through a mail order operation of his own, the Building Institute. "This market was being ignored by many publishers," Watkins explains, "and I was able to develop a profitable side business. Nontraditional markets like this are where packagers often excel."

Adler sees this style of packaging as a trend, boldly predicting that within five years "more than 25 percent of the nonfiction trade books published in this country will be packaged books. Publishers," he says, "are beginning to recognize that there are distinct advantages in having creative professionals deliver completed manuscripts that can be published with minimum editorial involvement and cost by the publisher." As far as her list for The World Almanac is concerned, Jane Flatt agrees: "A packager can do more for the book and for us than most authors. Every one of the books we wanted this year at Frankfurt was a packaged project."

Philip Lief of Philip Lief Associates, whose firm has had a number of bestselling humor books, points out: "Some editors still don't use book producers properly. We have the resources and the experience to give them things like fast production schedules, marketing information, research, choice in writing and art styles. They rarely ask about these things and tend to forget that we are not authors; we are full-service operations." Regina Ryan, packager and former editor-in-chief at Macmillan, supports this: "I think it is important that producers get involved in marketing and other parts of the process because they often know a lot more about the book, its audience, and the author than anyone else involved."

Jim Mann and David Cohn of Tribeca Communications emphasize the point by telling how an editor at one house told an author of a book on personal computers that he needed a packager before he needed a publisher. The editor turned the book down, but sent the author to Tribeca, which could work closely with him. The book, "Automating Your Financial Portfolio: The Investor's Guide to Personal Computers" by Donald R. Woodwell, was subsequently sold to Dow Jones-Irwin.

Crown is probably the publisher with the most experience and understanding of packagers. Alan Merkin, Crown's president, says, "We try to take advantage of the skills a packager has, be they editorial, design, production, special sales, or whatever." Citing "The Joy of Sex" as an example, he points out that the view of the book and its basic development came from Mitchell Beazley in London. Crown had a lot of editorial input, including the title, which was Nat Wartels's idea. "In short," says Merkin, "whether it is a packaged book or a coproduction with a foreign publisher, we try to have a joint effort by sharing the ideas and talents."

When Harmony, a Crown division, contracted for "Fabulous Fallacies," a Stonesong Press book by Thaddeus Tuleja, it elected to buy finished books. While Stonesong had the responsibility for all stages, Harmony made itself available and helped out on such things as content ideas, production specifications, and jacket design. Peter Shriver, Harmony's editor, stayed closely involved. Harmony solicited opinions on catalogue copy, and Stonesong provided sales kit materials. We depended on and worked with each other to produce the book. The point here is that this sharing of roles is a growing trend, particularly because many of the newer book producers have substantial prior "in-house" experience.

Sarah Lazin, whose Rolling Stone Press had three American Book Award nominations (two for "Destinations" and one for "The Beatles") feels that sharing is important, but she still wants to keep responsibility: "The TABA nominations resulted in publishers being much more receptive to our having the responsibility for the design and production up to mechanicals. Many publishers have approached us now that our rock reference books have track records for sales and quality."

Adler feels that the combined skills of publisher and packager were what made one of his many best-sellers: "Our most successful recent package was 'The I Love New York Diet,' which we packaged for William Morrow and which has sold over 130,000 copies in hardcover alone. This was a complete editorial package. We worked very closely, however, with Larry Hughes and the editorial and sales people at Morrow in developing it. With most successful packages there must be cooperation and trust between the publisher and the packager."

When the producer delivers finished books, it has already quoted a price (as with mechanicals) for delivering a certain number of bound copies to a publisher's warehouse at a fixed cost per copy. Technically, until those books are delivered in acceptable form to the publisher, they are owned by the producer. This is the fact that makes some individuals shy away from book production as a part of packaging. The investment risk in producing 25,000 copies of a book are great. One mistake in printing or paper or color could literally lead to the end of many a company. Because of that risk factor and the high cost of capital, a number of producers no longer deliver finished books. Indeed, this amounts to a fundamental change in the direction of packaging today.

More and more packagers, both foreign and domestic, have become quite flexible about what they will deliver. If the price for bound books is too high, an editor can ask about buying mechanicals or film. Sometimes the producer will prefer to deliver the edited manuscript and leave the design and production to the publisher. Aside from the cost of money, a key reason for this change—at least among the newer producers—is the time it takes for production. A small packager can make more money for the time invested by selling manuscripts or mechanicals, even though its production and overhead costs would be considerably lower than the publisher's. New contractual clauses about printing and binding are changing or being dropped because of this money factor, with the publisher handling the printing and binding. Judy Linden points out that she is able to use only slightly amended author's contracts when buying this way. "We usually don't need a long, complicated form with detailed specifications, since we are acquiring a manuscript or mechanicals."

Of course, when a considerable amount of color work is at stake or a large international print run is being put together, this will usually not be possible, and the producer's terms don't have much give.

Other parts of the standard contract are changing, too. Several packagers now negotiate for some unusual arrangements. John Monteleone of Mountain Lion Books will license a share of foreign rights to his sports and fitness books, with the understanding that they revert in full to his company if they have not been sold within a year of publication. "I figure the publisher has about a year and seven months from the time I deliver the manuscript, and that should be plenty of time," he says.

Exercising Editorial Control

Clauses specifying how the packager's name will appear are common, as are ones about what kind of sales kit material the packager will provide. Publishers these days are asking for tougher clauses about editorial control. Joan Sanger of Macmillan and Grace Shaw of Bobbs-Merrill are two of several publishers who said they are cautious about editorial control and want a strong say about what will become final copy. "Our contract will often state that manuscript material will be shared with us at a number of points in its development. That way there are no surprises," says Shaw.

In contrast, Sarah Lazin reports that "Rolling Stone always has approval of format and design of the books as well as all catalogue copy and complete cover design."

A random sampling of other nonstandard clauses includes the following:
- a full right-hand page announcing the book in the catalogue;
- an agreement to pay the packager an amount that will be used for newspaper and magazine publicity;
- an agreement wherein the packager has the right to print and sell a spe-

cial edition in mail order with *no* payment to the publisher;
● a clause that gives exact calendar dates for payments due, as opposed to payment after receipt of materials.

Authors and agents often ask about compensation offered by packagers, and the reply is that there are no set rules or standards for paying writers who work for packagers. It is important to understand that a producer's share of monies has to come from the unit cost paid by the publisher, from the royalties, or from both. That is the only way devised so far for a developer to earn a fair dollar. The range of payments to writers, therefore, goes from a flat-fee, work-for-hire arrangement wherein the writer gives up all rights, to an advance and royalties and rights for the author. Nothing is "normal" or "standard," and it is hard to see how it can be because there is so much variety in packaging styles and in the types of work needed by the packager.

If a producer is assigning parts of a work (a reference book, for example) to a writer, then a fee will be negotiated that covers the assignment as a work-for-hire. Some packagers use this kind of arrangement for all their books. Others might pay a small royalty after a certain number of copies are sold, or might go so far as splitting all income equally with the author.

It is safe to say that generally an author does not receive 10 percent, 12½ percent, and 15 percent royalties or subsidiary rights percentages that would be normal when working with a publisher. Ironically, however, an author can often make more money on a packaged book than on one that is not. The reasons will depend on the nature of the book, the reputation or skill of both packager and author, and the way payments are structured by the publisher. For example, when a producer delivers printed and bound books, *all* royalties for *every* copy are included in the amount paid per copy. And each time the book is printed, all royalties are inlcuded in the publisher's purchase price. Therefore, the author need not wait for royalties; he or she is paid when copies are printed—and that includes printings in foreign countries. Of course this would not be true if the producer were delivering a manuscript or mechanicals.

At the time of this writing the Stonesong Press is negotiating a royalty-inclusive sale of a quantity of books to a company that will resell them through the mails. Those rights were withheld from the publisher, and again, the author will see her royalties at the time of sale, not eighteen months to two years later, with a reserve withheld for returns.

Because of the huge number of books published each year and the ever-increasing burden of overhead (often created by mergers and acquisitions), many publishers, particularly the large ones, have begun to rely increasingly on the outside editorial and art sources that packagers can offer. Editors who have their own ideas for projects are routinely turning to book producers for the development of them.

Such out-of-house services are far less costly and time-consuming than in-house staff. How many trade editorial departments, for example, can afford staff people who can make calls (as my company recently did) to more than 150 manufacturers of do-it-yourself materials?

Mary Lee Grisanti of M. L. Grisanti Associates, for another example, was recently commissioned to produce a multivolume popular encyclopedia of science for both Encyclopedia Britannica and Fabbri. "This is the only project on which Britannica has ever put its own imprint that was produced outside its own facilities," Grisanti said. "We were equipped to do the twenty-eight-volume series the way both publishers wanted. Without any staff additions or extra overhead, both publishers will have a continuity series of high quality, written and produced by a team of professionals."

Limited Staffs

Jim Charlton, former editor-in-chief of Quick Fox, looks at the producer's out-of-house role a bit differently: "If there is going to be another Maxwell Perkins, he or she will be a packager. Most editors inside publishing houses just don't have the time that a packager does. A packager may spend days or weeks in direct, face-to-face contact with the author, shaping and molding a manuscript. In-house editors just can't afford to do that on too many projects."

While some American packagers have full staffs of people to handle editing, design, production, and accounting, most packagers still operate with one to three people. At the Stonesong Press, where I've been packaging for the last few years, I'm not only the editor and rewriter but also the production manager, bill collector, and receptionist, working with a part-time assistant and a wonderful Rolodex of freelancers. We small packagers will farm out copyediting or proofreading and have an accountant check the ledger and do our taxes, but one or two people will: do the typing and filing; research all the ideas and write out the initial proposal; find an author; sell a publisher; handle the accounting debits and credits; arrange for jackets, typesetting, paper, printing, binding, shipping; and pray. Typically, we'll have between two and ten projects under contract at any one time and others cooking on the back burner.

Trade editors inside publishing houses probably handle fifteen or more titles a year and simply do not have the time or the assistance to work closely and frequently on their own ideas for books. The editor may suggest an idea to an author, but will not stay personally involved with its development and maturation. An editor/packager, on the other hand, not only comes up with the idea and the writer but also is the mentor and the wordsmith who sees it to fruition. Perhaps that is the reason why many book producers come from former editorial positions in publishing houses. It is also a key reason why trade departments save time and risk capital by working with packagers.

The major difference between the in-house editor and the editor/producer is that the producer's time is spent almost solely on his or her books. "There are no ruffled feathers or bruised egos to soothe," says Jim

Charlton. "Simply put, it is nice to be on your own and to make the choices about whom to deal with, and which projects you will handle."

A couple of months after I took my imprint out of Grosset I realized I had not been to or called a single meeting; had not sought an approval for anything; had not written one memo, read a single printout, or phoned another department in the company. I was doing everything, and it was easier and took far less time. Time was the wonderful difference. Time to think an idea through, time to look things up, weigh alternatives, talk to others. What a luxury it is and how much difference it makes, particularly when starting out. Now, only a few years later, there are still no excessively long meetings or printouts, but the free time has started to erode as more projects come to fruition.

For the beginning producer the proposal to the publisher is all-important because he or she has no reputation. The novice producer must be able to prepare an enticing but accurate description of the book. And cost estimates must be right, because increases from the publishers are very unlikely after the contract is negotiated. Carter Smith of Media Projects, Inc., who started creating books in 1969, goes so far as to say, "For the first five years you had better be able to write exciting, attention-getting proposals, because your stock in trade is ideas until your finished books have sold well."

There are other significant differences between the producer and the publishing house editor. Here are just a few:

• The producer/editor creates almost all the book ideas he or she is working on.

• The producer/editor will share in the royalties received for the books—indeed, will *depend* on the money and will put up the money to get the project going.

• An in-house editor's project can be vetoed by the editorial board or the sales department, whereas the producer can take the project to many other sources until a publisher is found. It is almost axiomatic that packagers' projects are multiple submissions.

• A small producer's livelihood depends on his or her skill and knowledge of almost all facets of publishing: contracts, selling, rights, editing, production, design, finance, etc. The packager completes about 80 percent of the publishing functions, whereas the in-house editor handles 15 percent-20 percent.

• Another difference is money, and there the publisher's editor has the advantage. When one is backed by the budget of a large department or company, there is monetary room for alternatives and errors. But when one's own mortgage money or grocery bill is at stake, the perspective is more pragmatic, and each dollar in the budget is spent more judiciously.

• Last, the producer is usually motivated to be in business by the chance at the independence and authority that goes with being one's own employer. This was cited by almost every packager interviewed.

Richard Gallen of Richard Gallen Books was quoted in the June 13, 1980, *Publishers Weekly:* "If publishers were doing their job well, they wouldn't need independent book producers. . . . There aren't enough creative editors in-house to think up the ideas. So they need us!" I think that's partly true, but would add that we also make the job of the in-house editor easier because we deliver a manuscript or book that is already edited and designed, even tailor-made to fit an idea provided by a developing editor.

There are many risks and problems for book producers, particularly the very small ones, but as was true for the publisher of earlier times, it is basically easy to hang out a book producer's shingle today. Capital and competition are two obvious headaches for the producer. I had heard about and given lip service to cash flow when I was on the publishers' side of the fence, but I didn't really appreciate what it meant until I went into business for myself. I still detest doing my own bookkeeping, but it has taught me about the cost of money and given me a more hard-nosed and careful respect for where it will be spent.

Competition won't go away and probably will increase among producers. Already we are learning to be leery of trendy ideas that may be on the drawing board of other packagers.

Like publishers, packagers seem to be willing to discuss with each other what they are doing—with limitations, of course. The regular meetings of the American Book Producers Association sometimes feel like editorial meetings. We talk about each other's projects, gossip, share sources, and suggest solutions. This has resulted in a few cases already where two packagers with the same idea have joined together to produce one book instead of two. And it has even led to Philip Lief producing two books for another packager, Tribeca Communications, which will act as the publisher. Within five weeks they jointly produced two humorous parodies, capitalizing on what Lief calls "filling the need for a satire" created by best-sellers.

It isn't just the occasional similar book that makes things competitive, though. It is also the increasing number of new producers. An informal count came up with more than sixty in the New York metropolitan area, two in Chicago and seven on the West Coast. Richard Gallen, the current president of the American Book Producers Association, observes that "the recent growth in the number of book producers is the product of several factors: the recessions, the separation of management from ownership (conglomeration), the profit squeeze experienced by book publishers and the success of the book producers."

Certainly, book producers are a growing force in the industry. And, in reality, they are not "packagers" or "producers" in the usual sense of those words. Rather they are copublishers. The book producer has at least half the normal publishing responsibility and brings the project to the point where it can be "made public." The publisher in such a cooperative venture prints and/or sells the book. Both the responsibility and the risk are shared and that, to my mind, should be called copublishing.

Paul Fargis is the president of The Stonesong Press, Inc., 319 East 52nd Street, New York, NY 10022, a book development and publishing consulting company. This article originally appeared in *Publishers Weekly,* copyright © 1982.

Literary Collaboration Agreement

This Literary Collaboration Agreement (the "Agreement") made by and between _____ and _____ (collectively, both jointly and severally, "Authors") and _____ ("Collaborator") as of the _____ .

    1. SERVICES: Authors and Collaborator hereby agree to work together to research and write a book dealing with skin care and tentatively entitled _____ (the "Book"). While it is acknowledged that there may be some overlap in the type of services rendered by the respective parties hereunder, as a general matter it is expressly understood and agreed that Authors will be providing factual data and research material, while Collaborator will be primarily engaged in the casting of such material into its final prose form for the Book.

    2. COMPENSATION: Provided each party fully and completely performs all of its obligations hereunder and is not otherwise in breach hereof, each party shall be entitled to and hereby agrees to accept as consideration in full for its services under this Agreement, the following payment:
    (a) Collaborator shall receive the entirety of the _____ advance payable for the book by _____ & Company Publishers ("Publisher"), pursuant to the publishing agreement (the "Publishing Agreement") with Publisher regarding the Book.

    (b) Authors shall receive all of any royalties payable under the Publishing Agreement until Authors individually shall have received an amount equal to _____ minus the total amount of expenses each.*

    (c) After such date, if any, as Authors individually shall have received royalty payments in the amount of _____ , each and all further royalty payments made in respect to the Book shall be split equally among all three (3) parties hereto, one-third (1/3) thereof to Collaborator, one-third (1/3) thereof to _____ , and one-third (1/3) thereof to _____ .

    3. WARRANTIES AND INDEMNIFICATIONS: With respect to any and all material respectively furnished by each of them for use in the Book, each of the parties, separately and individually, that is, _____ and _____ , does hereby make to each and both of the other parties hereto the same warranties and representations with respect to such material as are made to Publisher with respect to the Book in the Publishing Agreement. Each of the Parties hereto, separately and individually,

does hereby agree to indemnify and hold harmless each and both of the other parties hereto for any and all breach(es) of its own said representations and warranties.

4. Each of the parties hereto hereby expressly agrees that the exclusive agent of all of them for purposes of obtaining and negotiating the Publishing Agreement has been and shall continue to be _____ Beverly Hills, California and all of the parties hereto expressly agree that any and all payments from Publisher with respect to the Book shall be sent to said agent care of his agency, and that he shall be authorized to deduct from any and all such payments an agency commission of ten percent (10 percent) thereof.

IN WITNESS WHEREOF, the parties have affixed their signatures herein below as of the date and year first above written.

_____

"Collaborator"

_____

"Author"

_____

"Author"

Publishing: Dealing with Tardy Authors

by Edwin McDowell

Burt Reynolds is more than a year overdue with his autobiography, so the actor's lawyer said this week they have notified Arbor House that they will return the six-figure advance.

When Jody Powell missed his deadline last October, the former aide to President Carter and his publisher, William Morrow & Company, agreed to extend it until later this year.

And St. Martin's Press recently went to court to recover a $14,000 advance from an author who never delivered a promised manuscript and apparently had no intention of doing so.

Most authors are late delivering manuscripts but some never deliver and some deliver manuscripts that publishers regard as unpublishable. In years past, publishers tended to write off advances paid to the last two groups of authors, particularly if the amount was less than $10,000.

But these days, with interest rates high and advances bigger than ever for established writers, publishers are making greater efforts than ever to reclaim money they believe is due them. "We've always done it to some extent, and we still do it with discretion, but we're absolutely moving more now to recover the cost of undelivered books," Roger Donald, executive editor at Little, Brown & Company, said. "We expect guarantees to be executed."

It May Be Worth the Wait

Mr. Donald and other editors say they ask for their money back only as a last resort, because they would much prefer to have a publishable manuscript. "Some of our very best books, in terms of either literature or commerce, or both, have been books delivered well beyond deadline," Samuel S. Vaughan, editor-in-chief of Doubleday & Company, said. "We waited for and we financed nine times the little number of Alex Haley called 'Roots.'"

Many houses have had similar experiences. Judith Thurman's biography of Isak Dinesen, which won the American Book Award this year, was about five years overdue, according to Thomas J. McCormack, president of St. Martin's. "But Judith was working on it all the time. She even learned Danish to do the book. In that case it's worth the wait."

The late Katharine Anne Porter started writing a short novel in 1940, changed the title several times, even changed publishers and did not finish until more than twenty years later. When it was finally published by Atlantic-Little Brown in 1962, it bore the title "Ship of Fools."

Publishers stand over you and breathe down your collar while you're working, Miss Porter complained. "They say, 'Why don't you finish that book?' as if you'd promised to turn one out every year. And I just say to them: 'Look here, this is my life and my work and you keep out of it. When I have a book I will be glad to have it published."

Mr. Vaughan of Doubleday said: "Patience is usually the best policy for a publisher, since authors cannot write and deliver like machines, and should not and are not expected to do so." But some authors respond only to deadlines, he said, including one temporizing novelist he recently put the heat on to deliver "by pretending that our business department was putting the heat on me."

"Some writers would polish forever if you didn't throw out that threat," Betty Heller, an associate editor at Doubleday, said. "Sometimes you have to force them to send it to you so they can go on to something new."

Problem of Late Delivery

A bigger problem than nondelivery, in the view of many publishers, is late delivery. That is because a house not only loses the interest it could otherwise earn on the advance money, but it also does not begin to collect on its investment until after the book is published, shipped, and sold and the money has been remitted several months later by the bookseller. "If an author with a $200,000 advance is twelve months late, at 15 percent interest that costs us $30,000—and many books I publish don't make that," Mr. McCormack said.

As a way of reminding authors of deadlines, St. Martin's, which has almost $4 million outstanding in author advances, sometimes stipulates in big-money contracts that for each month the manuscript is late, the amount of the advance payable on delivery of the manuscript can be delayed two months.

Procedures vary from house to house, but publishers generally review contracts outstanding every few months and ask editors for a progress report. If there is no visible progress, the editor, or perhaps someone from the contracts or the legal department, will ask the author for the manuscript or the money. Often it takes the form of letters, which "get tougher and tougher," one publisher said "like those dunning letters from a department store."

Illness, indolence, and writer's block get in the way of some authors, and others just lose their first enthusiasm. George J. W. Goodman, the "Adam Smith" who wrote "Supermoney," "The Money Game," and other best-sellers, returned a $100,000 advance to Atlantic Monthly Press a few years ago after he decided against writing a book about the Arab world. "He just thought it was the right thing to do," recalled Robert Manning, then editor-in-chief of the company.

In the case of Burt Reynolds, his lawyer, Charles Meeker, said that the actor was determined to write the book himself, "but he's done back-to-back pictures and just hasn't had time." The money would have been returned earlier, Mr. Meeker said, except for what he described as a "minor hangup"—specifically, the refusal of the literary agent Irving Lazar to return his 10 percent of the advance.

"I've done my job, I brought Burt and the publisher together," Mr. Lazar said yesterday. "Should the agent who did his job and got him a $1 million advance not get paid?" The $250,000 already paid to Mr. Reynolds represented the first installment on his advance.

A Conflict of Activities
Unlike Mr. Reynolds, some authors are late with manuscripts because, having pocketed the advance, they are working on books for other publishers. One author who had been under contract some years ago to St. Martin's was also under contract to six other publishers, Mr. McCormack said, using the advance money from one house to repay another. That is no longer so likely today. "If we're going to lay out big money for a book, we'll do some investigation to find out that the author doesn't have four or five other contracts outstanding," Phyllis Grann, publisher of G.P. Putnam's Sons, said.

Publishers also try to insure against nondelivery by taking out insurance policies on older writers—"if it isn't an emotionally painful subject with the author or agent," one publisher said. But sometimes it *is* painful; a well-known novelist and short-story writer left his longtime publisher in a huff a few years ago when the company's financial managers—much to the distress of the editors—insisted on taking out an insurance policy.

If nondelivering authors vex publishers, authors inveigh against the "satisfactory manuscript" clause that allows publishers to reject a manuscript if they find shortcomings in character, content, or form. Because the clause does not define "unsatisfactory," some authors say that publishers even invoke it to turn down an otherwise worthy book whose subject has been overtaken by events.

In such cases, publishers don't usually demand return of the advance, unless the manuscript is sold elsewhere.

Can Trade Publishers Ever Make Money?

by Barrows Mussey

Shouts and moans, mine included, greeted "The Blockbuster Complex," Thomas Whiteside's 1980 *New Yorker* study of how electronically generated dealmaking has transformed the trade book business. That quaint occupation has fascinated me ever since the summer of 1929, when I had my first job in publishing, and did not cease to do so after the unilateral love affair ended in 1950.

Mr. Whiteside confirmed my belief that "things ain't what they used to be; nor ever was." The only novelty today is that some really conspicuous money does change hands.

Predictions of doom for the trade publishing industry have of course been conventional in the English-speaking world at least since the interurban trolley, the nickelodeon, and the cat-whisker radio, and have been derided by hindsight with each new book boom.

The prophets were apparently wrong, but I suggest that the jeerers were little wiser. Trade publishing (as distinguished from reprints, school and law books, Bibles, and other more marketable fare) has never been an industry at all; it's a narcissistic craft.

Printing *is* an industry; in the 1930s various printers in New York and Boston unwillingly owned a flock of trade publishers that had died in hock to them. Chain book merchandising *is* an industry, starting with wholesaling to railway newsstands by the American News Company from 1862 on.

Trade publishing, however, is primarily an effort by the publishers to impose their authors, and thus themselves, on an undefined public—on suspects, not prospects, as the old direct-mail operators used to sneer. The trade business can be seen as a sort of vanity publishing, with the publisher rather than the author paying to see himself in print.

As Kenneth ("Wind in the Willows") Grahame said to the adolescent me, "The strongest human instinct is to impart information; the second strongest is to resist it." And a perennially drawn battle goes on between publishers who hope the author's name and work will move the book, and authors who (usually in vain) expect the publisher to do the moving.

Clifton Fadiman, once a prominent book editor with Simon & Schuster, very aptly called publishing "the world's most luxurious way of starving to death."

Schoolbook, technical and law publishing are, of course, radically different from the literary branch: those people won't even dream of a book until they have demographed and counted the potential buyers. And there is often public money at large—so much that in the 1920s rumors circulated of a rivalry between Ginn and American Book to buy the Texas legislature.

But the false confidence born of visible cash often combines with gambling spirit and "literary" aura to graft trade departments upon otherwise sober and thriving publishers of tax serivces (Prentice-Hall), newspapers (the *New York Times*), and magazines (*Time*), not to mention upon remainder dealers (Crown Publishers). In the '30s, when my office was next door to the Macmillan Company, word spread at intervals that George Brett was finally going to close down the feckless trade department. He and his son did summarily fire various senior editors from time to time. (The rumors subsided for a couple of years after the late Lois Dwight Cole sent head editor Harold Latham to see an old pal of hers in Atlanta who had an enormous script; it turned out to be "Gone With the Wind.")

As for reprints, their traditional function was to exploit the success of exceptionally lucky hardcover books. Allen Lane in England and Pocket Books in America did this so well with paperbacks that they put rental libraries out of business (I gather some are not coming back, thanks to soaring paperback prices), and soon chewed up all the titles worth reissuing, plus a good many more. They also generated such a big, industrial-scale cash flow that speculative guarantees on new books looked deceptively small by comparison.

Around my third year in publishing, say 1932, I reached the conclusion that an honest combined balance sheet of all trade publishers would add up to red ink.

This theory remained my private village-atheist bit for about 40 years, until I came upon the great Chicago economist Frank H. Knight's 1920 dissertation: "Risk, Uncertainty, and Profit." On pages 364 ff. of the Chicago University Press edition (1971) he says: "It may be objected that it is impossible that enterprise on the whole should suffer a net loss, but a little consideration will show that this is not true. The entrepreneur, as society is organized, is almost always a property-owner and must necessarily be the owner of productive power in some form. It may then well be that entrepreneurs lose more than they make, the difference coming out of the returns due them in some capacity other than that of entrepreneur."

For instance, as suggested above: in publishers' capacity as printers, periodical publishers, reformers, or simply wealthy young men with cultural amibitions. Real estate is said to be what kept the Philadelphia Lippincott family afloat during much of this century.

Knight goes on: "The writer is strongly of the opinion that business as a whole suffers a loss. The main facts in the psychology of the case are familiar. . . . The behavior of men in lotteries and gambling games is the most striking fact. Adam Smith pointed out the tendency of human nature to exaggerate the value of a small chance of large winnings. [Nassau] Senior thought that the imagination exaggerates the large odds in favor of either gains or losses. [E.] Cannan holds that both unusually risky and unusually safe investments are especially attractive to large classes of men and yield too small a return, while ordinary hazards are neglected and hence yield more. . . . It is certainly true that . . . most men have an irrationally high confidence in their own good fortune, and that this is doubly true when their personal prowess comes into the reckoning, when they are betting on themselves. . . . The prestige of entrepreneurship and the satisfaction of being one's own boss must also be considered. It therefore seems most reasonable to suppose that the prices of these are fixed at a level above rather than below that which the facts actually warrant."

One might add that nothing in the definition of that chimera, Gross National Product, rules out an entire economy in red ink. Looking at Penn Central, Chrysler . . .

Figures quoted by Whiteside from president Townsend Hoopes of the Association of American Publishers—173 publishers that had not existed before 1971, issuing over 4000 titles in 1972, 10% of the year's new books—tend, if anything, to support my thesis.

New small publishers have of course been sprouting like mad in California and elsewhere. Nearly all are amateurs, and it would be interesting to know how many of those 1976 imprints are still alive now, six year later. But as Hoopes also points out, the casualties will have been more than replaced by fresh enthusiasts.

What strikes me as a decisive though largely overlooked factor in the small-publisher boom is the almost total collapse of physical bookmaking standards brought on by photocomposition. You can now make books however you like, including keyboarding your own copy, and there's nobody left in authority to hold his nose.

Harsh words, but well considered. I have before me a work on philosophy from the Oxford University Press that would have disgraced a rural job printer 20 years ago. In Gutenberg's own country five years of photocomposition have sufficed to erase 500 years of accumulated tradition: the typographic point system is illegal; the trade of compositor has been stricken from the list of recognized occupations for training. Anybody can punch a keyboard, and anybody does.

Yet oddly enough when I was publishing in the mid-1930s we could count on getting an ordinary hardbound and jacketed novel from manuscript to the stores in five weeks; it retailed for $2 or $2.50. Twenty years ago the process took five months; how long it takes today I dare not guess.

I am tempted to misquote my friend C. Northcoat Parkinson: manufacturing expands to fill the time available; losses expand to consume the available financing.

There is much academic and professional handwringing about this state of affairs; I join in wholeheartedly. But what law says you must be able to make a living out of your favorite occupation? In my experience success is much commoner with your second dearest ambition anyhow.

Teetotaling was the true vocation of both Thomas Cook the travel agent and John Cassell the publisher. Conversely, Henry Garrity was a prosperous liquor wholesaler who believed a curse lay on profits from rum, so in 1911 he started the present Devin-Adair Company by reprinting an old book of essays that had caught his fancy.

Dedicated money-grubbers make the best church-wardens. (Did somebody say Rockefeller?)

Certainly the world of hype Whiteside so vividly described makes some authors richer than any have ever become before from writing, even allowing for inflation. What I wonder about is a different parameter, as I believe the management scientists call it: How many titles do the hypers need to draw on for the successes they score, and *how much do the nonsuccesses lose?* What about the overprintings of hyped paperbacks?

Are we back to Frank Knight and his unprofitable aggregate enterprise?

Reprinted from *Publishers Weekly* of November 12, 1982. © 1982 The Xerox Corporation.

Publish AND Perish: The Business and Perils of Putting Out Books

by Stanley J. Corwin

Several years ago in a New York publishing conglomerate, a young secretary was fired for incompetence. Her parting revelation was "I never knew that publishing was a *business*."

If book publishing was once disguised as a literary endeavor fashioned by "gentlemen publishers" like Alfred Knopf and Bennett Cerf, the conglomerateurs soon redirected the literary business from critical praise to credible profits. For better or worse, the bottom line dominated the editorial word as Bertelsmann acquired Bantam Books, MCA acquired Putnam's and Berkley and on and on ad literatium.

Publishing became a *business*, where its president was often an accountant or a lawyer and its new owner comprehended bricks better than books. Publishers became an almost dying breed. Only a handful of independent publishers escaped assimilation into giant corporate structures. The firms of Farrar, Straus & Giroux and Scribner's were the exceptions to rampant mergers and acquisitions while old-line houses like Lippincott and Crowell and Hawthorn were absorbed into surviving publishing companies. A giant literary monolith like Random House with its affiliate companies—Knopf, Pantheon and Ballantine—was acquired, then discarded by its new parent RCA. It is a sad irony that there were few bidders for today's Random House because profit margins had dwindled below conglomerate expectations. The U.S. Department of Justice intervened in conglomerate takeovers but didn't understand when and where to meddle. They condoned ABC's acquisition of Chilton and MCA's purchase of a second paperback house, Jove, but denied Harlequin's prospective purchase of Pinnacle Books. Their test case was not directed at RCA or Gulf & Western but at CBS for owning Fawcett *and* Popular Library. The smaller publishing house was caught in a paradoxical squeeze—to remain independent without the resources to compete in the best-seller marketplace or to be annexed by a larger corporate parent and lose its autonomy.

If you generated the big bucks to compete editorially and promotionally there still were no guarantees for success. If you didn't spend, your books experienced marginal national distribution. All the hoopla and hype was manifested over the million-dollar books sold to paperback and the movies, yet only 100 major films were released each year and 5,000 new paperbacks were published annually. Approximately 4,900 mass-market paperbacks were not movie tie-ins. Judith Krantz, Robert Ludlum and Ken Follett were isolated successes, "Kramer vs. Kramer" and "Rich Man, Poor Man" the rare media phenomena. Who was buying the thousands of hardcover novels and works of nonfiction that nobody ever heard of? They were being remaindered (sold at reduced sale price) at the national chain stores. Who was buying the 400 new paperbacks that reached the mass marketplace every 30 days? As in the record business, most were being returned—that is, only their covers were being returned to the publisher—for full credit. Some were never even distributed and all too often publishers listened to the author's lament, "I can't find my book anywhere."

Book publishing in America became a business of higher speculative advances for the "big" books, increased costs for paper and printing, advertising and promotion, freight and distribution, and the inflationary cost of money. The best-seller syndrome pervaded every corporate scenario, because marginal and secondary books didn't pay the rent or the overhead. The books were expensively produced and shipped to an oversaturated market that couldn't absorb them all. So most books were generally returned to the publisher. If you published "Princess Daisy" or "How to Prosper During the Coming Bad Years" or "The Mr. Bill Show," you had winners, and profits soared. If you just published books, even good books, they too often went unnoticed, unopened and fell onto the bracketed side of the bottom line.

The Dalton and Walden national chain stores acquired the smaller mom and pop bookshops across the country. They became computerized and microfiched to sell the books that were *selling,* since too many were being published. As publisher's costs soared due to proliferating returns of unsalable books, the retail prices escalated. The $9.95 hardcover became $12.95 and soon $15. The $1.95 paperback grew into $2.95, $3.50 and soon to be $3.95. The publishers and the chains could only profit from best sellers and the public could only afford to buy a few books a month. There were far too many books being published on running, tennis, losing weight, getting rich and living longer. The publish or perish syndrome of academia became for the conglomerate book companies, "publish best sellers or perish." Authors looked for the "formula" best seller. Judith Krantz inherited the mantle of Jacqueline Susann. Ludlum followed Graham Greene, and Michener, Shaw and Robbins kept right on satisfying the reading tastes of their public.

More people were reading books but each person was reading less of them. And they pondered the apocalyptic announcements from the literary world. Have we seen the demise of the traditional hardcover book? Will all first novels follow the European format of initially being published in a quality paperback edition? Will mass-market paperback best sellers soon sell for $5? Higher costs, higher returns, diminishing profit margins all cast a pallor over an industry that once upon a time was nurtured on the literary work while a controller with a green eye shade and suspenders rendered a balance sheet at the end of the fiscal year.

As the 1980s began, doom and gloom prophecies soon pervaded the publishing industry. Publishing houses were being bought, sold and mutilated. Smaller houses were putting up "going out of business' signs or being absorbed as an imprint or a backlist. The state of book publishing in

America was depressing—for the publisher, the author and the reader. Yet, prominent publishers like Ron Busch, president of Pocket, and Marc Jaffe, president of Ballantine, were optimistic. And Warner Books and Price/ Stern/Sloan enjoyed the most profitable years in their respective publishing histories. Smaller publishers like Melvin Powers of L.A.'s Wilshire Book Co. achieved high profit margins because of low overhead. Major hardcover authors were selling more books at higher retail prices than ever before. The Literary Guild and Book-of-the-Month Club were thriving extraordinarily well. Gulf & Western was more than satisfied with bottom-line results from Simon & Schuster, while Avon was delighted it had acquired the small hardcover firm of Arbor House.

Were the publishing forecasts optimistic or pessimistic? Rampant problems were increasing in a troubled industry. But opportunities are often created out of problems, and numerous enterprising publishers, authors, agents and the emerging independent book producers and packagers are creating significant books and profits. Like other industries in these times of spiraling inflation and excess, survival of the fittest challenges all publishers today.

For survival, change must occur. Fewer books must be published; retail prices must be stablizied; greater editorial judgment must be exercised; and every book can't be hyped and promoted as a best seller. "Soon to be a major motion picture" and "the $14.95 bestseller now only $3.95" must be translated into a good reading experience for the buying public. Print runs and forced distribution must reflect realistic numbers of copies that can be sold and won't be returned to the publisher in unopened cartons. Fewer books published with judicious editorial selection can mean fewer returns. An emphasis on quality and publishing and printing that will fulfill a market need still can simultaneously enhance a publisher's pride and profits. A blend of the publisher's vision and the accountant's slide rule can effect literary harmony and financial success.

The secretary's revelation about publishing being a business was a harbinger of the future of the industry. There is pessimism about the present state of publishing in America today. There is also hope that the literary visions of Alfred Knopf and his peers will be sustained for a while longer. Marked change must take place. The publishing industry will thrive and succeed in the ensuing decades if we reorient our thinking to the market needs of our public. Publishing can continue to be exciting and stimulating and profitable—for the publisher, the conglomerate, the bookstore, the writer, the reader and for you and me. Like Xerox and IBM and the corner grocer, it *is* a business, whose books have to be arranged every once in a while.

The Self-Published Bookshelf

by Michael Scott Cain

Here is a basic list of information sources for prospective self-publishers.

Book Publishing: What It Is, What It Does, 2nd ed., by John Dessauer, R.R. Bowker, 205 E. 42 St., New York City 10017, $23.95 hardcover, $13.95 paperback.

A standard introduction to the publishing industry. Dessauer discusses the industry's practices in detail. The self-publisher will find many tips on how books are published.

Cataloguing in Publication: Information for Participating Publishers, Cataloguing in Publication Project, Library of Congress, Descriptive Cataloguing, Washington, D.C. 20540, free.

You can get your book into libraries more easily if it is already catalogued. Through the Library of Congress's Cataloguing in Publication program, you can catalog it before publication, with the information appearing on the copyright page of the finished book.

How to Get Happily Published, by Judith Appelbaum and Nancy Evans, Harper & Row, $9.95.

Appelbaum, formerly managing editor of *Publishers Weekly,* and Evans, a successful freelancer, have put together the single most valuable book on how to get your book onto the market. Their chapters on small press and independent publishing are insightful and wise. The 50-page resources section at the end will lead you to nearly every piece of information you could need.

How to Publish, Promote, and Sell Your Book, by Joseph Goodman, Adams Press, 30 W. Washington St., Chicago 60602, $3.25.

Adams Press is a short-run commercial printer and this book was, I gather, originally put together for its customers. The information on layout, design, and so forth is sound.

How to Publish Your Book, by L. W. Mueller, Harlo Press, 30 W. 16721 Hamilton Ave., Detroit 58203, $4.95.

Another book put out by a commercial printer. Overlook its biases and you will pick up some good tips.

The Publish-It-Yourself Handbook, ed. by Bill Henderson, Harper & Row, $4.95 paper.

Bill Henderson originally self-published this book under his Pushcart Press imprint; the revised edition is a Harper & Row title, thus making this inspirational volume a success story in its own right. Here you will find articles by self-publishers explaining why they chose this route.

Printing It, Clifford Burke, Wingbow Press, distributed by Book People, 2940 7th Ave., Berkeley, California 94710.

Burke takes the mystery out of offset and other printing techniques. He teaches you how to get it done cheaply and easily.

American Odyssey: A Book Selling Travelogue, by Len Fulton and El-len Ferber, Dustbooks, Box 100, Paradise, California 94969, $4.95.

When Len Fulton's novel, *The Grassman,* was published, he and his friend, Ellen Ferber, loaded up the car with copies and crossed the US to sell them. This book describes the journey. It will teach you how to deal with retailers, reviewers and the like.

The Book Market: How to Write, Publish, and Market Your Book, by Aron Mathieu, Andover Press, 516 W. 34th St., New York City 10001, $19.95.

Aron Mathieu has a lifetime of experience in the book business. Espe-cially good if you have a commercial book.

Guide to Women's Publishing, by Polly Joan and Andrea Chesman, Dustbooks, $4.95.

The Self-Publishing Manual, by Dan Poynter, Parachute Publications, Box 4232, Santa Barbara, California 93103, $9.95.

For my tastes, Poynter's information on writing is a little naive, but the fact that he has sold a couple of hundred thousand books tempers my criticism. One thing that definitely helped sell those books is the systematic and organized approach to the business of marketing that he describes here. Poynter's book is strong on the nuts and bolts of setting up and oper-ating a publishing business from your home.

The Book Book, by L. M. Hasselstrom, Lame Johnny Press, Box 66, Hermosa, South Dakota 57944, $6.95.

In a series of alphabetical entries, Hasselstrom describes the entire process of design, layout, paste-up, etc. As I said on the cover blurb I wrote for the book, I'd recommend it even if my name wasn't in it.

Publish It Yourself, by Charles Chicadel, Trinity Press, Box 1320, San Francisco 94101, $4.95.

Chicadel, a long time self-publisher and graphic artist, has put togeth-er an attractive and inexpensive volume. His goal is to teach you to do the same thing.

The Writer-Publisher, by Charles N. Aronson, Charles N. Aronson Writer Publisher, Rt. 1, Hundred Acres, Arcade, New York 14009.

Aronson had a bad experience with a vanity publisher, which led him to set up shop as a self-publisher. He offers advice to others who want to take their destinies in their own hands.

A Manual on Bookselling, The American Booksellers Association, Harmony Books, $4.95.

Designed to aid the beginning book retailer, this covers most of the major concepts operating in the retail industry. It will help you keep your expectations about selling to stores realistic.

Paperback Parnassus, by Roger H. Smith, Westview Press, 1898 Flat-iron Court, Boulder, Colorado 80301, $12.75.

A delightfully witty study of the growth of paperback distribution in this country, this volume will, if nothing else, teach you why mass-market paperback distributors cannot help you.

Book Traveler, by Bruce Bliven Jr., Dodd, Mead and Co.; $4.95.

A profile of George Scheer, one of the legendary publisher's representatives, this title shows you how publishing salespeople operate. You will learn how new books actually get into stores and why, as often as not, they don't.

The Co-Op Publishing Handbook and *Book Marketing: A Guide to Intelligent Distribution,* by Michael Scott Cain, Dustbooks, $3.95 and $6.95 respectively.

It isn't simply ego or a desire to boost sales that leads me to include my own books in this list. Both contain useful information for the beginner. *The Co-Op Publishing Handbook* is the only book devoted solely to collective publishing, a strategy where you share skills and resources with other publishers, all of whom are equal partners in the endeavor. People who have successfully developed these models discuss them with an eye toward helping out newcomers. *Book Marketing* is the only title devoted exclusively to getting your book out to its audience.

The Making of a Bestseller—Hollywood Style

by Charles Trueheart

"Word of mouth," that elusive element of book publicity, seems almost quaint as a term to describe the launching of David McClintick's sensational nonfiction bestseller about the wicked ways of Hollywood: "Indecent Exposure."

The prepublication circulation of pirated photocopies of the book in galley form, principally in New York and Los Angeles, was unprecedented in its swiftness and its impact. It turned relatively modest plans for an initial printing of 25,000 copies into a scramble to put upwards of three times that many books into stores, well in advance of pub date. The wonder—and perhaps the lesson—is that the publisher, William Morrow, orchestrated none of this advance momentum, and for a time the author struggled to fight it.

"Indecent Exposure," of course, is the day-by-day, revelation-by-revelation account of the so-called David Begelman scandal at Columbia Pictures in 1977-78. David McClintick was the *Wall Street Journal* reporter who first documented what the stir was all about: Begelman, as president of Columbia, had requisitioned, endorsed with forged signatures, and cashed some $69,000 in company checks for his personal use. McClintick left the newspaper in 1978 to reconstruct the story from beginning to agonizing end, and the resulting narrative is as he intended it—not an aberrant drama, but a sobering distillation of what the entertainment industry thinks and believes.

McClintick submitted his manuscript to his editor at Morrow, James Landis, last December, about a year and a half late and several hundred pages longer than planned. Landis recalls that the book had not stirred much passion therefore. "It was too long, too expensive, and it was about Hollywood. People were yawning. Who wanted to hear that story again?" But when they read it, editors and marketing people recognized right away what an exciting property they had on their hands. Even so, admits Morrow's marketing director Allen Marchioni, "We had no idea the storm was coming."

Landis was gingerly in sending out galleys for advance comment in April. In covering letters, he admonished the select list of recipients that the contents of "Indecent Exposure" were newsworthy and therefore for their eyes only. But one of them, McClintick learned almost immediately, "had taken it upon himself to hand it to someone in the L.A.-N.Y., N.Y. pipeline."

McClintick polled the field of recipients—which included Jay Presson Allen, David Halberstam, Joseph Wambaugh, Tom Wolfe, John Updike, John Kenneth Galbraith, Norman Mailer and Andrew Tobias—and at last identified the culprit, whom he asked to cease and desist. For a while, Mc-

Clintick says, "I labored under the illusion that I had plugged the leak."

No such luck. The copying machines at either end of the bicoastal pipeline were already churning out photocopies made from photocopies made from photocopies, a xerographic virus impossible to contain. The potential for the kind of advance publicity publishers pay oodles to contrive, McClintick says, "didn't occur to me." His main feeling was of "chagrin that someone had violated the moral request for confidentiality and had done so in a casual and cavalier manner." Moreover, McClintick was concerned that this privately published version, as it were, had no epilogue, no source notes or explanation of methodology, and was uncorrected besides.

McClintick's phone began ringing after the Memorial Day weekend. The calls generally were from people he had interviewed for the book, and they were of a piece. "I read your book over the weekend," the caller would begin, lavishing praise on McClintick for writing; even the encomium was a constant: "a real page-turner." *Then* the caller would offer a "comment" or two, invariably a complaint about his own portrayal in the book. "I didn't make a single change because of these calls," the author says.

As McClintick was fielding telephone calls from injured parties and, by early June, a ravenous press, plans were being made at Morrow to move the pub date from September 14 to August 23, and to get the books to the stores as quickly as possible. The first printing was doubled, to 50,000 copies. On July 7 the *Los Angeles Times* broke pub date by nearly seven weeks for a review.

By this time, "Indecent Exposure" was a hot item in Hollywood and something of a status symbol in a community where power rides upon such ephemera. Studio underlings were being told to bind the cumbersome photocopies like scripts for the reading ease of their superiors. One agent was seen perched on a sink in the men's room of a Beverly Hills restaurant, devouring the book on what was presumably a brief loan.

"I could have gotten it from any number of people," says one studio executive who was given a copy for his Fourth-of-July-weekend-reading pleasure. "There was never any question of copyright infringement, either. The irony is that there is such a big outcry in the industry about the privacy of films and cassettes and disks. But because it was about Hollywood, the feeling was, 'It's about us, so of course we get to read it.' "

The first printed books were rushed from the factory in Harrisonburg, Va., to Fifth Avenue stores in New York on July 15. "Indecent Exposure" reached the West Coast a week later, and some stores here reportedly were paying air freight costs just to have the books in stock. Yet photocopies of deteriorating quality were still circulating. McClintick even heard from readers complaining that their copies were hard to read, and one boldly asked the author to read him a passage he couldn't make out.

Will this true story of Hollywood be made into a movie? McClintick, for one, believes it would make "a wonderful multipart television movie;

but who's going to stick his neck out and make it?" He has had inquiries from studios, producers and talent agencies, as well as from "wealthy women with millions of dollars who want to go Hollywood." The real motive of some would-be purchasers, others have speculated, may be to suppress the story by buying it and burying it.

McClintick went on the road to promote his book during August. "It's amazing," he told PW in Los Angeles, "how many people have asked me, 'Is this fiction or nonfiction?' When a book is about Hollywood there's a tendency to think that it has to be a novel. People don't think of Hollywood as attached to the real world, and in many ways, of course, it's not." Had "Indecent Exposure" not proved the point dramatically, the heated commerce in photocopies surely does.

Index

Other Books of Interest

General Writing Books
Beginning Writer's Answer Book, edited by Polking and Bloss, $14.95
Getting the Words Right: How to Revise, Edit and Rewrite, by Theodore A. Rees Cheney $13.95
How to Become a Bestselling Author, by Stan Corwin, $14.95
How to Get Started in Writing, by Peggy Teeters $10.95
International Writers' & Artists' Yearbook, (paper) $10.95
Law and the Writer, edited by Polking and Meranus (paper) $7.95
Make Every Word Count, by Gary Provost (paper) $7.95
Teach Yourself to Write, by Evelyn A. Stenbock $12.95
Treasury of Tips for Writers, edited by Marvin Weisbord (paper) $6.95
Writer's Encyclopedia, edited by Kirk Polking $19.95
Writer's Market, edited by Bernadine Clark $18.95
Writer's Resource Guide, edited by Bernadine Clark $16.95
Writing for the Joy of It, by Leonard Knott $11.95
Writing From the Inside Out, by Charlotte Edwards (paper) $9.95

Magazine/News Writing
Complete Guide to Marketing Magazine Articles, by Duane Newcomb $9.95
Complete Guide to Writing Nonfiction, by the American Society of Journalists & Authors, edited by Glen Evans $24.95
Craft of Interviewing, by John Brady $9.95
Magazine Writing: The Inside Angle, by Art Spikol $12.95
Magazine Writing Today, by Jerome E. Kelley $10.95
Newsthinking: The Secret of Great Newswriting, by Bob Baker $11.95
1001 Article Ideas, by Frank A. Dickson $10.95
Stalking the Feature Story, by William Ruehlmann $9.95
Write On Target, by Connie Emerson $12.95
Writing and Selling Non-Fiction, by Hayes B. Jacobs $12.95

Fiction Writing
Creating Short Fiction, by Damon Knight $11.95
Fiction Is Folks: How to Create Unforgettable Characters, by Robert Newton Peck $11.95
Fiction Writer's Help Book, by Maxine Rock $12.95
Fiction Writer's Market, edited by Jean Fredette $17.95
Handbook of Short Story Writing, by Dickson and Smythe (paper) $6.95
How to Write Best-Selling Fiction, by Dean R. Koontz $13.95
How to Write Short Stories that Sell, by Louise Boggess (paper) $7.95
One Way to Write Your Novel, by Dick Perry (paper) $6.95
Secrets of Successful Fiction, by Robert Newton Peck $8.95
Writing Romance Fiction—For Love And Money, by Helene Schellenberg Barnhart $14.95
Writing the Novel: From Plot to Print, by Lawrence Block $10.95

Special Interest Writing Books
Cartoonist's & Gag Writer's Handbook, by Jack Markow (paper) $9.95
The Children's Picture Book: How to Write It, How to Sell It, by Ellen E. M. Roberts $17.95
Complete Book of Scriptwriting, by J. Michael Straczynski $14.95
Complete Guide to Greeting Card Writing, edited by Larry Sandman (paper) $7.95
Complete Guide to Writing Software User Manuals, by Brad McGehee (paper) $14.95
Confession Writer's Handbook, by Florence K. Palmer. Revised by Marguerite McClain $9.95

Guide to Greeting Card Writing, edited by Larry Sandman $10.95
How to Make Money Writing . . . Fillers, by Connie Emerson $12.95
How to Write a Cookbook and Get It Published, by Sara Pitzer, $15.95
How to Write a Play, by Raymond Hull $13.95
How to Write and Sell Your Personal Experiences, by Lois Duncan $10.95
How to Write and Sell (Your Sense of) Humor, by Gene Perret $12.95
How to Write "How-To" Books and Articles, by Raymond Hull (paper) $8.95
Mystery Writer's Handbook, edited by Lawrence Treat (paper) $8.95
Poet and the Poem, revised edition by Judson Jerome $13.95
Poet's Handbook, by Judson Jerome $11.95
Programmer's Market, edited by Brad McGehee (paper) $16.95
Sell Copy, by Webster Kuswa $11.95
Successful Outdoor Writing, by Jack Samson $11.95
Travel Writer's Handbook, by Louise Zobel (paper) $8.95
TV Scriptwriter's Handbook, by Alfred Brenner $12.95
Writing and Selling Science Fiction, by Science Fiction Writers of America (paper) $7.95
Writing for Children & Teenagers, by Lee Wyndham. Revised by Arnold Madison $11.95
Writing for Regional Publications, by Brian Vachon $11.95
Writing to Inspire, by Gentz, Roddy, et al $14.95

The Writing Business

Complete Handbook for Freelance Writers, by Kay Cassill $14.95
Freelance Jobs for Writers, edited by Kirk Polking (paper) $7.95
How to Be a Successful Housewife/Writer, by Elaine Fantle Shimberg $10.95
How You Can Make $20,000 a Year Writing, by Nancy Hanson (paper) $6.95
Profitable Part-time/Full-time Freelancing, by Clair Rees $10.95
The Writer's Survival Guide: How to Cope with Rejection, Success and 99 Other Hang-Ups of the Writing Life, by Jean and Veryl Rosenbaum $12.95

To order directly from the publisher, include $1.50 postage and handling for 1 book and 50¢ for each additional book. Allow 30 days for delivery.

Writer's Digest Books, Department B
9933 Alliance Road, Cincinnati OH 45242
Prices subject to change without notice.

INTRODUCTORY OFFER
SAVE $3.00

Since 1920 *WRITER'S DIGEST* has been showing writers how to write publishable material and find the choice markets for it. Each monthly issue features:

- Hundreds of fresh markets for your writing. We list the names and addresses of editors, what types of writing they are currently buying, how much they pay, and how to get in touch with them. Get first crack at the new markets, while they are hungry for manuscripts.

- Professional insights, advice, and "how to" information from successful writers. Learn their techniques for writing and selling publishable material.

- Monthly expert columns about the writing *and* selling of fiction, nonfiction, and poetry.

A $3.00 DISCOUNT. Subscribe through this special introductory offer, and you will receive a full year (12 issues) of *WRITER'S DIGEST* for only $15 — that's a $3.00 savings off the $18 basic subscription rate. If you enclose payment with your order, and save us the expense of billing you, we will add an *extra issue* to your subscription, absolutely *free*.

GUARANTEE: If you are not satisfied with your subscription at any time, you may cancel it and receive a full refund for all unmailed issues due to you.

(Detach and mail today)

SUBSCRIPTION ORDER FORM

Yes, I want to know the techniques that professional writers use to write and sell publishable material. I want the latest market information, "how to" advice and other information that will help me get published. Start my subscription to WRITER'S DIGEST today.

Please check appropriate boxes:

☐ Send me a year (12 issues) of WRITER'S DIGEST for only $15 (a $3 discount off the basic subscription and cover price).

☐ I want to save even more. Send me two years of WRITER'S DIGEST for *only $29 (a $7 discount).*

(Please remit in U.S. dollars or equivalent. Outside of U.S. add $2.50 per year.)

☐ Payment Enclosed *(you get an extra issue for saving us billing postage).*

☐ Please Bill Me.

☐ Extend My Present Subscription

☐ New Subscription

Send my subscription to:

Name

Address

City   State   Zip

Please allow 5 weeks for first issue delivery.

205 West Center Street
Marion, Ohio 43305

VBA84-1

THE WORLD'S LEADING MAGAZINE FOR WRITERS

Would you like to:

- get up-to-the-minute reports on where to sell what you write?

- receive the advice of editors and professional writers about what to write and how to write it to increase your chances for getting published?

- read interviews with leading authors that reveal their secrets of success?

- hear what experts have to say about writing and selling fiction, non-fiction, and poetry?

- get a special introductory price for all this?

(See other side for details.)